QUEST FOR CIVILITY

An Insight into Indian Babudom

V K BAHUGUNA

INDIA • SINGAPORE • MALAYSIA

Notion Press Media Pvt Ltd

No. 50, Chettiyar Agaram Main Road,
Vanagaram, Chennai, Tamil Nadu – 600 095

First Published by Notion Press 2021
Copyright © V K Bahuguna 2021
All Rights Reserved.

ISBN 978-1-63957-462-9

Contents

AN Prasad
Former Principal Chief Conservator of Forests
And Chief Wildlife Warden,
Government of Jharkhand

Foreword

I feel greatly privileged to write the foreword for this fascinating book written by one of my closest friend and batch mate Dr V K Bahuguna. We have been together in the service since 1979 and despite being allotted to two different States – Tripura and Bihar (later on Jharkhand), we had the opportunity to work together very closely for almost last 20 years of our service together in Delhi. Dr Bahuguna is known in the service for his professional maturity and for being outspoken and firm in his professional views and opinion. He has another great knack and quality of being able to express his views by writing papers in journals and of late writing regular columns on contemporary issues in national newspapers.

The demand for Civil Services, Judicial and Electoral reforms is without fail the need of the hour. Several Commissions and Committees have been constituted in last 20-25 years for the purpose but unfortunately not much headway has been made and most of the reports containing very important suggestions are gathering dust in the Ministries. Dr Bahuguna with his wide experience of working in different fields and places has very aptly captured these lacunas and shortcomings, especially in civil services, that is hampering the delivery of justice to government officers and employees as well as delivery of various Government schemes and programmes to the people and society in general. The systematic failure has adversely impacted the growth and development of the country. His narration of case studies based on his personal experience are an eye opener and clearly brings out failure of the system and how the powers are used and misused to undermine the fair governance by a few and no one bothers to take notice of such events. Although on paper the checks and balances provided by government circulars and guidelines appears to be foolproof but reality is something else as true events narrated by the author frankly. The author has the advantage of not only working in different departments and heading big organizations across the country but since his cadre was Tripura, a relatively small State, his interaction with the other civil services officers, political bosses and public in general was much more than others service mates. This definitely helped him to understand and analyze the shortcomings of the civil services more closely and comprehensively.

I am sure this book will generate a debate among the citizens of the country and will be particularly very useful to the policy and law makers in understanding the problems and correcting them for the benefit of the society in general. As the author has himself said the trigger of writing the book was the recent criticism of civil services by the Prime Minister of India in the Parliament, the book *ipsofacto* should attract the attention of political masters, students of public administration, constitutional experts and policy analyst not only in India but also at the international level. It will also be useful for our young officers joining the different civil services to shape their career in right trajectory. The fundamental thing is to root for genuine public interests.

Acknowledgement

I would like to acknowledge with gratitude all those civil servants and political executives with whom I have worked and shaped my career over the years. A few I could remember who helped me in my grooming during early part from the Indian Forest Service were Mr RN Chakraborty PCCF Retd and late D Nag PCCFs Retd Tripura who were both very hard task masters and professionally very committed dynamic officers who enthused in me the love for the profession, to be frankly argumentative on professional matters and boldness in taking quick decisions. In the government of India I had worked with very outstanding IFS officers like Mr GP Maithani, Mr JB Lal of MP Cadres and Mr MK Sharma former Director General of Forests. Among others in forest service with whom I interacted on professional matters and issues in performance of civil services are; Dr DN Tewari former Director-General, Indian Council of Forestry Research and Education (ICFRE) & Chancellor of FRI University and Member of Planning Commission government of India, Mr AK Mukherji former Director-General of Forests and Dr Ram Prasad former PCCF of MP. I am particularly indebted to late Mr Shyam Sunder the former PCCF Karnataka for being a role model for a large number of IFS officers all over India. He had always professionally guided me and recently prompted me to write this book and was waiting for it but unfortunately, he succumbed to covid-19 in the month of April 2021 during the peak of Covid-19 second wave in the country. I thank all my junior colleagues in IFS as well as all other professionals of other organizations who worked with me during my career and enriched my experience.

I closely interacted with and learnt from many senior IAS officers also in my formative years in Tripura. Among them the late SR Shankaran as Chief Secretary (CS) Tripura was always supportive of young officers of all the services. Mr NP Nawani former CS Tripura and Secretary Government of India who acted as our mentor (as Secretary Forests) during the initial years in Tripura and also later on whenever there was an opportunity. Mr M Damodaran was another dynamic officer who as CS Tripura forcefully supported us on forest conservation issues and warned the politicians to no to fiddle with Protected Forests. I am grateful to late Padam Shri AM Gokhale former Secretary Government of India and a great botanist and naturalist for his compassionate way of dealing with situations and who also became a partner in evolving lot of good ideas for nature conservation. I would rate him as one of the best IAS officer I have met in my career who had a practical sense of administration, reading the pulse of people, had vision and an inclusive approach on dealing with conflicting issues.

I am grateful to my parents, Father late SN Bahuguna and Mother late Manorama Bahuguna, for the value system and convictions inculcated by them which shaped my personality. I thank my wife Usha Bahuguna, children and other family members for supporting me in all my ventures during my service period and now in my activities post retirement in social service for taking up issues of public interests.

I am thankful to all my colleagues, subordinates and public in general with whom I worked for fabulously enriching my experience in public service and without them it would have been difficult to act in the way I handled various difficult situations in my career.

I thank the Government of India and British Council for nominating me under Colombo Plan for the MSc Resource Management Course in the University of Edinburgh during 1987. This course converted a traditional forest officer into a practicing and thinking resources manager/ administrator. A resource administrator always foresees the consequences of his and others actions before taking decisions. This happens only if away from the professional bias one can ask questions to himself and uses his or her common sense.

I am thankful to my batch mate Dr MH Swaminath IFS Retd and former Secretary Forest, Ecology and Environment Department, Government of Karnataka for agreeing to write the 'Chapter on Horses Mouth' narrating his experience with bureaucracy to lend more credibility to the issues germane to this book as well as bringing a different perspective and variety to the issues discussed in the text.

I am grateful to Shri AN Prasad (PCCF Retd Jharkhand) my batch mate and a close friend for agreeing to write the foreword for this book. He has worked with me very closely and knows everything about my work. No one can write a better foreword than a close friend who is acquainted with your work.

Last but not the least; I am thankful to the Notion Press and the publication manager Mr. Sarvesh Sriram for bringing out the book in great shape and quality.

In my narrations I am always reminded by the following quote of Leslie Stephan the famous British intellectual and historian.

"Every man who says frankly and fully what he thinks is doing a public service"

Preface

The Trigger: I have had a wide range of experiences during my 37 years of career in the Indian Forest Service. I had been fortunate enough to get exposure in varied fields of administration. I had over the years' interactions with large numbers of civil servants, ministers, scientists, academics, national and international experts, social activists and media persons during my postings under the government of India, State government, public sector undertaking and autonomous institutions. My hands-on experience and free mingling with common people during my service period demolished the traditional 'Ivory Tower' image I carried about the civil services before joining the service. Nearer to my superannuation, I had firmly believed that all organized civil services cadres need to look inwards to inspire the confidence of civil society about their overall image relating to their performance in delivery to people, honesty and devotion to public cause, compassion, commitment, fairness and of course professional competence. Whereas, the entire world is looking for innovation to achieve the goals of development, the civil servants barring a few generally face criticism for resisting changes and nipping in the bud even the *insitu'* new ideas or reforms. The people however, immensely love and respect those civil servants who work with devotion and compassion. *My experience tells me that let any government of any party or ideology rule in 80 to 85 % of cases it is the civil servant which matters and takes decision on schemes and issues relating to common man. It is here that creates the need of a neutral, efficient, just and transparent civil servant.*

I have therefore, for quite some time after my retirement in 2015, been toying with the idea of writing a book on the needs of reforms in all the Indian Civil Services as well as in the overall governance machinery. But I involved myself more on taking up issues of public importance with the concerned government agencies and social media as well as writing columns in the national and regional newspapers on behalf of a non-profit Trust I registered under the Indian Trust Act 1882 namely "Foundation for Integrated Resource Management" now renamed as "Centrefor Resource Management and Environment". I also established an informal confederation of grass root level NGOs in Uttarakhand "Jan Vikas Manch" to help these voluntary organizations to articulate their demands. There are senior retired civil servants and NGOs who guides these organizations.

However, early this year the trigger to ultimately write the book came when the Hon'ble Prime Minister Shri Narendra Modi himself vehemently raised the issue of reforms in civil services in his speech in the Parliament and his clarion call to civil servants to perform or perish. Soon after I started writing the book and finished it during the present covid-19 pandemic.

Focus of the book: The book tries to analyze the functioning of Indian governance particularly the bureaucracy and bring out those facets which are not known outside the four walls of these institutions. It aims to put up a case for reforms in it with an innovative approach. There are a lot of long-dead issues in the functioning of civil services in India which still guide its working and tells upon its character but the majority of civil servants steadfastly adhere to these and oppose any talk of reform. Many times, civil servants without accountability unduly influence, misguide and impose their selfish agenda on the political masters many of whom are beholden to them and thus misuse their clout of being close to the seat of power. The common citizens immensely suffer at the hand of such unconstitutional powers enjoyed by a few civil servants which is an antithesis to the classical definition of the role of bureaucracy.

At the same time the increasing browbeating of civil servants or developing cosy relationships with them for ulterior motives by the political executives to meet their selfish ends is giving a serious blow to rule of law in the country. The '**Netadom**' as this writer would prefer to call this all pervasive increasing tendency now among the Indian political executives is similar the way Indian bureaucracy is sarcastically called as '**Babudom**' for their redtapism, arrogance and lack of unaccountability. Netadom as well as Babudom both are detrimental to the fair, lawful and transparent governance. The net result of this is suffered by the people and the pillars of democratic polity get weakened.

The civil services have, however, played a key role in the journey of India during different stages of it being administered by different actors from ancient time to the present time. The role played by the All India Services in uniting the country as one nation despite regional and linguistic barriers in the aftermath of partition soon after independence is laudable. After more than 70 years of independence, there is a long-felt desire to change the format, structure of composition, style of functioning and control over it so that the actions of civil servants mirror the aspiration of the changing society in a democracy. However, for the sake of unnecessary writing the detail history of civil services (which has been written umpteen number of times by several authors), the writer would like to primarily concentrate on how Indian civil services have contributed and bring out many unknown facets of their working style before the public so far and flag issues for action by the society and policymakers.

The objective here is to also scan through the minority negative elements in the top levels of civil service who are ensconced in their cosy surrounding of government power and the general public does not know what types of white-collar crimes this minuscule bunch of civil servants has been perpetrating on the people. In this process, they are bringing bad names to the civil services. The activities of this minuscule section of civil servants are unless exposed, the people will continue to suffer, create chaos in governance and the country's development and freedom will be in jeopardy.

The main intent of the author's arguments on civil services is thus to mobilize public opinion and strengthen the administrative capacity of our system to perform important government functions with a view to raise the quality of services to the citizens that are essential to the advancement of sustainable economic and social development.

One of the key failures of the criticism of civil servants all over the world during the present time is their lackadaisical attitude towards environmental issues knowing full well that all of humanity had to swim or sink together with our environment. The dishonesty in international meetings between the delegates of different countries on environmental issues is palpable and that is because of the poor vision and poor strategy drafted by their civil servants and knee bending half baked experts. The climate change negotiating juggernauts of the international community enjoy their foreign visits more than genuinely caring for arriving at decisions for the climate change mitigations. It is routinely noticed in the various meetings of most of the United Nation's bodies which have become the fiefdoms of a few powerful countries at the cost of less powerful developing countries. The countries must not waste time and think of meeting the global challenges together as united humans by treating the globe as a single village to bring happiness to the faces of billions of world population and ensure the survival of the human race on planet Earth. The breakdown of covis-19 pandemic in 2020 is grim warning by nature to humans on earth to behave rationally otherwise remain ready to face the heat. The collective genius of mankind must rise to the occasion and set rules how the countries and the world should govern now and it is here that the role of good civil services becomes paramount. Let us positively hopes Indian people lead in this venture.

THIS BOOK WILL BE A CALL TO OUR CITIZENS AND POLITICAL MASTERS TO BRING REFORMS IN THE ADMINISTRATIVE CULTURE OF CIVIL SERVICES AND OTHER GOVERNING INSTITUTIONS. THE REFORMS HAVE EVADED US FOR A LONG TIME AFTER INDEPENDENCE.

Introduction: The Preamble   01

The art of governance is to exercise control over people, resources and their distribution and utilization. It may be a country, or an organization or a company run by few individuals. The governments of the countries are run by the rulers as per the constitution of the country. In the past, the feudal system usurped all powers in the hands of kings and their henchmen. The modern era, however, is the era of democracy in most parts of the world. All nations and their rulers in the modern world have evolved organized systems of rules and regulation for administering their countries per their nation's political aspirations reflecting the will of the people, constitution and other supportive institutional apparatus. This task is achieved through administrators who are appointed as part of a permanent system to help the rulers is generally termed as 'bureaucracy'. The bureaucrat can serve any organization or field or enterprise. When they serve the government, they are called civil servants. The bureaucracy is very powerful because it takes most of the decisions in the government within the overall umbrella of policies framed by the elected representatives.

The civil servants are well-trained professionals and are supposed to have three basic traits viz. domain knowledge, human resources management skills and the capacity to organize, visualise and see through the functions and roles of an organization. They must execute the programmes and policies of their rulers and provide regulations. A better administrator would recognize and assimilate the aspiration of its political forces to meet overall social and economic obligations. The conceptualisation skills of administrators thus set the tone for success in the implementation of the decisions. The conceptualisation involves analysing all pros and cons of a subject on which decisions are to be taken. For example, allocation of funds to a particular sector would require the situational knowledge of why and what for the fund is needed and of all those who would receive the funds, as also the assessment of the productivity of the fund allocated so that the objectives of the programme are achieved successfully. Once you have your priorities clear, the next thing required is adequate technical or domain knowledge and resources mobilization. The third important aspect is pooling up and management of human and other resources to effectively implement the decisions.

Whatever be the form of government, be it in ancient time or modern times, the civil service is the single most important institution affecting the lives of the citizens of a State and competence of the governance. They can make or break the future of rulers. The conduct and competence of civil servants' influence are all-pervasive in the modern world where most States perform extensive functions in providing social services and regulating the economic life of people.

The top echelons of administration in most countries today are occupied by the politicians who mostly rule the nations. The civil service serves the Government of the day and they are responsible to their Ministers for their actions and conduct. Civil servants must serve their Ministers with integrity and to the best of their ability. The ruling class in most countries come to power now through democratic means where the people give their mandate to the ruling parties' or a leader for a fixed period.

In Indian conditions, the constitutional provisions have laid down a fool proof mechanism of administering the country. The three wings of the government are i.e. 'executive' (consisting of heads of government at Centreand States and Ministers in charge of specific subject departments and the permanent bureaucracy is its part) which administers the country; 'legislature' (consisting of elected representatives in Parliament and State Assemblies which makes the laws of governance to be implemented by the Executive's apparatus); and 'judiciary' which is to interpret the implementation of the laws of the country for the benefit of society. All three wings collectively form the government and are referred to as 'Organs of the Government'. These three wings of government in working democracies are interdependent, complementary but independent of each other in performing their task. The 'Press' has assumed the status of the fourth estate as the watchdog of public behaviours of these organs. One social activist in a discussion smilingly told me a few years ago if press is the fourth estate why not call civil services as a fifth or sixth estate or estate in itself! Generally fifth estate is referred to outliers view point like journalist or bloggers and mainstream media but I will club them with the fourth estate. We have to decide if it is a compliment?

Indian Civil Services: An Historical Perspective

02

All kinds of ruler need a bureaucracy. It may be hired in a personal capacity or an organized one to run the establishment. The civil services thus essentially evolved with the human civilization. The Egyptian civil services can be described as the forebears of all form of bureaucracy.

The earliest reference of civil services is found in the ancient Egyptian civilization which was flourished by its civil servants. Initially, they recruited and trained people for waterways management and as business prospered, civil services gradually took over the entire country. The primacy of civil services and their role in the administration was established in one form or the other. Even in the Indus Valley Civilization, which is a Bronze Age Civilization (3000 BC to 1300 BC), there appeared to be a well laid out system for planning the cities which could have been done only by a developing civil administration. The Roman Empire outlined their civil service structure in the '*Notitia Digmtatum*'a work by 'John Lydus'. The appointments of civil servants in ancient times were not made on merit but entirely by inheritance or patronage. It was also possible for officers to employ or second other people to carry out their official tasks but continue to draw their salary themselves.

Similar parallels are available in other countries. The establishment of the modem civil service, however, is closely associated with the decline of feudalism, the growth of national autocratic States and with the advent of democracy.

India is one of the countries which had well structured and the oldest civil services during the Mauryan period. The Prime Minister of Chandragupta Maurya, the wily Kautilya, better known as 'Chanakya', established the civil services in India during 313 BC when he created the treatise 'Arthsastra' in which he laid down the rules of governance and educational qualifications of civil servants. India was one of the most admired civilizations in the world, as, during the ancient time, it had prospered in all fields like philosophy, art, music and science. The modern civil services and public administration framework with proper institutional and operational arrangements were brought about much later by the British. The Arthsastra is the forerunner of how to organise Statecraft and how to make the king superior, control his subjects and appoint ministers and civil servants to carry out the duties of running administration like law and order, defence, education, taxation etc. At times, Kautilya recommended unorthodox manners and Machiavellian ways of doing things, but only in cases of dealing with criminals and those recalcitrant people who were acting against the interest of the State, people and king.

According to Kautilya, the fundamental duty of the State is to think about the welfare of its people and the king's prime duty is to serve the people and country with honesty and effectiveness. In the Mauryan period, like in today's system of governments, the '*Amatyas*' (Ministers), Secretaries and Heads of Departments were the important functionaries. The key civil servants were '*Samahartr*' who was supposed to prepare the budget and '*Sammdhatr*' who was responsible for tax collection and of the stores. There were seven basic features of administrative machinery. These elements are mentioned in the doctrine of the *Prakrits, Swamm*(the ruler), *Amartya*(the bureaucracy), *Janapada*(territory),*Durga*(the fortified capital),*Kosa*(the treasury),*Danda*(the army), and *Mitra*(the ally). According to *Arthasastra,* the higher bureaucracy consisted of the *mantrms* and the *amartyas.* The *mantrms* were the highest advisors to the King and were chosen from among the *amartyas who* were the civil servants. There were three kinds of *amartyas* --the highest, the intermediate and the lowest; based on the qualifications possessed by the civil servants. A similar system continued in the Gupta period which is also known as the Golden period of Indian history. The key civil servant was *Samahartx* who was responsible for preparing the annual budget, kept the account of expenditure realization of taxes and other revenue etc.

The Arthsastra also gives vivid details of the law and order authorities. It systematically narrates the manner of police action on an investigation, crime and punishment. The police force was divided into two. The regular one and the secret one akin to present intelligence set up. The regular one consisted of three tiers of policemen. The *Pradesta (rural police), Nagaraka (the urban police)* heading their forces on the top, while *Sthanikas* headed the middle level and *Gopas* at the field level. The secret police were again divided into peripatetic (a moving intelligence) and the stationery. The intelligence organizations were a great handle in detecting crimes and investigation. Today's police stations were the *Sthanikas* of ancient time. There were *Sthamkas* who used to function as executive officials. The highest-ranking officers in the administrative hierarchy were the *Mantrms* who were chosen from amongst the Amatyas. During the Gupta period too, it is said that civil administration was under the charge of the *Mantrms* and broadly similar to the Mauryan period in its content. A new office of *'Sandhmgrahika'* who was in charge of foreign affairs, however, came into existence as an independent office during the Gupta period only.

In the Mauryan period, foreign affairs were the exclusive domain of the Prime Minister and the King. We thus see that during the Mauryan and Gupta period, the broad contours of the administrative pattern as far as its format is concerned, it is similar except for the nomenclature and the manner of recruitment. In ancient times, recruitment to these offices was done on the basis of heredity and family background. The recruitment on the basis of an open competitive system was not known during that period though in China such a system was in vogue since 120 BC.

The character of civil services changed with the advent of foreigners coming to India. Muslim invasion led to the establishment of Delhi Sultanate and later on setting up of Mughal rule by Babar. The key objectives of both were to keep the annexed territories under control and expand their rule and therefore the civil services were part of the Military establishment and overall administration was centralized in the hands of Sultans and Emperors. The Mughal administration was a mixture of Arab, particularly Egyptian pattern and some classical Indian system features.

The Delhi Sultanate ruthlessly subjugated the native population and established control and they brought about revolutionary changes in the civil services compared to Mauryan and Gupta periods. During the Sultanate period, the priority of all the rulers was to enforce their writ and consolidate their authority over the newly won territories and their subjects. This was done by assigning land temporarily to their henchmen and confidents who became the civil servants and formed an elite class. The rulers retained the right of transferring these rights quite frequently so that they can effectively control these right holders and keep them on the tenterhook and prevent rebellion. This was one of the reasons that the

Sultanate was successful in ruling the country efficiently. Later on, one of the most successful Hindu kingdoms the Vijayanagar Empire during the Mughal period adopted this system and ruled Southern India for a long time and expanded their territories.

The Mughal administration drew a lot from the past and civil services were essentially on the lines of the Sultanate period. There were four important officers in the Central government; i) the *Diwan or Vazir* equivalent to present-day Chief Minister but mainly looking after Finance department apart from other general responsibilities; ii) Mir Bakhshi who was head of both Military as well as civil services; iii) Mir *Saman* the in charge of *Karkhanas* (manufacturing units), communications, stores etc; and iv) *Sadr* looking after charities and religious matters. The magnificent grandeur and stability of Mughal rule was due to its selection of better people for the top posts. The organization of administration and delivery of public services was best at the time of Akbar whose bureaucracy was, based on the *Mansabdari* system which he borrowed from Persia. Each Mansabdar was given a rank in the hierarchy, was part of an imperial cadre and, were supposed to be responsible for both civil and military jobs and liable to serve anywhere in the empire. The Mansabdars were appointed by the emperor based on the recommendations of military leaders, State governors and his courts. Some very important administrative reforms were brought about by the Sher Shah Suri during his brief tenure of five years especially in land revenue records, infrastructure like roads, public buildings, new currency, and postal services. The staff dedicated to all departments' streamlined law and order machinery. These reforms were adopted by Akbar also to efficiently run the Provinces and ensure peace and tranquillity.

During Akbar's regime, the Provincial government were better organized in terms of their boundaries with a set of trained civil servants under the control of governor known as *Sipah Salar*. At the district and city levels, two other important officers were *Faujdars and Kotwals to* look after general administration and law and order. At the village and panchayat level, the Mughal did not intervene too much and allowed the village panchayats to function and deal with local issues. Mughal, especially

Akbar, paid attention to improving the land and revenue system created by Sher Shah Suri as it was one of the important sources of income and the Emperor closely monitored its functioning. Indian revenue records still are based on the same pattern as the British also followed it.

After the East India Company took over the reign of the governance in India, upon winning the Battle of Plassey in 1757 and Buxar in 1764, the need for a modern civil administration was felt and the foundation of modern civil service started in India. Its structure and practices derived from that of 'Whitehall' in the middle of the 19th century. It started with career civil servants who would work subject to satisfactory performance till attainment of retirement age. The British civil services initially focussed on exercising control over vast tracts and a large potentially hostile population of natives. The modern Civil Services were started by Lord Cornwallis and he is rightly called the "Father of Indian Civil Service". Cornwallis who was the Governor-General of Bengal Presidency realised that to consolidate the British rule in India, it was felt essential to organise a systematic civil administration with trained civil servants. In 1793 he started the new revenue system of permanent settlement of records and transferred all rights to Collector and thus the seeds of Indian Civil Service were shown by him. According to Jerry DuPont, Cornwallis was responsible for *"laying the foundation for British rule throughout India and setting standards for the services, courts, and revenue collection that remained remarkably unaltered almost to the end of British India"*.

The British appointed Lord Macaulay as Chairman of a committee to recommend a suitable structure of the civil services and consequently the British Parliament passed the civil services Act in 1853. The committee defined the ideal administrator "as a gifted amateur who moving from job to job was capable of taking a practical view of any problem irrespective of its subject matter on the basis of his knowledge and experience in the government. The British laid more emphasis on grooming generalist civil servants to tackle the primary concern of the British to control the territories and oversee a wide variety of issues so the civil servant was supposed to have interests in a variety of things and to pursue these interests. The aim was to widen the horizon of the young civil servants so that they can deal with the issues without too much emphasis on knowledge. The specialists were treated as 'narrow' specialists with technical skills who were just only paid for their skills. The generalists back home in Britain compared to specialists at that time were having more prestige like Barristers and Bishops and hence the generalist civil service in India became a lucrative profession for the public school educated youth. The civil servants were trained to focus on broader community welfare than individual achievements and it was considered as one good attempt to win over the masses, which had to suffer at the hands of many exploiters.

After the Government of India Act of 1858, the higher civil service in India came to be known as the Indian Civil Services (ICS). The Indian Civil Services Act of 1861 provided that certain posts under the Government of India were to be reserved for persons who had been a resident of India for 7 years or more. The Indian Civil Services gradually was opened for Indian and this small group became the backbone of the British Empire. Satyendranath was the first Indian to be selected for the Indian Civil Service in June 1863. Gradually other services like Indian Forest Service/ Forest Engineering Service, Indian Police Service, and Indian Medical Services etc came into existence. These services set the pattern of today's Indian bureaucracy which is guiding the destiny of our administration. The British did not tamper much with the Mughal system but modernised it in all fields and today most of our rules, Acts etc are the legacy of the British period.

Many of these Acts have become archaic and not relevant in today's situation. The present government headed by Prime Minister Narendra Modi had weeded out 1,200 old laws during the last five years and has identified 1824 more Acts for repeal. Before this, 1301 obsolete laws were repealed by the previous governments. It is a welcome sign and as the saying goes change is a must and change is inevitable. The Indian system of administration especially the bureaucracy and judiciary must change to mirror the aspiration of the changing society and be effectively accountable for bringing happiness to the people. The civil service is today composed mainly of career bureaucrats hired by the governments on their professional merit whose institutional tenure is permanent and who are the key advisors of political leadership.

Before the British came, the judiciary was the weakest link in the civil administration as they neither had set procedures of dispensing justice nor proper organizations of courts. Both the Mauryan period as well as the Mughal period lacked it. The process of litigation for Hindus was performed either by the caste elder or village Panchayats or zamindars whereas for Muslim Qazi dealt with the litigations. Disputes were handled by the Kings and Emperors. The first reforms were undertaken by Warren Hastings from 1772 to 1785 by establishing, two courts for resolving disputes – District 'Diwani Adalats' for civil disputes and District 'Fauzdari Adalats' for criminal disputes. Then Lord Cornwallis during his regime from 1786 to 1793) the District Fauzdari Court was abolished and 'Circuit Courts' were set up at Calcutta, Decca, Murshidabad and Patna. It acted as a court of appeal for civil as well as criminal cases which were led by European judges. **William Bentinck during his tenure** made the Persian and a Vernacular language for the court proceeding in the lower court and made English the official language for Supreme Court proceeding. During his reign, the Law Commission was set up by Macaulay which codified the Indian laws. Based on this commission, a civil Procedure Code of 1859, an Indian Penal Code of 1860, and a Criminal Procedure Code of 1861 were prepared. By the High Court Act of 1861, the High Courts were established at Calcutta, Madras and Bombay. The Government of India Act, 1935 changed the structure of the Indian Government from "unitary" to that of "federal" type. To avoid disputes the distribution of powers between the Centreand the Provinces to contain disputes between the States and the Centre. It also provided for the establishment Supreme Court, which was set up in 1937 with appellate and advisory jurisdiction. Its appellate jurisdiction was extended to civil and criminal cases. Today, we find a lot of Tribunals running in the country dealing with various issues.

Role of Civil Servants: In Today's India

03

In a democracy, people are supreme and the government of the day is elected by the people. In India, people elect their representatives right from village panchayat-level to District to State Assemblies to Parliament through a single transferable universal adult franchise. The elected representatives exercise the power through legislatures by enacting laws and by the executive which consists of a Council of Ministers headed by the Prime Minister in the Centreand the Chief Ministers in the States. To advise the Ministers, the career civil servants are appointed, trained and posted at different levels and to implement the decisions of the government faithfully. The civil servants are supposed to take decisions based on the rules and precedence and use their quality of knowledge; experience and assessment of a situation concerning public interest. The civil servants have therefore, a herculean task to honestly fulfil the promises made by their political masters. In parliamentary democracies, civil services have a massive grip on the politicians as they help in policy-making for the political executives by providing inputs. Apart from Constitutional provisions of governance Indian democratic institutions have been well served by a free press and have complemented the executive, judiciary and legislature. These institutions play their role in strengthening governance.

One of the basic components of Indian constitutions is to have very fair, impartial, honest and well qualified and well-trained civil services in diverse fields. The civil services are mostly recruited by the Union Public Service Commission, State Public Service Commissions and other such independently authorised bodies. The Indian Civil Services as an institution is, therefore, a very potent and powerful institution actively engaged in the governance of the country. The real power and influence of civil servants far out weight their position on paper as mere advisors and file pushers. In many ways, due to their knowledge of the system and closeness to the seat of power, they become the *de-facto* arbitrators of dispensing justice to people on behalf of democratically elected public representatives. They form a permanent institution of governance and lend continuity to the administration. The functioning of civil services especially the All India Services has immensely contributed to the stability of our democratic fibre and ensuring unity in diversity in the administration. The importance of All India Services has been proved time and again in protecting the unity of India along with Armed forces especially during the period of instability and uncertainties. In uniting India as a nation and lending stability and continuity in administration the All India Services are still playing a very vital role and their contribution is no less than any elected constitutional post.

As Stated in India there is thus immense importance of the civil services in the administrative system as the most vital clog in the governance. In post-independent, Indian civil services were reorganised. There are three tiers of administration that include Union/Central Government, State Government, and Local Government. The civil service includes three All India Services, namely the Indian Administrative Service (IAS), Indian Forest Service (IFS), and Indian Police Service (IPS). Besides these, there are other organized Central Services such as the Indian Revenue Service (IRS), Indian Foreign Service (IFS), Indian Audit and Account Service (IA&AS), Indian Railways Services, etc. under the Central Government. The State Governments have their own set of services like State Civil Service/State Police Service and State Forest Service etc. During the British period, consolidation of territories, enforcement of law and order and collection of revenue was the major work of civil services officers. After the independence of India, the civil services are seen as an agent of social welfare apart from other duties they performed during the British period. They have a role in planning the development process and implementing national and State policies of welfare. The civil servants are supposed to give non-partisan advice to political leadership and their advice to constitutional authorities becomes crucial during times of uncertainties.

Need for Reforms

The civil services have a responsibility to achieve the development objectives of the political leadership and welfare of the State. These days due to poor exposure of many political leaders the failure of delivery to people is considered as either a failure of civil servants or their handiwork. Such criticism is quite reasonable considering the way a vastly unwieldy vast administrative structure is maintained at a very high cost to the exchequer and perceived to be a burden on taxpayers. The public perception of Indian civil services is that it is inefficient, arrogant, inherently biased, and insensitive to public feelings, unaccountable, selfish and corrupt. Such criticisms keep coming at regular intervals especially when a few civil servants do not conform to the high traditions of neutrality and honesty and become subservient to politicians in power and also blatantly misuse their position for selfish gains or partisan ends. The number of such civil servant is rising steadily and putting a question mark on the entire bunch of civil servants across the spectrum and is not restricted to a few services. The main criticism of today's civil services is the gradual erosion of essential service values like fairness, compassion, ethics, morality and self-esteem. However, it is also a fact that without the dedication and hard work of different civil services including engineers, doctors and scientists, Indian democracy would not have been what it is today in the comity of nations as a vibrant stable country marching ahead toward progress in all directions despite huge population, hindrances and divergent interests and consequent conflicts.

Though the seminal contributions of civil services in nation-building cannot be denied, at the same time it must also be noted that the degradation in the civil services cannot be ignored anymore. The role of the civil service as a tool in a State's socio-economic, cultural and political development is indisputable. Compared to India, in some parts of the world, however, the civil service are either incapable or too much politicised to meet the sociological, political and economic aspirations of the people and have failed to have a vision of change and foresight and lack of management innovations along with the poor institutional capacity building. And because of poor governance strife, civil wars, conflicts and socio-political disturbances are witnessed in these countries. Many countries are now introducing major changes in the structure and content of their civil services. However, the changes in civil service format need political will, as well as the support of the well, informed public to carry forward the vision of change and overcome the resistance to the changes.

In the Indian situation, though civil services are playing an excellent role in national development, nevertheless, for a better tomorrow we must be ready to bring in necessary changes in the functioning of our civil services so that this vast country can be managed efficiently for better public services and to create a society where every citizen get justice with equity and fruits of development are enjoyed by all. The biggest problem is the '*status quoist*' *and selfish* mindset of our civil servants.

The objective of civil services reforms, therefore, is to mirror the challenges for the future and to strengthen the administrative capacity to effectively implement the decisions of the government and to raise the quality of services to the citizens. This is necessary for the advancement of what we call today sustainable development with peace and happiness for the people. In fact, there is a continuous need for the review of our public services for the larger good of society. The good thing about civil services is that they have an organized thinking pattern, analyse well and work systematically but their biggest weakness is that they are biased, and protective of their and their cadre's interests. We need to convert this weakness into strength. Now a day's their aloofness to public welfare and insensitivity to the sufferings of people at the hand of criminals and perpetrators of corruption is another emerging criticism. Because of deficiencies in the governance by the Executive the Supreme Court and High Courts are stepping in occupying space of the Executive. The judicial assertion started from the Keshvanand Bharti case when it ruled that basic features of the constitution cannot be changed. The enunciation of the doctrine of Public Interest Litigation (a relaxation on the traditional rule of *locus standi*) by Justice PN Bhagwati opened the courts to socially disadvantaged sections of society and opened doors for course correction by it in the functioning of the Executive. In the recent past, many landmark judgements in the field of the environment have endeared Judges to the people of the country notable among them were Justice Kuldeep Singh and Justice AN Verma. The 1996 Godavaram case turned the trajectory of forest and wildlife management in the country. Despite the enactment of the Forest Conservation Act in 1980 and the Wildlife Protection Act 1972, the lackadaisical attitude of the Central and State governments had put the forest and its biodiversity at great risk. The interventions of the court for the last 24 years had forced the executive agencies to act to a certain extent for the smooth implementation of the constitutional provisions for the conservation of our forest and wildlife resources. India was one of the earliest countries in the tropical world to implement working plan provisions for managing the forests sustainably. The working plans were almost forgotten all over India till the Supreme Court interventions. The Supreme Court through its intervention streamlined the forest management in the country and forced the governments to prepare and regulate the management of forests through working plans. Now the results are visible on the ground. Similarly, the rampant mining in forest areas is being closely monitored by the Court. This positive action of the Supreme Court struck a balance in restoring the constitutional obligation of the Executive. Yet another instance of excellent intervention relates to declaring River Ganga a live entity by the Uttarakhand High Court. Such decisions of the Apex Court have touched the lives of millions of our citizens. What is most significant in this regard is the recognition of the rights of those who cannot speak like trees, animals and rivers which are crucial for sustaining life on Earth. The establishment of the Compensatory Aforestation and Planning Authority (CAMPA) in the country which now have a collection of whopping more than Rs 75,000 crore was possible due to the direction of the Supreme Court. I was closely involved in creation of the CAMPA and had weathered a major bureaucratic road block in its creation.

In yet another epoch-making intervention, the Supreme Court came down heavily on real estate thugs masquerading as builders in connivance with the political and bureaucratic mafia in Noida. The bureaucracy in Central and the UP government completely failed in checking the real estate scam in Noida. For the last three years since October 2017, a Supreme Court bench had sent a stern message to these thugs operating the Amrapali housing projects. The builder in league with officers of Noida Authority and political patronage swindled more than Rs 8000 crore hard-earned money of the home buyers akin to a daylight robbery perpetrated under the nose of all those who were supposed to protect the interest of people. The problem with our governance system is such that it gleefully ignores the sufferings of the people at the hands of such criminally minded people in powerful position and the inherent corruption. The Supreme Court in an unprecedented manner has been relentlessly trying to restore faith in rule of law among forty thousand home buyers where the executive in all its power and vacuous announcements have failed miserably. The Court had appointed a Receiver for the case and tied up funds from Banks and asked the National Building Construction Corporation to complete the projects. The Amrapali promoters are cooling their heels in jail for the past several months and their properties are under auction.

The question before the country is why the Executive repeatedly fails in its duty and why the judiciary had to step in? The answer lies in the lopsided democracy we follow wherein only vote fetching and government formation is the only priority of political leaders and public interest takes back seat. Because of this, the remits of the judiciary are being redefined with great public support.

There are several books written by retired civil servants on the contribution of civil services and the need for reforms. Most of the books barring a few are at best statement in self-praise, in the praise of their service and personal glorification. After independence, two administrative reforms commission were set up and voluminous reports had been submitted by them for action. The government, however, have not taken any action on these reports because of the deeply entrenched interests of the bureaucracy and primarily of the IAS. There is an Administrative Reform Department in the Central Government which is responsible for implementing the reports of these commissions. However, nothing substantial happens primarily because of two reasons. First, the constitution of the commission is itself full of those who will never recommend the fundamental changes in the structure of civil services and guard their hold over the administration. Secondly, there is nothing in these reports for bringing major changes to be initiated. Most of the recommendations are flippant and even if some are there to be acted upon for better efficiency are killed in the red tapes and buried in records. This author had after more than 37 years of experience in diverse fields as an Indian Forest Service officer have realized that there are so many hidden aspects of Indian civil services which are not known to the public and unless we mobilize the public, media and political leadership the *status quoist* will continue to neglect the needs for reforms. The present system of governance is so much symbiotic that a small group of political masters and civil servants serve each other's interest, based on *quid pro quo.* In every department, there is a coterie of few people. Today, there is a need to have a new civil service structure that is futuristic, transparent, accountable, people-oriented, fair and respected by the masses. The author, therefore, based on his personal experience brings to the notice of people how the civil servants work and why the reforms are essentially needed.

Civil Services and the Executive

Today, the countrymen often ask if the civil service is a part of the Executive organ of the government. The Constitution under Article 311 gives protection to the civil services in the country both under the Central as well as State governments; while Article 312 empowers the government to create All India Services. However, going by the Constitutional provisions they do not derive any *de jure* authority which the executive or judiciary does in any constitutional framework in democratic governments, though they had over the years accumulated enormous clout, influence and defacto powers under delegation by the elected executives mostly by the Ministers and the Cabinet. Being the permanent organ of the government, they advise the public representatives who are not permanent. But yet their authority is not the authority conferred on them by the sovereign will of the people. The public representatives are accountable to their voters while the civil servants are accountable to the government since civil servants are supposed to implement the policy of the government. They cannot be blamed by people for failures of the policy unless they are held responsible for deviating or sabotaging the policy. The responsible government to deliver its policies require a competent, accountable and independent civil service staffed by persons capable of advising successive ministers based on their long administrative experience and who are a permanent part of the system. In today's scenario it boils down to the question of lack accountability for their actions though it exist on paper but practically non-existent.

It would be interesting to note how the All India Services were made part of the constitution. The experience of then Prime Minister Jawaharlal Lal Nehru and the majority of members were very bitter about Indian Civil Service (ICS) and Indian Police (IP). Nehru felt the ICS and IP though consisted of Indians as well as European, were more loyal to the British and, therefore, the first draft of the constitution did not have any provision for the All India Services (AIS). Jawaharlal Nehru felt that the Indian component of these services tried to prove themselves more loyal than the king and argued that none of the political leaders had sympathy for them. The ICS and Indian Police according to them were though efficient and competent but their loyalties were with the British Crown. All along the course of freedom struggle the role of these All India Services had been to be indifferent to the freedom movement and many a time, this machinery was used by the British to suppress the freedom struggle and freedom fighters had suffered at the hands of the ICS and the Indian Police.

It was, however, on the insistence of Home Minister Sardar Patel that the constitution recognized the civil services as its part. He wrote a letter on 27th April 1948 to the Prime Minister and stressed the need for civil service more in a democracy than in an autocratic rule. He wrote in his letter to Nehru: *"I need hardly emphasize that an efficient, disciplined and contented service, assured of its prospects as a result of diligent and honest work, and is a sine qua non of sound administration under a democratic regime even more than under an authoritarian rule. The service must be above party and we should ensure that political considerations either in its recruitment or in its discipline and control are reduced to the minimum, if not eliminated. In an All India Service, it is obvious; recruitment discipline and control, etc. have to be tackled on a basis of uniformity and under the direction of the Central Government, which is the recruiting agency. You will recall that all these matters have been settled at a conference of Prime Ministers convened in 1946 and the details have been settled by correspondence with Provincial Governments. No criticism, therefore, can be made that either in the formation of these Services or in the preparation of necessary Rules and Regulations Provincial susceptibilities and views find no place. Indeed, there was a remarkable unanimity between the views of the Provincial Governments and those of the Central Government throughout on these questions. Any pricking of the conscience on the score of provincial autonomy or on the need for sustaining the prestige and powers of provincial Ministers is, therefore, out of place"* (B. Shiva Rao, The Framing of India's Constitution, Select Documents, Volume 4, Universal Law Publishing Co. Private Limited, Delhi, Pages: 332-333.).

But while the matter came up for discussion in the constitutional assembly no one (including Prime Minister Nehru) except BR Ambedkar, the Law Minister supported this as they did not want an independent civil service. To this Sardar Patel thundered to resign and said without independent All India Services the solidarity and unity of the country cannot be maintained. It would be interesting to quote his speech" *"As a man of experience I tell you, do not quarrel with the instruments with which you want to work" he said. "It is a bad workman who quarrels with his instruments. Take work from them. Every man wants some sort of encouragement. Nobody wants to put in work when every day he is criticized and ridiculed in public. So once for all, you decide whether you want this service or not. If you had done with it and decide not to have this service at all, I will take the services with me and go".* (From a lecture by LP Singh in South Gujarat University on 15th December 1986)There upon, Pandit Nehru melted down and the other members of Constituent Assembly finally agreed to accord Constitutional status to these Services at its meeting held on April 30, 1948, and made provision in part 14 of the Constitution of India with regards to Services under Union and Sates and the All India Services. The civil servants of all hues must be told to remember these words of a great visionary leader who had the vision and almost staked his job for making the civil services a part of the constitution and gave them constitutional status. This status impinges upon the civil servants a responsibility to act as per the spirit of constitutional norms to be independent, neutral and fair.

From the debates in the constitutional assembly, it is clear that the constitutional status given to the All India Services was done under tremendous pressure from Sardar Patel supported by Dr B. R. Ambedkar against the wishes of a majority of the members of the Constituent

Assembly. With great difficulty, Sardar Patel could convince the Constituent Assembly in getting the All India Services incorporated in Part-XIV of the Constitution of India. However, the nitty-gritty of their control, manner of working and their relationships with political masters and accountability etc was left to the future parliamentarians. Had Sardar Patel lived for few more years he would have worked for a new work framework/structure for civil services to work efficiently, honestly and independently and would have made it part of the constitution. But soon after the politicians in power developed a cosy relationship with civil servants and became experts in using them for their self-interests and in turn the powerful civil servants set an example for their juniors. Soon a culture of 'you scrap my back, I will scrap your back' took over the lofty ideals of objectives of governance. The politicians, therefore, became used to control over the civil services and government machinery.

The civil services especially the AIS were created to function as an organic link between the Centreand the States to safeguard the unity of the country and to act independently in the discharge of their duties while serving the political masters. Considering the need for safeguarding our environment, a third AIS was created in the form of the Indian Forest Service (IFS) in 1966. It was in fact a revival of the old British time Indian Forest Service the recruitments for which was stopped after 1932 due to imminent transfer of subject 'Forest' to Provincial list after the implementation of Government of India Act 1935. Now the question is what next after safeguarding the national solidarity and unity after 70 years of independence. Sardar Patel's emotional speech clinched the deal for All India Services and Union and State Civil services under Part-XIV-Article 310 to 313. To insulate them from undue political interference, the constitution made provisions for an independent body for their recruitment in the form of Union and State Public Service Commission. The AIS has gradually assumed developmental responsibility. But the question is, are civil servants serving the people with commitment, honestly and efficiently? Are they behaving as servants of the people or masters of their destiny? Is there a need for reviewing the structure of civil services in India if yes in what manner? How are the institutions of UPSC and State Public Service Commission's working and discharging their duties?

We need to examine these issues because the experience shows that gradually almost all institutions of the country have undergone changes some with good results but many have been deteriorated and misused by the individuals in a position of power. These will be examined by the author in the form of case studies. The case studies will throw light on how the civil servants are working in this country and how they are being abused and, in the process, a nexus works to the detriment of public interest but it works fine for the selfish interests of politicians and the civil servants. They are increasingly being joined by a few in the judiciary for the post-retirement sinecure.

Some of the best examples of downfalls in the quality of officers in civil services can be seen from the way a select few posts like Cabinet Secretary are chosen for a fixed tenure beyond retirement age and granted repeated extension. Such extensions and appointment of civil servants beyond retirement may be justified only in case of Prime Minister's office due to strategic reasons considering the vastness of the problems the Prime Minister has to face in India and the need for suitable reliable assistance or in cases of national emergencies like wars, pandemics diseases and natural disasters and not as a routine matter. It may be a good argument for having a minimum tenure of two or three years for the senior posts like secretaries but it should be across the board and not for posts like home and defence Secretary or Cabinet Secretary alone and a few IPS cadre posts. The repeated extension of chosen few also reflects that no one is suitable down the line to hold these posts based on their seniority and merit. It one way or the other degrades other similar rank posts and gradually may give a serious blow to the morale of civil servants as it gives undue advantage to the extra smart lobbyist to scamper through to top posts. However, there is another view that such appointments at senior Secretary level posts for the best performers among their peers are necessary to promote efficiency in administration. I would like to fully support this view provided there is a fair and transparent mechanism is establishment to do this exercise so that the non-performers are weeded out and outstanding performers are rewarded.

More often than not, political parties are openly taking political advantage by using the civil servants especially in the States to meet their political ends. Such tendencies are thus a violation of high moral and constitutional democratic values and now after 70 years, we must think of when and how to reverse the trend. It is considered necessary also as few people argue that not only bureaucracy but the whole gamut of executive apparatus should be considered for reforms because the way nepotism is being openly resorted to in the name of democracy and people's will, nothing substantial would be changed by simply changing the formats of bureaucracy. No one could imagine even 35 years ago that a father while occupying the post of Chief Minister would have thought of giving his young son a ticket to fight the election and appointing him as the Cabinet Minister in his own Cabinet; the way it has been done in one State last year. The Atal Bihari Vajpayee led NDA Government had appointed a Constitutional review panel with great fanfare but it proved to be a non-starter due to the prevalent political climate in the country and stiff opposition from the entrenched political interests. The present government has the clear mandate to make positive changes and the intention of the Prime Minister is forthright on this.

How to Ruin Institutions: A Case Study

04

The Indian Council of Forestry Research and Education (ICFRE) is the apex body looking after forestry research and education in the country. One of its institutions and its predecessor, the Forest Research Institute and Colleges (FRI & Colleges), is responsible for introducing scientific management of forests in India as it developed all the technologies of managing the natural forests, use of the timber and minor forest produce and, raising nurseries and plantations techniques for umpteen numbers of species in the country including the agro forestry/farm forestry and social forestry. Today most of our river catchments and watersheds are viable, well protected and providing water and food security for a population of 139 billion and still growing. The FRI was the fountainhead of forestry research in the entire tropical world during British time. It rooted the forest management ethos deeply in India, guided its spread in other parts of the British Empire and also helped in the creation of the American Forest Service. It acquired a massive reputation in entire Asia for its quality of scientific work and experience. In the early 1960s, it was given the task to set up Malaysian Forest Research Institute which today is a leading forestry research institution in Asia.

The narration here will lead the reader to an untold story of how the systems of governance in the country are being sabotaged by bureaucracy and neglect by political masters. It would be appropriate to discuss the history of the creation of the Indian Council of Forestry Research and Education before we discuss how far it has achieved or failed in its mission. The author was its head from May 2011 to June 2013 and occupied the post of Director-General of ICFRE and Chancellor of FRI University (a post equivalent to Secretary to the government of India in pay scales). ICFRE has around 12 Additional Secretary level and more than 45 Joint Secretary level officers and Scientists guiding its work.

The people today must know how the FRI became capable and famous in the British Empire in promoting scientific forest management. During the early days, the avowed purpose of forest management was to conserve soil and water conservation and to promote agriculture in the Indian sub-continent and also to garner revenue. British realized that to exploit the rich forest resources, counter frequent famines and ensure water security for the people it would be necessary to protect and conserve the forests in the catchments of more than 450 rivers and rivulets in the country. They recruited trained officers and appointed them into the forest service. A trained Botanist Dietrich Brandish was appointed in 1864 as the first Inspector-General of Forests and thus the journey of Indian Forest Departments started in India. Brandish while travelling to Burma on appointment as Conservator of forests. He brought two trained German foresters Schlich and Ribbentrop to India and both succeeded him (first Schlich (from 1881 to 1884) and after him Ribbentrop (from 1884 to 1889) as Inspector General of Forests. These three Germans foresters laid down the foundation of forest management in India during their 25 years of combined tenure. It is on his insistence that equal to two-third of forests declared as reserved forests were retained as a buffer for the use of villagers. These early foresters founded the department all over India and a systematic scientifically trained and well-equipped organization came into existence.

The Forest Research Institute (FRI) was set up in 1906 at Dehradun to provide scientific backup to forest managers in the field through research work. In 1920, the Government of India decided that the IFS Probationers may be trained at the Forest Research Institute at Dehradun. The training started in India in the year 1926 and FRI was renamed FRI & Colleges. The present iconic building of FRI was inaugurated in 1929. After independence, the working of FRI was reviewed from time to time by several expert committees (Sir Harry G. Champion in 1956; Prof MS Thacker the then Member Planning Commission in 1964; FAO Advisory Mission led by EP Cliff and JD Ovington in 1977; Task Force headed by Dr TN Khoshoo in 1981 and finally by a Panel led by Dr Hari Narain in 1982). All these reports argued for granting functional and administrative freedom to FRI so that it can equip itself to solve the emerging problems of forest conservation in India.

But the establishment of the Ministry of Agriculture and Cooperation (with which the Forestry wing was attached up to 1985) and the forestry wing headed by the Inspector-General of Forests and ex-officio Additional Secretary did not give much credence to these reports and nothing happened as it continued to be short of scientific manpower and leadership except for a brief period when Mr KM Tewari was the President of the FRI during the early eighties. He gave purposeful direction and leadership to it.

Then in 1985, when the Department of Environment and Forest came into existence and Mr TN Seshan joined as Secretary. A dynamic and visionary officer of IAS (known more for his overbearing way of doing things- perhaps he learnt how to move the musty rusty labyrinth of bureaucracy to work) he set himself into reforming the newly carved out offices of Environment and Forest Ministry. Under his roving eyes, he bulldozed the naysayers and the government of India after carefully analysing the recommendations of various committees decided to reorganize the FRI. It separated the training of IFS officers and other ranks from Research and thus from FRI. The FRI was thus reorganized in January 1986 through a government notification for better planning, execution and monitoring of forestry research in the country and created a pan Indian research infrastructure in the country for meeting future goals. The training was assigned by upgrading the Indian Forest College to the National Academy of Forests (now known as IGNFGA). The President FRI was re-designated as DG ICFRE and FRI became part of the Indian Council of Forestry Research and Education. The Council now today has a network of nine Institutes in different agro-climatic conditions of the country i.e., at Dehradun, Shimla, Ranchi, Jabalpur, Jodhpur, Jorhat, Bangaluru, Coimbatore, Hyderabad (this Centrewas upgraded by me to the level of Institute of Bio-diversity in 2012) and three research Centres at Allahabad, Chindwara, Mizoram and Agartala. Mr TN Seshan moved out to other Ministries soon after in 1988 and could not grant it autonomy as decided by the government till 1990 when after so many hiccups the cabinet approved to grant it autonomous status. He, however, must be credited for bringing into existence the regional offices of the Ministry to monitor the implementation of the Forest Conservation Act 1980 and the Environmental Protection Act 1986. These regional offices are today the greatest strength of the Ministry and act as field arms and watchdogs of the Ministry. It along with Forest Conservation Act 1980 and Environmental Protection Act

1986 is considered one of the biggest positive reforms in the field of Environment and Forest governance since independence.

The agenda of revisiting the reorganization of FRI & Colleges as per the 1986 resolution of the government was moving at snail's pace and both IAS and IFS officers sitting in Ministry were weighing how not to let loose the control over this organization. However, because of the pressure of imminent scientists like MS Swaminathan and some scientists and foresters, the Ministry ultimately agreed to bring in a cabinet note. Thus, in a cabinet note dated September 5, 1990, it was proposed to grant it full autonomy for effective functioning in achieving its mandate on the pattern of Indian Council of Agricultural Research (ICAR) and Council of Scientific and Industrial Research (CSIR) and thus Government of India vide F.No 1-8/89-RT dated 22.06.1990 conveyed the approval of Union Cabinet declaring ICFRE as an autonomous body. The cabinet mentioned the pattern of CSIR and ICAR, however, the Ministry cleverly side-tracked the issue of full genuine autonomy while communicating the cabinet decision and skirted the issue of creation of a Department of Forestry Research on the pattern of ICAR and CSIR. The officers who were in ICFRE's helm of affairs at that time in the euphoria of getting autonomy forgot how the entire organization was fooled by granting a truncated autonomy which demolished the existing government structure and converted a world heritage institution into a society under the Societies Act of 1860. Immediately after the creation of ICFRE as an autonomous body, a second cabinet note should have been initiated by the ICFRE to the Ministry and most probably it could have been accomplished if piloted properly. It is also a fact that during that time granting autonomy to get rid of red tapes in the government was a fashion among the heads of departments of such institutions. In one sense, it became a win-win situation for both the heads of the institution (for getting rid of rushing to Ministry for small things) and for the Ministry official to get unwritten perks like car etc from the autonomous bodies and at the same time, keeping the organization under their thumbs. With this truncated autonomy, in a nutshell, the powers of spending money by ICFRE without approaching the Ministry increased (it is another matter that the institutions were then slowly choked off government funds after the World Bank project). It, however, opened doors for getting international funding and thus the DG became a little more independent in taking decisions and for lining up funds from external sources but he could still not plan anything without keeping even the junior-most officials of the Ministry into the loop.

The ICFRE, however, during this period after months of haggling got a dynamic DG in Dr DN Tewari who had wide-ranging experience in government of Madhya Pradesh, Central Secretariat and in the academics as Vice-Chancellor of Bilaspur University. He realized the limitations in infrastructural institutional deficiencies' in ICFRE and started to focus his energy on taking advantage of its being an autonomous institution and eligible for World Bank funding (The World Bank was insisting for long that for funding the institution should have autonomy). A project proposal for creating ICFRE infrastructure was approved by the world through a project on forestry research, extension and education which created the much-needed infrastructure for its newly-established institutes and the exposure visits of scientists to international institutions as also some technical programmes on tree improvements. Dr Tewari managed to get University Grant Commission approval under section 3 of the UGC Act to declare FRI as a Deemed University. The University started the MSc courses in four disciplines of forestry and environmental subjects and PhD courses. This was a landmark achievement and could be done by Dr Tewari due to his tenacity and networking skills, despite the several hurdles created by the bureaucracy. After his retirement, the Ministry ensured to post only those officers who could be tamed and that too only after keeping the organization headless for a pretty long time in between (when I was appointed DG in 2011, I found that since its creation 24 years ago the post of DG was kept vacant for more than 8 years). While working in the Ministry for long eight years I could very well understand the type of politics this Ministry is ridden with and why such institutions are stagnating and the sector is not able to show results to the extent it should have.

How I Landed Up as DG ICFRE

In the meanwhile, by a quirk of fate, a well-qualified visionary Minister in Mr Jairam Ramesh was appointed as Minister of Environment and Forests after the 2009 elections. Mr Jairam Ramesh soon after taking over visited the ICFRE several times and realised what ails it and ICFRE's capacity to improve the forestry and environment sector. So, he set his eyes to reform it. As destiny would have it, I became its DG ICFRE in May 2011, selected by a committee headed by none other than Dr MS Swaminathan the world-famous agriculture scientist.

But before I write how it could happen, it is necessary to write how the IAS and a few IFS officers joined hand and tried all nefarious tricks in the world to stop my selection twice. The main reason for opposing me was my strong professional background, clear vision for the sector and an 'informal' decision among the bureaucracy was taken after I left the Ministry in June 2004 to never allow 'my type' anywhere near the Ministry as I was named as 'change monger' since in 8 years in the Ministry I created several new schemes and changes by deft handling which were not liked by many senior officers including the Secretaries. As I was already working in the Planning Commission at the Additional Secretary level in the National Rainfed Area Authority, I was not very keen to move to Dehradun but was prompted by many forest officers to apply for the post. The other reason for my applying was to fulfil my professional desire of revisiting the Forest Types of India which Champion and Seth had stressed while publishing the revised forest types of India in 1968 to see their present status. A Department of Personnel and Training (DoPT) approved search committee was set up by the Ministry headed by Dr DN Tewari former Member Planning Commission and consisted of other regular members. The committee after taking interviews of candidates selected two candidates me and Mr Ashwini Kumar (who later on became DG ICFRE after me and after two DG Forests of the Ministry held the charge for more than a year). However, when the minutes were written the then Secretary plotted to ease me out and engineered a letter from Secretary Science and Technology (who had earlier signed the minutes) that he wanted to add a third candidate in the Panel. After getting the letter from Secretary Science and Technology, the Secretary wrote a note to the Minister to accept his nominee also in the panel. He planned to then pull wires in the Department of Personnel and Training (DoPT), Cabinet Secretariat and Prime Minister Office (PMO) to get his nominee appointed. The Minister Mr Jai Ram Ramesh accepted the proposal of Secretary and included the name suggested by him in the Panel. He at the same time saw through the game as after visiting the FRI campus several times was determined to post a professional with proven credentials. He asked for the Bio-data (CVs) of all the three candidates and after perusal of the CVs in his detailed speaking order only recommended my name to the Appointment Committee of the Cabinet (ACC) for appointment as DG ICFRE and Chancellor FRI University based on my credentials. The proposal was sent to the Appointment Committee of Cabinet (ACC) which is chaired by the Prime Minister. Now the theatre of conspiracy to undo the selection begins and shifted to DoPT (DoPT's unwritten mandate is to guard IAS supremacy in governance and, in this process, they create imaginary ghosts and threats to the system. It is said about the DoPT that it operates on the principle "you show me the face I will show you the rule"). The candidate Secretary wanted to appoint got a letter written from a member of Rajya Sabha to the DoPT Minister and asked for stalling the process. The Secretary also prompted one of the candidates who appeared in the interview to write to DoPT questioning his omission. It was a well-planned and well-orchestrated plan to make the selection process controversial and to be fit to be rejected. The stage was thus set for rejection. The DoPT proposal in this direction was sent to ACC and PMO did oblige and the proposal came back with a terse comment to *redo the entire processes* after sitting over the proposal for six months. One of the issues for the country's democratic rulers for reforms should be to unshackle the country's appointment process from the cesspool of DoPT's biased stranglehold. Several IAS officers are also the victim of DoPT's coterie (part of Lutyen's Delhi group) and its unrestrained, unaccountable and arbitrary style of functioning.

Once the proposal came back after several months the Minister Mr Jairam Ramesh constituted yet another search committee headed by Dr

MS Swaminathan long with Dr Kasturiranjan, Member of Planning Commission and renowned space scientist and other usual members (Secretaries of Environment, DoPT, Science and Technology and the Director-General of Forests). By this time the Secretary had retired and Dr TT Chatterji an IAS officer of Andhra Pradesh Cadre had joined as Secretary in the Environment Ministry. Dr Chatterji being a straightforward fair-minded well-read environmentalist infused fresh air of fairness in the Ministry. This Committee interviewed several candidates and unanimously recommended only my name for appointment as DG ICFRE. The Ministry initiated the proposal for ACC approval in February 2011. Now the DoPT and Cabinet Secretariat had no other option but to consider the proposal as the panel contained only one name. In the meanwhile, I had taken disciplinary action against one notorious Under Secretary of my office in the National Rainfed Area Authority (NRAA) who was found indulging in corruption and was extorting money from the infrastructure and man power service providers. This Under Secretary was called by few officers of the Ministry and promised from top levels of bureaucracy that he will be let off from the charges if he writes against me to challenge the award of Commonwealth Forestry Association (CFA) the United Kingdom sponsored 'Queens Award' for Forestry. (CFA is an affiliate organization of the Commonwealth Secretariat and India is a member). This Under Secretary obliging immediately wrote to Prime Minister, Forest Minister, Planning Commission, Cabinet Secretary, DoPT and all-over Central Secretariat that I am a British agent as I have got the Queen's Award for forestry without permission of the government. This ludicrous allegation was lapped up by the DoPT and Cabinet Secretariat. The Minister Mr Jai Ram Ramesh called me and inquired about these allegations. I showed him all communications between CFA and Secretary Environment and Forest, DG Forests etc. I also showed him papers of government approval like granting me political clearance and official Passport for travelling to receive the Award in 2001 in the IUFRO World Congress in Malaysia (though a government order itself had Stated in a notification that international prizes in scientific fields from foreign countries can be accepted without approval of the government). Thankfully, a well-meaning Joint Secretary from IFS of the Environment Ministry wrote to me and asked for submitting all the records on the Queen's Award. In my reply to the Joint Secretary of the Ministry I submitted the full records of the communication from the Commonwealth Forestry Association intimating the Secretary of the Ministry about the conferment of the award and the Ministry then intimating me and allowing me to travel abroad to receive the award at Kualalumpur in Malaysia in 2001 world IUFRO Congress.

Then suddenly appeared a retired forest officer of Tripura cadre into the scene who was charge-sheeted by the State government based on my report of 1994 'Jampui' timber scam in which as Conservator of Forest he was found involved in illicit felling of trees and creating a scam of more than Rs 280 crore in 1991 to 1992. The scam was exposed by the Indian Express in its front-page report. To escape from the charges, he filed an FIR against some IAS and IFS officers including me which were inquired into by police and found baseless. He was contacted from the top and (through a candidate who lost in the interview for DG's post) asked to write a letter to DoPT and Cabinet Secretary that an FIR is pending against him. He duly obliged and wrote but, in the meanwhile, due to unreasonable delay of four months the Minister Mr Jai Ram Ramesh and sensing the sinister game of wires being pulled by hidden hands in the PMO and Cabinet Secretariat he protested to the Cabinet Secretary and met the Prime Minister on this deliberate attempt to second-time foil the selection process. He got the file cleared from ACC and ultimately willy-nilly I was appointed as the DG ICFRE on 19th May 2011.I was however, surprised to see the appointment order only for two years as instead of giving me a full tenure as per rule for the Secretary level post for the All India Service officers, in contravention of this rule, I was given only 2-year tenure to keep me on tenterhooks. In the meanwhile, the Tripura police intimated that the FIR has been closed a few years back and no truth was found in the complaint.

After joining as DG ICFRE on 20th May when I met Mr Jairam Ramesh, he candidly told me that "your service did not select you and I had to tell the Prime Minister whose officers were sitting on the proposal and deeply involved in the conspiracy to derail the selection done by none other than Dr MS Swaminathan led committee and only after I spoke with the Prime Minister your file for the appointment was cleared. Please lead the organization well and sort out the mess created by some people who were heading it for last few years". Yet again later after a few months one disgruntled forest officer who missed being selected funded the Under Secretary to file a case against my selection in the Delhi High Court. The case was dismissed after the court examined the search committee minutes and other records and verbally observed during the hearing that "an eminent panel has selected an eminent person". The Court was about to fine the applicant but he was allowed to withdraw the case on an unconditional apology and the case was thus dismissed.

An Attempt to Achieve the Mandate of Creation of ICFRE

Mr Jai Ram Ramesh after taking over as Minister had comprehensively examined the functioning of ICFRE and wanted me to complete the unfinished agenda of converting it into a Department and to bring a massive thrust in its strategy so that it gains its lost position as a world-recognized institution and solve the emerging problems in the field of forest and environment; as potential exists but vision is lacking and is languishing in incompetence and so many avoidable conflicts. He had asked me to set the institution to correct trajectory and to solve all problems created by the previous incumbent Deputy Director General who held the current duty charge as DG. He clearly said that the ICFRE should be converted as Department of Forestry Research as indicated in the 1990 Cabinet decision and asked me to submit the proposal. I was preparing for a presentation before him and a group of expert-led by Dr MS Swaminathan who had a role in the creation of ICFRE but suddenly on August 30, 2011, Mr Jai Ram Ramesh was transferred from the Ministry. Mr Jai Ram Ramesh had created a hornet's nest as an activist Environment Minister which ruffled the feathers of those seeking easy environmental and forests clearances and the bureaucrats in the Ministry also found his intellect a problem to push him to their biased way of decisions. He was promoted as Cabinet Minister and transferred out of Environment and Forest Ministry to the Rural Development Ministry.

After some time, however, after discussing the matter with Secretary and the DG forests, I submitted the Cabinet note to the Ministry and proposed *'interalia'* creation of a Department of Forestry Research to realize the original idea of creation of the Council and to meet emerging needs of the sector and, in fulfilling the 1990 Cabinet decision with a proposal to shift the Headquarter of ICFRE from Dehradun to Delhi as there was no logic of having it in FRI premises in a corner of the country when we have institutes all over India. For this, I had already got the approval of the UP-forest department as well as Minister Ms Jayanthi Natrajan for the transfer of 25 acres of forest land in Noida. But this proposal was buried in the files of the Ministry and a fresh bid started to oust me as a concerted attempt was made to create a wedge between me and the Minister by few IAS and IFS officers. The matter regarding an attempt to provide autonomy as per the previous decision of the cabinet is being discussed in a separate chapter.

At the ICFRE I had initiated drastic changes swiftly and worked to alleviate its image as a premium institution outside the country. Before my joining the institution was in disarray, the post of DG ICFRE was as usual lying vacant for more than one and half years. One DDG was holding an additional charge for more than a year, was abruptly removed by the Minister for gross mishandling the institutions in January 2011 for harassing the scientists and officers including other serious misuses of power and corruption. There was, therefore, a lot of mistrust in the organization between the management and the employees. I soon after joining purged the nefarious personal staff from the DG's office as they were creating a lot of misunderstanding and behaving super DGs. After joining I immediately visited all the Institutions and took a review of activities and noted the grievances of scientists, technical and other staff. I then decided all pending matters strictly on merit and fairly and transparently. One such matter I had to face related to the withdrawal of 'Grace' for PhD degree of one of its former DDG who working as in-charge Vice-Chancellor of the FRI Deemed University (during his earlier stint in the FRI), appointed examiner for examination of his thesis, changed the examiner mid-course who adversely commented on the quality of research. He as Vice-Chancellor approved his PhD degree in violation of all standards of fair play and morality. A UGC sponsored inquiry materialised after I joined. The Vice-Chancellor and Director FRI proposed his case to be put up before the University's Board of Management. The Board of Management of the Deemed University meeting is chaired by DG as Chancellor of the FRI deemed University. I as Chancellor based on the decision of the Board of Management has no alternative but to agree to the recommendations to withdraw the grace for his PhD degree. However, as Chancellor, I wanted to give him a chance to defend the thesis. I promised him a fair decision when he approached me and requested to reconsider the decision of the Board. I asked the Registrar to issue him a notice and put up his defence Statement immediately on the decision taken by the Board of Management. But instead of replying to the notice, he went back to his State (as after a few days of my joining I relieved him on his request for premature repatriation) and foolishly filed a case in Madras High Court against the notice issued to him. The Madras High Court during the hearing was surprised to notice that a Vice-Chancellor has approved his PhD degree, dismissed his petition and as such the case was also beyond jurisdiction. He then filed a case in the Uttarakhand High Court. It has been learnt now that after eight years the Uttarakhand High Court suddenly ordered that without going into the merit of the case allowed his PhD degree with the direction that the ICFRE can order a fresh inquiry into it. It is not understood why the High Court did not decide on the merit of the cased and how it suddenly decided the case and allowed the petitioner conditional relief that too after sitting for eight years. It raises the question mark on how sometimes justice is delayed and how the judiciary is functioning. Now the matter is again hanging fire before the Board of Management of the Deemed University. If this officer had not filed the writ in Madras High Court perhaps, I would have certainly found a way out to spare this 'ignominy' to him if his explanation had substance by again re-examining his degree by appointing fresh examiners. On re-examination the thesis could be modified. In fact it could have been done much earlier. But after he went to the court the Chancellor of the University had no alternative but to withdraw the degree soon after the court dismissed the writ to implement the Board's decision. This decision also gave a clear signal to one and all that the University will not spare anyone if found indulging in malpractices and is one of the unique instances in the annals of higher education.

My Two Years Tenure as DG ICFRE

I would like to narrate an incident immediately after taking over as Director-General of the Indian Council of Forestry Research and Education (ICFRE) and Chancellor of FRI University in May 2011, I went to meet a senior IAS officer working as Advisor Environment and Forests in the Planning Commission in June 2011. He told me that the reason for poor funding for ICFRE is a strong impression in the Planning Commission that ICFRE has not done anything good in the field of forest conservation. He said it is better ICFRE prepares a presentation on the work done by the FRI and ICFRE over the years to educate the officers in corridors of power. Though I strongly refuted the allegation and told it is an insult to those foresters and scientists who had done great work in the past and present, I was not surprised by this Statement as during my eight years of stint in Delhi in the Ministry of Environment and Forests, I had noticed that there was a calibrated gradual choking of funds for the forestry wing and its institutions by the Budget division of the Environment Ministry controlled by the IAS officers. In this task, they were helped by all the Planning Commission Advisors and smaller cronies in the commission. From 1997 to the early 2000s, the Forestry Wing of the Environment and Forest Ministry used to get 55% of the share of Ministry and Environment Wing's share would be around 45%. By the time I left the Ministry in 2004, the share became less and finally, when I left the ICFRE in 2013, the share of the forestry wing was even lower than 45% of the total budget.

So, after returning to Dehradun, I called a meeting of all the senior scientists and we decided to bring out a solid publication giving details of the technologies developed by the ICFRE and the FRI (and their application in the field) which was the fountainhead of forestry in India and elsewhere in the British Empire. I involved myself in collecting material, monitoring and editing the material and in the next six months before the end of the year 2011, we published an 800 pages Book ***"ICFRE in the service of***

Nation" in which we gave in comprehensive details on the technologies developed and their applications in the field. I presented the book to the Finance Secretary and all other important officers of government including the Planning Commission Advisors and officials. I also gave a presentation in the Planning Commission. However, though everyone I presented the book lauded the attempts but barring a few exceptions, very few came up to assist the ICFRE and the forestry sector in real terms but it did keep their mouth shut during my tenure.

One of the reasons for me to run around the corridors of powers was to get through the road block created by the bureaucracy on the 'one-time grant' of Rs 100 crore announced by the then Finance Minister Mr Pranab Mukherji in his budget speech of 2009. Strangely enough, the release of this amount was held up for almost 4 years and trapped in the internal bureaucratic politicking of the Environment Ministry in tandem with support from the Finance Ministry and the Financial Advisor of the Environment Ministry. Bureaucracy blatantly tried to dishonour the budget passed by the Parliament and the Director-General of Forests, the head of forests service could do nothing on this. The one-time grant was sanctioned due to the efforts of Mr Jairam Ramesh who was the only powerful, dynamic, knowledgeable and ebullient Environment Ministers this Ministry got since its creation. Mr Jairam who had been in the Planning Commission previously had the experience of handling the Bio-diversity in Karnataka State and was aware of the history of forest management in India. He soon after taking over as Environment and Forest Minister in 2009 visited ICFRE and FRI several times. He after visiting ICFRE convinced the Finance Minister to sanction a one-time grant of Rs 100 crore for developing the modern infrastructure for forestry research and extension. The bureaucracy, however, had another plan to derail it and get it trapped in the red tape and Mr Ramesh for almost three years allowed the Ministry officials to play with this grant. He was also annoyed with the then top levels of ICFRE functionaries and did not intervene because the matter was not brought to his notice. Instead of releasing the money to an autonomous institution, the officers of the budget section and the Financial Advisor started rejecting the proposals on flimsy ground *suo motu* arrogating themselves the powers of technical evaluation. The procrastination in implementing the decisions of the Cabinet and the Parliament was a clear case of breach of privilege of Parliament but no one could take up the matter and the decision remained unimplemented. Over the years there may be many such incidents of bureaucrats trampling over the decisions of the parliament in other Ministries and now it has become a routine. On one occasion when I met with an Additional Secretary of the Finance Ministry in early 2012 on this issue he said "there is sufficient money with your Ministry to release this grant as around 800 crore earmarked for Externally Aided Projects (EAP) is available to be used in other activities as the EAP projects are based on utilization of the funds and there is no ground to block the whole sanctioned money for EAP for the whole year and every year due to this the Environment wing was surrendering a sizeable amount of the unutilized funds". It was thus a calculated attempt at the instance of the Environment Secretary to reduce the budget of the forestry wing so that the wing under performs in critical areas and to allow ICFRE to languish for funds and then make these institutions as symbols of foresters' incompetence. The Director-General of Forests who is the head of the forestry wings either never seriously takes up these issues or his advice is scornfully ignored. This was the result of uncalled for inter-services strife between the IAS and IFS and those who control the resource are the winner. Gradually the IFS officers posted in the Ministry have accepted this without a murmur. In the case of MoEF, the secretaries taciturn manner deal with such issues by first agreeing to a proposal that will benefit the forestry wing and then pull wires in the Planning Commission, DoPT, Cabinet Secretariat and the PMO with the help of their service colleagues by acting in tandem to derail the proposal initiated with their approval.

Had Mr Jairam Ramesh continued in the Ministry many such issues would have been solved. The fact is in less than three months of my joining Mr Jairam Ramesh was shifted out of the Ministry as Rural Development Minister. Notwithstanding the problems, soon after joining I quickly formed a cohesive team of scientists and IFS officers constituted a task force for revisiting the 'Forest Types of India' to assess the changes in the vegetation as the composition of Forest Types of India in the field have changed a lot since last revision in 1968. The revision was long overdue as Champion and Seth had called upon the future foresters to monitor the changes periodically. Forestry extension had always been the weakest link as most of the research work is seldom taken to the field immediately and therefore, a 'Direct to Consumer' programme was started with nodal officers appointed for each subject and institute for immediate transfer of technology on completion of research projects. This innovative scheme was an enormous success and faced problem of scaling up due to fund restrictions, it nevertheless worked very well in taking the research done to consumers.

I opened access to all staff even at the cost of a senior officer's complaint that they cannot discuss important matters as initially a lot of time was spent by me in interactions and meetings with aggrieved staff. Soon, a semblance of peaceful working returned. I instilled a sense of confidence, unity of purpose among the Scientists, IFS and other officers and staff in the ICFRE and its institutes and removed most of the grievances and pending matters of irritation to the individuals and groups in the ICFRE in 30 days. On review of research advisory committee meetings, we found that hardly 10 crore rupees are available for research work and what to say of innovations. I had then given a presentation to the Advisor of Planning Commission an IAS officer of clear conscience Mr Ranjan Chatterji, who told me that ICFRE will have to bring out a clear case of its contribution to convincing officers in the Planning Commission for better finances. As Stated, we, in the next six months released an 800-page book entitled "*ICFRE in the service of the nation*" giving in details the technologies developed by FRI and ICFRE for the last 100 years with their use and application in the field and industry. This book was widely circulated. I made a presentation before the Parliamentary Standing Committee on Science and Technology and stoutly defended the criticism that the forestry sector has not contributed much with solid facts and figures. It is the old foresters and scientists who developed all the technologies of growing trees in India and utilization of forest products and all other innovations in the sector. But it is also true that no organization can live on its laurels and ICFRE need full backing financially and politically to come up to the task of meeting the future challenges for which it was established. The Chairman of the Standing Committee Mr Subba Rama Reddy was very happy with our presentation and Stated that all kinds of criticism are fed to them against the forestry institutions and forest officers. He then wrote letters to the Planning Commission, Prime Minister and the Environment and Forest Minister defending the contribution of the forestry sector and requested the government to infuse more resources to the research institutions. We also calculated the contribution of the forests to the Gross Domestic Product (GDP) and published a paper in January 2013 fixing the tangible and intangible benefits from forests to more than 6.5 percent of the GDP. These figures were later on accepted by the Dr Kasturi Ranjan Member of the Planning Commission who informed about it in lecture to the Probationers of the IGNFA.

I had to deal with problem of non-release of Rs 100 crore special grant announced by the then Finance Minister as Stated in the preceding paras. Shri Pranab Mukherjee in his budget speech of 2009-10 had announced this grant. As Stated to scuttle it both the Finance and Environment Ministries kept on inventing one argument after another to delay the release. This is a glaring example of procrastination and a case in point how a few bureaucrats without any accountability effectively muzzled the Parliament approved budgeted scheme and tried to brazenly dishonour the mandate of Parliament for more than 3 three financial years; a classic case of undermining the decision of Parliament by the executive the other wing of the government. After so much running around, I could convince the finance Ministry to release the money but it came in trickle till I was DG. During the financial year 2012-13, in the fourth quarter, one impartial and honest IAS officer Mr Shasi Sekhar who was Additional Secretary and Financial Advisor in the Environment and Forest Ministry after realizing that some politics is going on in the Ministry despite the opposition by the politicking Secretary, sanctioned 30 crores to ICFRE (a part of the Rs 100 crore grant). His decision was backed up by the letters of Mr Subba Rama Reddy, Chairman of the Parliamentary Standing Committee, who also raised the issue of non-release of Rs 100 crore approved by the Parliament.

However, this Additional Secretary was promptly shifted from the Finance Division by the Secretary and ultimately posted elsewhere. The Secretary did not release the balance of 70 crores and kept on poisoning the air of the then naive Minister Jayanthi Natrajan against me as he was conspiring to ease me out with the help of DoPT, PMO and Cabinet Secretariat. This Secretary instigated the same Under Secretary who was used by DoPT to torpedo my selection first time in 2010 to write false complaints against me on one hand, and on the other hand, Ministry's Research and Training (RT) Division which looks after the administrative matters of the ICFRE informed that these are false malicious complaints without an iota of doubt was side-lined and Forest Establishment Division was asked to ignore the notes of RT Division. Strange but true and the match was fixed. What happened is discussed in another chapter.

The working of FRI Deemed University was streamlined and 10 MSc Fellowships were announced for the students of SAARC countries by the Prime Minister Dr Man Mohan Singh in 2011 in Thimpu, Bhutan, when the SAARC countries met after I proposed to Secretary External Affairs. Within a week, I got a call from one Joint Secretary of the External Affairs Ministry informing me that the proposal has been agreed upon and wanted details so that during the SAARC summit in Bhutan, Prime Minister can announce it. Had I routed the proposal through Ministry, it would have never seen the day.

The other significant decision during my tenure was to upgrade the Forest Research Centre, Hyderabad into a full-fledged Institute and rename it as the 'Institute of Forest Biodiversity'. Yet another major initiative was restructuring of the erstwhile Project Formulation Division into the Panchayats and Human Dimensions Division, for ensuring 'interface' with Panchayat Raj Institutions in the country with a special focus on developing a baseline of forest and non-forest land-use practices. I had specifically sanctioned six crores to FRI when I was in the National Rain Fed Area Authority of Planning Commission for resource inventory of forest and adjoining non-forest lands for better planning of rural developmental activities in around 170,000 forest fringe villages situated in 32 million ha of forests with special focus on land vested with tribal people under the Forest Right Act 2006 (one all India coordinated Project under Conservation of Biodiversity and enhancing livelihood options for Tribals and other Forest Fringe communities was launched). We organized the first-ever and last 'Forestry Congress' during November 2011 to chalk out a charter of forest and tribal development in the country with the involvement of 700 delegated which included village Panchayats and the Joint Forest Management Committee members also apart from national and international experts. I launched All India Coordinated Projects in different fields and one project on Non-Timber Forest Products (NTFPs) with 12 Agricultural Universities. An agreement was signed between ICFRE and ICAR for cooperation between Krishi Vegan Kendras and Van Vigyan Kendras for the transfer of technologies to farmers.

The national media during 2010-2011 was agog with Karnataka mining scam and the Supreme Court was hearing a Public Interest Litigation (PIL) on this. The ICFRE was assigned by the Supreme Court to conduct the Environmental Impact Analysis (EIA) of Bellary, Tumkur and Chitradurga Districts and a task force was constituted in August 2011 and the task force was headed by me as DG ICFRE. The report was submitted in record time and was very well received by the Apex Court. For this purpose and to augment the revenue I strengthened the Environment Management Division of ICFRE. ICFRE thus soon became a lead mining consultancy organization in the country under my direct supervision and immediately the Karnataka government awarded it 15 crores for preparing the Mines rehabilitation plans.

These are some of the steps taken by me in brief and for lack of space; it will not be possible to mention each one. However, the most satisfying was to solve the problems of the staff especially relating to medical reimbursements for retired and serving employees and the festering issue of pension sustainability fund beyond 2014. All cases of harassment were reversed, scientists were exposed to foreign visits (more than 54 Scientists were sent abroad within 2 years of my tenure) and their postings in ICFRE management as ADGs were started. The technical staffs, that are the backbone of all research support structure, were agitating since fifth pay commission for their salary structure. A proposal for the creation of

Technical Services on the lines of ICAR was initiated with the Finance Ministry and pursued vigorously. This proposal was approved after my departure and also the pension issue was settled as the government of India agreed to support the pension of all those who were working as Central Government Employees before the creation of ICFRE were. This was one of the unrelenting focuses during my tenure to ensure the safety of life of the people in their twilight years who had given their prime for the institution.

After sorting out all frictions the ICFRE for the first time started working as a team and had produced credible publications for the stakeholders apart from releasing important tree varieties for agro-forestry and block plantation. The important publication apart from the book "ICFRE in the Service of Nation" and release for 487 pages monumental work 'Revisiting Forest Types of India' included, "Vision document for the forestry research and education for the next 25 years", publication on "Voices from the field", "Forest Sector Report India- 2010", Coffee Table book on "Forest Biodiversity in India" "Forestry Research – ICFRE Supporting Rural & Tribal Livelihoods" and "Forestry Statistics India-2011" etc to mention a few. One of the long-pending matter hanging fire was the creation of a 'Foresters Memorial' and with mobilization of funds its foundation stone was laid by the then Governor of Uttarakhand Mr Aziz Qureshi in October 2012 near Brandish road and was nearing completion before I left. Considering that 25% of India's forests are in the north-eastern State (which is also one of the bio-diversity hot spots) and considering the forest-based livelihood, I established the "Centreof Forest based livelihood" at Agartala in Tripura. Being my home cadre, I signed a memorandum with the then Chief Secretary Dr SK Panda for transfer of a building in the forest training school complex, permission for carrying out trial plantation on forestland in collaboration with the State forest department, and assurance for granting accommodation for the Centrein charge. I posted a hard-working young scientist from the Jorhat Institute as Director of the Centreand also got one Assistant Conservator of Forests from the State on deputation. As of today, this Centre is the best functioning Centrewith credible evidence of success in its mandate. For better research work we appointed four Chairs of excellence in Forest Genetic Planting and Research Management Network Forest and Climate Change, Biodiversity and Ecology.

In recognition of my contribution during the 'World Forest Week Event' during COFO meet in September 2012, the Food and Agriculture Organization (FAO) of the United Nations invited me as DG ICFRE to Chair a session on "Strengthening forestry in land-use decisions". It was the first invitation to India in many years. The session was attended by Forest Ministers of 70 countries and heads of forest administration of more than 120 countries. I received a special appreciation letter from the FAO Director-General for crystallizing solid recommendation during the session based on Indian experiences. I was elected as Vice-Chair of the Asia-Pacific Association of Forestry Research Institutions (APFRI) during its sixth general assembly at Guangzhou, China on 31st August 2012. I was also elected as a Member of the 11-member Executive Body of the International Poplar Commission of the FAO (United Nations) in November 2012. The conference was organized successfully by the ICFRE in November 2012. These two last positions, however, were more of recognition of India than as an achievement of an individual.

So, in nutshell, during my tenure ICFRE worked achieved significant progress as a team and while emphasizing and enlarging the scope of scientific research on key theme areas, ICFRE also extended its reach by working on the livelihood of the tribal and rural people and created a separate Division for Interface with Panchayats and Tribal people and posted a separate Assistant Director-General Panchayats. To promote the forest-based handicrafts of tribal and rural people we opened a souvenir shop to provide marketing linkages through ladies' club self-help group and it worked very well as a lot of tourist visit to see the FRI building. We also provided two electric cars to the tourist for travel from the FRI gate to the main building on payment of a nominal fee to check pollution in the complex. One of the few last duties I performed was the release of the book '***Forest Type of India – Revisited***' on 17th May 2013, a monumental treatise on the existing conditions of forests. The creation of a Pensioners Health Welfare Scheme on the pattern of Central Government Health

Scheme which was one of the major demands of the employees in the Council.

My performance and popularity at ICFRE was an eyesore for the Ministry officials. They have already set a plan to evict me from the Institution by withdrawing my proposal of extension till superannuation. What role the Ministry played and how I tackled the white-collar crimes committed by these people with high sounding designations but behaving like 'Lilliputian's fuehrer' is discussed in other case studies on the Ministry of Environment and Forest. I had to leave the Council and Joined the State of Tripura on 18th July 2013. After my departure, a rollback of all good things started and harassment of officers and staff had begun. Unfortunately, at that time, the Minister who was sarcastically named for imposing 'a tax after her name' by the then opposition Prime Ministerial candidate for charging this tax for clearing the files for environmental and forestry clearances. This Minister came into conflict with me as she asked the Director of our Institute at Coimbatore to appoint 18 people to technical posts without any interview. She also asked me to appoint a fresh PhD candidate as a Scientist against a post for which nine years' experience was required and which was equivalent in ranks with the Deputy Secretary of the government of India. When she knew that Rs 30 crore had been sanctioned in March 2013, she sent a message through the Coimbatore Institute's Director to give an order of Rs 10 crore for the purchase of scientific instruments. These requests were politely declined. However, some of her requests like the distribution of high-quality seedling worth one crore of a tree species to cyclone-affected farmers of Pondicherry developed by our scientists were complied with.

Before joining ICFRE as DG, I was working in the grade of Additional Secretary in Delhi in the National Rainfed Area Authority (NRAA). The authority was set up at the behest of then Prime Minister Manmohan Singh in 2006 as an attached office in the Agriculture Ministry to act as a policy formulation body to boost stagnating Agriculture productivity in the country and work for convergence in the management of natural resources. The authority was earlier with the Ministry of Agriculture but was transferred to the Planning commission later on due to the uncooperative attitude of Secretaries of the Agriculture Ministry.

The authority was headed by a very committed well-known agriculture Scientist Dr JS Samra in the grade of Secretary. The authority now is back in Agriculture Ministry and is headed by an IAS officer as CEO. In NRAA, I tried a few innovative works for the convergence between forest and non-forest lands for the development of holistic natural resources management. When the post of DG ICFRE was advertised it was at the level of Additional Secretary only but I applied for it as I had a clear vision for this Institution and desire to implement my ideas based on my previous experience in the profession and of more than seven years working at the FRI and ICFRE (from May 1985 to September 1990 and again from October 1995 to June 1997). I have closely watched the creation of ICFRE after the 1986 resolution of the government of India (when the then President FRI used to get papers made from us and running to Delhi and back) and while serving as ADG ICFRE from 1995 to 1997. As ADG, I implemented the World Bank project on forestry extension and in this process, we virtually dug out some excellent research works buried in the files for more than 30 years like one on Rubber Wood treatment and successfully transferred this technology to Tripura State. I had to shift to the Ministry only after one and a half year of my second tenure in June 1997 when I found it better to leave the place as I was not appointed to the post for which I was recruited and left for Delhi when I was offered the post of Deputy Inspector General (DIG) of Forests in the Ministry of Environment and Forests. The deterioration of ICFRE was witnessed soon after the World Bank project as the last year budget syndrome choked research activities of funds as Planning Commission and Ministry did not give it the funds it needed to keep up the momentum after the World Bank Project was over and funds dried up. A unique way of depriving the ICFRE of funds and the Forestry wing of the MoEF was designed by the officers of MoEF looking after the budget in tandem with a Director in Planning Commission. In 2011 when I met the Expenditure Secretary for release of 100 Crore one time grant when the Ministry's Additional Secretary and Financial Advisor told me that Finance Ministry has not yet released sufficient funds; the

Finance Secretary informed me that the MoEF is the culprit in this as they are blocking the entire 800 crore Externally Aided Projects (EAP) funds which are released based on a reimbursement basis and the entire amount allocated to Ministry should not be blocked for the whole year.

It may be remembered that the purpose of this was to gradually reduce the budget of the Forestry and Wildlife Wing. Till June 2004 the forestry wing's budget was around 55% compared to the environment wing. This was when National Ganga Cleaning Programme was part of the Ministry. By 2011 when I was appointed DG ICFRE, the forestry wing budget was reduced to less than 45%. In 2008, the finance minister during his budget speech announced a one-time grant of Rs 100 crore which was not released as Stated before. After I joined in May 2011, only Rs 37 crore was given in two years, though the Ministry had been on an average surrendering Rs 500 crore every year for the last few years regularly. Naturally, Finance Ministry and Planning Commission would cut down the budget under such a situation. The Inter and intra-services rivalry in MoEF does not allow several policies, administrative and planning decisions on merit. The senior officers in MoEF have no time for ICFRE and forestry institutions are becoming the fiefdom of junior functionaries like section officers, undersecretaries and deputy secretaries. These minions are past masters in sabotaging anything good in the files because senior officers are otherwise busy or encourage them and they thus gleefully enjoy the senior officers of subordinate offices to run around them.

It is this kind of blatant mismanagement just for indulging in futile self-defeating antics by some individuals with bloated self-ego aided by a false sense of superiority and, in the process, causing great damage to the office they work for and for the mandate of Ministry. The inter-services strife, due to imaginary fears, is getting importance over promoting better work culture.

After I departed from ICFRE, during the next regular incumbent's tenure there was zero budget left for research and extension. He survived only on externally funded projects. Now, however, the situation has improved slightly what I noticed during my two years tenure from 2018 to 2020 as the Member of ICFRE Society, the apex policy-making body headed by the Minister of Environment, Forest and Climate change.

The Ministry officials have been milking the ICFRE with various demands by ensuring the posting of professionals of dubious distinctions. In one case, during a foreign visit of a former DG ICFRE for less than a week, the mobile bill was more than sixty-five thousand as Secretary and other delegates used his phone. His average monthly mobile bill during his tenure of three years was more than Rs 22,000. So after my joining after one month, I got a call from the Secretary requesting me to provide him with a Maruti SX4, a new high-end sedan, as his vehicle was giving trouble. I agreed with the request and asked the Director of the Institute of Temperate Forests, Shimla, to send the recently purchased Maruti SX4 vehicle under one consultancy project to Secretary Office in Delhi. In any case, it was a spare vehicle and the Secretary as the Chair of the Board of Governor and was genuinely helping the Council and needed a vehicle to replace the old car. After Secretary, a few other officers also wanted a vehicle which was politely refused but I agreed to provide it as and when required. After some time, I was told by Secretary ICFRE that one Director level officer of Establishment Division (ED) is willing to help ICFRE on pending matters and would require help in getting some additional staff on a contract basis. ICFRE paid for the salary of three staff engaged by them so that he could help sort out some long pending issues. After one year, I found the demand increasing and these staff being used by them for their personal use. I refused to extend the option at the beginning of 2013 as instead of helping initially in revising the recruitment rules this Director of ED after getting '*insitu*' promotion started behaving as super DG on my DDGs and other officers. The situation turned in his favour as, after the retirement of Mr Chatterji, the next Secretary, a poor specimen of IAS, managed to join as Secretary by having an understanding with Tamil speaking Minister to fulfil her targets in the Ministry. His one-point agenda was to make things difficult for me as he was jealous of my performance as IGF when he was JS in the Ministry during the Vajpayee government (1998 to 2004). This shows how national institutions are ruined by inferior caricatures who occupy senior post by a quirk of fate by entering the premier All India Services.

One of the deficiencies in organized services is that they believe their fellow servicemen blindly and start hunting the targets in packs causing immense damage to the fairness in decision making and IAS being a powerful group all-pervading in the Centre and State governments, it ultimately affects the performance of the system and also gives a bad name to their service at the hands of such undesirable members of service. Even when the institution is not having sufficient funds for carrying out research but demands keep increasing from these minions lording over in the corridors of power. One of the reasons why Indians fail at the global level in scientific excellence and delivery to the public in administration is this type of mindset which the present-day politicians ignore and allow this cancer to eat into the vitals of clean and efficient governance. Like when the ICFRE was created in 1986 its Head Quarters should have been in Delhi but the then President Research Institute (the post was renamed as Director-General after the creation of ICFRE) wanted to stay in big Bungalow at FRI campus Dehradun for the fringe benefits of agriculture that accrue from such residences of British period.

A Failed Attempt

05

As Stated, the 1990 Cabinet decision created the ICFRE as an autonomous society but it was a stillborn child as several times the issue was raised by several scientists and other professionals for completing the unfinished agenda of upgrading it to the desired level on the pattern of CSIR/ICAR. The matter need to be dealt with in detail for better public perception though I have mentioned it in previous chapters briefly in between when the context arose.

When I joined as DG ICFRE on 18ᵗʰ May 2011, I met Mr Jairam Ramesh in his office, who candidly told me that my ''appointment was being blocked by the entire bureaucracy with the support of a few IFS officers acting as pawn". It was as if I was an anti-national on the prowl. Officers acted in tandem in the Department of Personnel, Environment Ministry with the active help of some forest officers, Cabinet Secretariat and the Prime Minister's office to stall my appointment. Mr Jairam Ramesh himself had to step in the end to protest to Prime Minister Manmohan Singh as how the PMO is sitting on this on the frivolous ground when the selection was done by a search committee headed by renowned scientists, Dr MS Swaminathan and Dr Kasturiranjan. He told me "do not think that your service has brought you here and please conduct yourself as a fair and competent leader" and asked me to concentrate on two things immediately. First, remove all the grievances of the scientists who were harassed by the previous incumbent; and Secondly, to come up with a proposal to create the Department of Forestry Research as envisaged in the 1991 cabinet note proposal to grant autonomy on the pattern of ICAR and CSIR, when the ICFRE was declared as an autonomous institution. He asked me to discuss it with Dr MS Swaminathan, DG Forests Mr PJ Dilip Kumar and the Secretary Dr TT Chatterji and come up with a presentation within July 2011 before a select group of officers/ experts and eminent persons for which he will request Dr Swaminathan to Chair the meeting. Dr TT Chatterji an IAS officer of Andhra Cadre, for a change, was a well-qualified environmental professional with fairly a neutral disposition. He was specially brought by Mr Ramesh to give better professional orientation to the Environment Wing. Dr Chatterji and the DG Forests and Special Secretary Dr PJ Dilip Kumar both supported the idea. Dr Chatterji informed me that he had already discussed this matter with Dr MS Swaminathan as the Minister had already briefed him about this and asked me to proceed and bring a cabinet note. I then met Dr MS Swaminathan in his official MP's residence in Delhi. He informed me that ICFRE was created through his efforts and lamented that it is languishing as a stillborn child in the absence of genuine autonomy at the policy-making level and this institution's health is crucial for the food and water security of the nation.

Mr Jairam was of the opinion that once it is elevated to a department under the Ministry, it will have its budget and freedom to promote and plan new research initiatives and extension activities with accountability to Parliament. He suggested a date for the discussion on the presentation and a tentatively fixed date in the last week of June 2011. Mr Ramesh was aware of the unfinished agenda of the 1991 cabinet decision on the creation of ICFRE and the fact that the decision taken in the meeting of the National Wildlife Board sometime in 2009/2010 or so for the creation of the Department of Forests and Wildlife is pending in the PMO on some specious ground. Incidentally, the Wildlife Board has not met after 2014 and since then more than 900 developmental projects have been cleared by its Standing Committee Chaired by the Minister of Environment, Forest and climate change. This information on the meeting of the board was given to the Parliament while answering a question by the Minister in February 2021.

After returning to Dehradun, I appointed a committee headed by the then Director FRI Dr SS Negi to propose changes and briefed the committee members about the mandate on the Minister and meetings with Dr Swaminathan, DG Forests and the Secretary Dr TT Chatterji. I asked them to prepare the presentation in time and then I left for the tours of all Institutions to apprise myself of the conditions of work. However, this committee did not come up with the report as they started assessing the future long-term scientific man power also with the result that I sought to postpone the meeting to last week of July 2011 and Dr Swaminathan agreed to this. However, on the stipulated date, unfortunately, Dr Swaminathan became indisposed and could not travel to Delhi from Chennai on the appointed date and the Minister's office informed me that the meeting has been deferred for the last week of August 2011. However, when we were about to travel to Delhi, the Assistant Private Secretary to the Minister telephoned me and confidentially informed me that the Minister is going to be shifted this weekend from the Ministry and therefore, the meeting may be postponed. It was a big setback not only for ICFRE but for the Ministry and conservationists as Mr Jairam Ramesh, for his independent style of thinking, dynamism and intellect was becoming an eye sore in the eyes of the corporate world and the officials of PMO as well as the Bureaucracy for his independent way of taking quick decisions. In this regard, I must also add that the concept of 'Go and no go' propounded by Mr Ramesh for release of forestland under the Forest Conservation Act for mining s in the opinion of many experts was perhaps an over reactive approach and not a pragmatic action, because all the forestlands are already a 'no go land' because of the Forest Conservation Act 1980 and there was no need to further divide the forests. According to them it only created chaos and fuelled the suspicion of the powerful corporate and development lobby which won and he was shifted by promoting him to Cabinet rank. Soon after the new Minister Mrs Jayanthi Natrajan joined and after meeting her I realized her focus in becoming Environment and Forests Minister is not to run it to achieve its mandate but to grind her own axe. To meet her objectives, she brought one of her political assistant, a lady congress worker of Coimbatore as her Officer on Duty (OSD). She gave us a sufficient hint of running down her predecessor when once I was invited by Mr Jairam Ramesh to attend the United Nation Development Programme (UNDP) sponsored conference on climate change and rural livelihood. She questioned me and the one Joint Secretary who also attended the conference for attending the meet and criticized Mr Ramesh for promoting the UNDP. It is interesting to note that such attendance by officers on professional matters arranged by other ministries are routine affairs but a few IAS officers were trying to poison her air against some of us from the very start and monitoring our movement rather than doing their job. On Joint Secretary was often called by her before meeting me whenever I went to meet her and he used to be present in her OSD's room always giving a crooked smile to me when I went to meet her. This Joint Secretary was tactfully getting orders from minister to take a scientist on foreign tours every time during international meetings without consulting the DG ICFRE office only to carry their papers and do other sundry jobs. I had however, never objected to this. According to her UNDP is opposing the policies of the Indian government. It is a fact that international agencies have their own agenda, but on this, her allegation was quite unsubstantiated and on many environmental projects UNDP has partnered with the government of India.

After the departure of Mr Jairam Ramesh I discussed the proposal about the cabinet note with the Secretary Dr Chatterji who however, requested that I should send the cabinet note as decided for the creation of the Department of Forestry Research. It may be mentioned that before submitting the cabinet note, to take the then Director-General of Forests Dr PJ Dilip Kumar again into confidence I arranged a meeting of Forest Scientists Association and the Establishment and Research and Training Divisions of the Ministry in his chamber and discussed the issues pending for the smooth functioning of this organization. It was decided in this meeting that a comprehensive cabinet note may be submitted. The ICFRE prepared the cabinet note and send it to the Secretary proposing the creation of the department of Forestry Research and Education and shifting the Headquarter of ICFRE to the NCR region at Noida. I firmly believed that the headquarters of the ICFRE should have been in an easily accessible and central place like Delhi or NCR and irrespective of whether ICFRE is made a department or not, hence I made attempts to create infrastructure in Delhi/NCR by first getting land. For the purpose of ICFRE HQ with the help of my batch mate, Mr JS Asthana, who was the Principle Chief Conservator of Forests and Head of Forest Force (PCCF and HoF) at that time in UP, the Uttar Pradesh government agreed to hand over 25 ha of forest land in Noida for which under the Forest Conservation Act 1980 we had to pay only around 2 crores as Net Present Value of the land. I also took the approval of the new Minister Mrs Jayanthi Natrajan who readily agreed to the proposal. I also made arrangements for the funds and directed the Director FRI to take steps for taking over the land.

However, after about a month the Secretary telephoned me and said that one of the Additional Director-General of Forests came to him and told him on some specious and funny ground that there is no need to create the Department and hence the cabinet note need not be processed. I was not surprised with this U-turn from the Secretary as it appears to be a ploy to kill the proposal on flimsy ground and did not try to verify the Statement of the Secretary blaming the ADG. But considering the way in the year 2001 creation of Department of Forests based on the 'Promotion of Agro-Forestry' report submitted by a Committee under the Chairmanship of Dr DN Tewari, Member Planning Commission was torpedoed by the then Secretary minutes before the then Prime Minister Atal Bihari Vajpayee was supposed to release this report and accept the proposal for the creation of the Forest Department to be headed by the DG Forests. At that time both ADGs in the Ministry after meeting the Secretary submitted a note opposing the creation of the Department on the ground of loss of synergy with the Environment wing and the Secretary rushed to PMO and submitted the note to the Principal Secretary to PMO, who briefed the Prime Minister that senior IFS officers are opposing this report. I was witness to this happening as I was working as DIG Forests and was also representing the Ministry in DN Tewari Committee. My immediate boss the ADG told me when I opposed the note being signed by him in my presence as I happened to be in his chamber. He told me "friend forget creating the department as Secretary says IAS lobby does not want it and had asked both of us to write this note". I told him "why both of you are dancing to his tune and should instead take a professionally correct view and argue with the Secretary that it will have better results in garnering more funds for the Ministry and bringing more professional approach in forestry matters and the Ministry would be strengthened". He blamed the other ADG for initiating the note. This is the way things are orchestrated in this Ministry for a long time and decisions arrived at. It is like a squint eye as if it is looking here but appears to be seeing there!

Going back to my conversation with Secretary on that day, I told him that DG ICFRE has been delegated full powers by the government (as per the ICFRE compendium) more than a Secretary but I have no financial autonomy to guide the Council to achieve its objectives and hence the main purpose of creation of Department is to get a separate budget to meet the requirements for the efficient functioning of the organization and settle several issues festering it for long from 1991 like pension, creation of technical services, medical and other benefits and funds for research and extension which remained unfinished since the days of creating a lame-duck autonomous body. The truncated autonomy only deprived the status of a Government servant from the employees and instead of strengthening the research setup, it unsettled it as many as 600 scientists and other staff did not opt for the Council and were declared surplus and posted in other departments by the Department of Personnel's (DoPT) surplus cell. It a classic case of loss of trained man powers by a half-backed policy decision. It is also a well-known fact that forestry and the environment cannot generate sufficient resources from the market as per the new guidelines of the Finance Ministry on the funding pattern of autonomous institutions. In the interests of the nation's food and climate-resilient agriculture, water and ecological security Forestry Research and Extension had to be supported by the government in a big way. So, I suggested to Dr Chatterji that the Secretary Environment can also be initially made Secretary of Forestry Research so long I occupy the post of DG ICFRE and instead DG ICFRE should be declared as Special Secretary and made Chairman of the ICFRE Governing Board. The DG ICFRE should also have a small skeletal office in the NCR for processing the papers and better coordination. With this at least the council will get a separate budget and its employees' same status as ICAR and CSIR. The Secretary asked me to send the proposal on these lines. After this, I sent the other proposal as discussed with Secretary. The Ministry, however, again torpedoed the proposal initiated by me. The IAS lobby backed by a few IFS officers had taken a conscious decision after the retirement of the then DG Forests and the Secretary to remove me from the post by engineering fake complaints in an organized manner so that proposal of extension of my tenure which was wrongfully initially approved only for two years can be torpedoed. The Secretaries of Environment, Department of Personnel, Cabinet Secretariat and the Prime Minister's office were directly involved in planning to remove me.

To execute their plan the Joint Secretary level officers were given different tasks in a coordinated manner. The IAS bureaucracy had termed me as a 'Change monger' and a threat to their supremacy and their cronies in the forest service (incidentally they will create cronies amongst the foresters who can be suppressed in no times for their foolish actions). This strategy serves the twin purpose. First ensures control over the sector and secondly make them showpiece of the inefficiency of the sector to retain their control and supremacy in this Ministry. This is a patently poor and myopic view of things and a sign of professional weakness. Some of these people have been running this Ministry since 1985 when it was created by dividing the IFS officers and promoting incompetence in all our institutions.

Except at the time when TN Seshan was the Secretary of the Ministry when some real reforms of far-reaching dimensions had happened like setting up of Ministry's regional offices, creation of ICFRE and Indira Gandhi National Forest Academy, nothing substantial had been done to strengthen the environmental governance further. Apart from Seshan only Dr Pardipto Ghosh and to a certain extent, Dr TT Chatterji acted reasonably during their tenure as both of them were also having a good grip on the subjects of the Ministry. Today some of the IAS officers ensure that DG Forests and his wing are deprived of basic resources and there is always a whispering campaign to defame the forest officers as anti-people. The Ministers and the Prime Ministers fall to this campaign and treat the forest officers with disdain. In this process, the IAS brings some pliable forest officers and posts them to good position provided they help them in containing their colleagues. The Central Civil Service (CSS) officers are very wily and play their part in harassing the officers in one form or the other to keep the pot boiling for IFS officers particularly on service matters at the behest of their bosses. For the past several years, though the service conditions of IFS have improved, their effectiveness as a cohesive, confident All India Service with élan (with energy and enthusiasm) has been severely dented.

Considering the overall situation and the gigantic task ahead at ICFRE I realized that in its present shape the ICFRE cannot meet its obligations, I decided to make one more attempt to bring ICFRE at least back as a government organization and spoke to the Secretary Mr Chatterji who was soon retiring in November 2012. He agreed to constitute another committee to propose types of changes. Dr PL Gautam (an Agriculture Scientist who was the former Chairman of the National Bio-diversity Authority and member of ICFRE society) was nominated to head it by the Ministry. The committee was therefore set up by the Ministry in 2012 which also recommended granting full autonomy to ICFRE on the pattern of CSIR/ICAR and making it a department. Before this, Dr Ram Prasad Committee also recommended the same in 2011. The 12th Five years Plan Environment and Forest sub-group report on 'Forestry Institutional and Technology Management' recommended providing ICFRE autonomy by an ACT of Parliament. It also recommended bringing all the forestry training institutions under one umbrella by re-designation of the post of Director Indira Gandhi National Forest Academy (IGNFA) as Director-General of Training. This subgroup was chaired by me, with Mr AK Mukherji, the former DG Forests and Special Secretary as co-Chair and DG Forest Survey of India, Director IGNFA, Director Wildlife Institute and Director Indian Institute of Forest Management Bhopal among others (a few NGOs) as Members. It constituted the top professional leadership of forestry at the national level. The report was accepted by the Planning Commission and made part of the main document for implementation. Sadly, all these recommendations have proving like "***casting a pearl before swine***".

After I left ICFRE yet another Committee was set up headed by a Secretary who just retired in August 2014 and who wreaked havoc on ICFRE during his tenure as Secretary of the Environment Ministry ostensibly to undo the recommendations of previous committees. That is the way we allow a few madcap and mischievous elements in bureaucracy to run our institution and the government. Had the forest officers of the Ministry supported me apart from the creation of a department of forestry research the department of forest and wildlife already approved by the then Prime Minister in the National Wildlife Board meeting would have seen the days. It is necessary to have these two departments for better growth and functioning of the environment and forestry sector. And the story goes on and we do not know how long it will go like this in many offices of Centre and States administration.

Unmasking White-Collar Crimes

06

The Ministries of the Government of India are the ultimate source of power in India and have a very well-structured system provided it works honestly and purposefully. The British did not have such a huge Central Secretariat as we have now but it served them well in ruling India with committed loyal English educated Indian civil servants. They created organized civil services and a system of checks and balances which served them well. After independence, the Central Secretariat grew many folds and many offices were created under them but the power remained concentrated in the Secretariat. This too much centralization of power in Secretariat now is becoming a road block for smooth administration and enforcement of accountability among the civil servants. This also percolates to subordinate offices and a chain of unaccountability and irresponsible actions is noticed when we see too much red-tapism in deciding simple things. It also deprives the scope for innovations and creativity. It will be worth reading the book on government's delegation of financial powers to heads of departments which is full of mundane items. Why we cannot the government adopt some of the good practices of corporate sector. Gradually, the Prime Minister's Office (PMO) also assumed more powers and until recently till a few years ago even the power to approve the appointment of even Director level officers on deputation was with the Prime Minister. The rut started some 50 years ago when over and above Departments PMO was created with no direct access as the focus of even routine matters was taken over by the PMO. A country of India's size and dimension keeps the Prime Minister busy the power is assumed by the officers and this grows into a coterie culture. Similar things are happening at the State level in the Chief Ministers offices. So, the objectivity, neutrality, honesty, fairness, accountability is fast disappearing from Indian bureaucracy and governance.

There are however, positives aspects of all organized civil services; they operate in a rational, systematic and logical way and the experience in the service enlarges their perspective and knowledge base. This explains the good work of the organized civil services especially after independence in strengthening the federal set-up as a vital link between Central Government and State Governments. India did produce imminent civil servants who contributed to making the Indian federation a reality by ensuring unity in diversity. They have contributed tremendously in the field of development and even today many are working consciously and honestly in the task of national development. However, the organized cadres are groomed in a particular tradition over the years and their mind gets attuned to a particular pattern which is often resistant to change and assimilation of new ideas. The excessive self-important mindset cuts them off from the ground reality; develop bias and many live in an ivory tower of their perception of things.

In this book, there is no intention to underrate the importance and achievements of all the civil services created in the country but it is an effort to provide true feedback to the policymakers and the people on their increasingly emerging negative work culture which is generally kept under the carpet due to lack of reporting and to improve their functioning so that they can once again play their legitimate e role effectively. However, as I have narrated, they are groomed in a particular way of thinking and have a tradition to admire their way of dealing with things. This is the main cause of the peculiar mindset of Indian bureaucracy. This mindset is responsible for resistance to any change which they perceive as a threat to their position and takes them away from the rational way of deciding things. It gives rise to a bonhomie culture among them and prompts them to take illogical, self-serving and biased decisions at the cost of public interest. This has given rise to several malaises in their behaviour and performance. In such a situation they get embroiled in a set of cobwebs. Today a large group of Indian civil servants are afflicted with a self-serving mindset and indulge in blatant misuse of their positions bordering on criminality. The nexus between civil servants and political masters have further aggravated the problem of fair, transparent, and accountable governance in the country.

An IAS, being closer to the seat of power than other services, has to share the maximum burden for poor governance of the country. This book aims at unfolding the hidden aspects of the functioning of the Ministries of the Central government which are causing serious damage to the sanctity of our institutions of governance. The book will expose the dirty tricks played by the top-ranking civil and public servants so that society knows the facts about how the white-collar crimes are committed by the bureaucrats and some politicians in gross violation of democratic values enshrined in the constitution. Action must be taken to reform the languishing structure after more than 70 years of independence. Unless this is done the country will continue to suffer and the democracy may become an aristocracy of civil servants in which the gullible politicians become an active partner knowingly or unknowingly in their hands and vice-versa and the public interest suffers and people's welfare takes back seat.

India is so huge in its size and diversity that most of the time the government offices remain busy tackling the emerging problems of governance and in their cocooned environment of mutual praise they feel that everything looks honky dory. The country's politicians think the ring of chosen few around them possess all the brains of the nation with all 'they know' syndrome, trust them and delegate to them. The hard fact is that many of them are the real cause of killing nice and innovative ideas in the bud. It is also equally true about the rising number of cases in which the narrow-minded and corrupt politicians play a reverse card of civil servants and in the process destroy the integrity of civil services, a spirit of fairness and the constitutional provisions. In modern days in Indian administration, there are umpteen numbers of cases to reflect on this condition. However, having said this I would also like to State that whenever committed, fair-minded civil servants have occupied the top posts in the government, fair decisions are taken but such examples are fast shrinking with time.

I had been in the Ministry of Environment and Forests from June 1997 to June 2004 for around 8 years and observed its functioning from closed quarters. The Central Secretariat is one place where a positive, honest and committed person, no matter in what position he works, can contribute significantly to the implementation of the government's policies and programmes. This is the beauty of working in the Central Secretariat. I had along with other officers of positive attitude played a key role in creating Forest Development Agencies (FDA) as a federation of village committees to manage afforestation activities, creating a Joint Forest Management (JFM) cell (This cell issued the February 2002 and December 2002 guidelines which opened good density forest cover to the JFM and a JFM network in the country for cross-sector dialogue), created a Forest Protection Scheme with peoples involvement, Innovative monitoring of forest fires in the country, streamlining the implementation of Forest Conservation Act 1980, starting the Bhopal-India process with IIFM Bhopal for evolving criteria and indicators for sustainable forest management; and creation of the Compensatory Afforestation Management and Planning Authority (CAMPA). The CAMPA has more than 75,000 crore rupees corpus which is being operated now through an ACT passed by the Parliament.

In the creation of FDA, the then Additional Secretary National Afforestation and Eco-development Board (NAEB) Mr Vinod Vaish IAS, played a key role (well assisted by one IFS officer Mr Arvind Kumar), accepted and pro-actively acted upon the report of a committee set up by the then Minister Mr Saifuddfin Soz to propose changes in the Afforestation programme (and the JFM) in the country. I was the member-secretary of this committee and drafted the report along with Mr AK Mukherji (former DG Forests) who was the Chairman of the committee. The creation of the FDA and JFM Cell was one of the most important reforms undertaken in the forest administration of the country after the creation of the Ministry of Environment and Forests and after the 1986 reforms by the then Secretary TN Seshan. It is because of my contribution in the profession in bringing policy changes in forest governance I was conferred with the ***'Queens Award for Forestry 2000'*** the most prestigious international award available for forestry professionals in the Commonwealth. The award is personally signed by the Queen of Great Britain on behalf of the Commonwealth Forestry Association which is an affiliated NGO of the Commonwealth Secretariat of which India is a member country.

I joined this Ministry in June 1997 as Deputy Inspector General of Forests and was given the charge of a defunct Forest Fires Division and Director of Air Operation Wing which has two grounded Helicopters and debris of Piper Seneca aircraft of the Ministry which crashed in 1994 ferrying the OSD of Kamal Nath the then Minister from Bhopal to Delhi. The two helicopters were repaired before I joined and were ready for flying during fires season. Soon I found they are still not in good shape and the aerial spray of foam is of no use in Indian conditions and the fire fighting scheme was also a non-starter only giving some obsolete ground equipment to the States. I convinced two successive Ministers who were in charge to have a broad-based approach on forest protection involving people of villages adjoining the forests and creating infrastructure for the field formulations of the forest departments to meet the emerging needs specific to each site. The use of aerial spry by helicopters cannot be done routinely as it is impractical in Indian conditions where almost 1,70,000 villages are located in the fringes of forests and whose activities lead to forest fires. The aerial spray is only resorted to in countries like Canada, the USA and Australia where they have dense forests over long stretches and in these countries also the aerial foam spray is a failure without the latest ground infrastructural support. I for the first time assessed the loss from forest fires which was presented to Parliament and convinced the planners to create a new scheme of forest protection. The forest protection division was created and a new forest protection scheme launched to provide infrastructure support to States like vehicles, wireless sets, mobiles, buildings etc with a component of 25% funds earmarked for involving the JFM Committee members in forest fire control. We also funded the Forest Survey of India (FSI) to provide instant messages to the territorial DFOs after tracking the forest fires through satellite to mobilise fire prevention activities quickly. The Ministry also issued guidelines for mobilization of the government manpower as per the provisions of section 79 of the Indian Forest Act 1927 which is seldom resorted to by forest officers as well as district administration. I replied to more than 150 pending Parliament Assurances successfully within two years of my joining this division.

Whatever I had contributed professionally in the Ministry is bearing rich fruits for the sector and the forest department today.

However, I was from the very beginning, an eyesore and thus a target of envy by a group of officers led by the then Secretary in the Ministry for fearlessly pursuing what is good for the sector which came in conflict with the way bureaucracy led by the IAS wanted to run this Ministry. This conflict of interest was just a figment of their imaginations and attempts were made to browbeat the officers of forest service to silence with the help of some selfish forest officers. In other words, it was selfish groupies that were responsible for such a situation. These self-proclaimed guardians of the IAS while acting as ears and eyes of Cabinet Secretary and Prime Minister's Office (PMO) would whisper that to ensure the hold of the IAS lobby and to prevent the creation of the Forest department (which was the legitimate demand of the IFS Association whose Secretary-General post I held for quite a few years), it is necessary, in their view, to control the activities of some of the forest officers like me. It is this mindset which gets some support from extremely ambitious forest officers and is the root cause of derailing the smooth functioning's of the system and damaging the institutions. The then Secretary used to lament from the very beginning of my joining the Ministry in June 1997. It had set a chain reaction among officers of DoPT as they will sit on proposals for the appointment of senior post on one pretext or the other. In one file DoPT sat for more than almost 18 months for the posting of IFS officers including me and Mr MK Jiwarajika to the post of Inspector-General of Forests. The file was cleared only when we raised a hue and cry; at that time some fear of the then PM was felt in the corridors of power. As per the rules of the system, the ACC is supposed to clear the file within two months. I left the Ministry on 30th June 2004 after 7 years and joined Tripura State, my parent cadre.

During my career in the Ministry, I had realized that forest conservation needs straight thinking, better professional experience and knowledge to grasp the situation. It also needs inter-sectoral cooperation and convergence. There has been a long-pending demand that the Department of Forest and Wildlife should be created with DG Forests as Secretary. A decision to create the Forest and Wildlife Department was taken some time in 2010 in the National wildlife Board meeting Chaired by the then Prime Minister Manmohan Singh. However, this is still pending in the PMO for implementation and it may be the rare case where a PM's announcement was minuted and then not implemented. Before that during the Atal Bihari Vajpayee regime as Stated earlier by me in preceding pages in the year 2001, a task force of the Planning Commission headed by the then Planning Commission Member Dr DN Tewari (who was also the former Director-General of ICFRE) on Agro-forestry and medicinal plants had also recommended the creation of Department of Forests to be headed by the DG Forests. But lo and behold just one day before when Prime Minister Atal Bihari Vajpayee was about to declare the creation of the Department of Forests, the Secretary called both the ADGs and sought their cooperation to kill the proposal. Once he got a note from them, he rushed to PMO with his note that the IFS officers of his Ministry do not want to create a separate Forest Department. The meeting with PM was cancelled and in retaliation, Dr Tewari did not allow the Medicinal Plant Board and Bamboo Mission to be housed in the Environment and Forest Ministry. While working in the Ministry I had been closely observing the functioning of ICFRE and felt that it was being ruined by apathetic handling by the Ministry's IFS and IAS officers as well as by the subservient DG's of ICFRE and other incompetent officers of ICFRE who failed to transform the idea sown by TN Seshan while ordering the reorganization of the forestry sector.

The Ministry of Environment and Forests has, therefore, always been in the vortex of the dirty tussle between various groups. At one level turf war between the IAS and IFS groups; and on another level, all those who are occupying even the lower-level posts in the Ministry unite to keep subordinate, attached and autonomous offices subjugated to unchallenged compliances of their whims and fancies, no matter what is desirable in the public interest. The cardinal principle is no one should be given any liberty beyond the 'unsaid' code of conduct and questions the unwritten laws of 'pseudo values' attached to this sacrosanct group, lest a firm hand be set out to put them at their place through minions working under them. At the same time, those who comply with their whims are rewarded with choice postings and other favours which also sent a message to other service members to do what they are asked to do. This is the way at least a few postings in senior levels are made in this Ministry and outside.

The Central Secretariat is the last seat of power and all are supposed to act with utmost honesty and devotion to rule of law as a permanent implementing organ of the political executive. Gradually, however, the value system and ethics, honesty and commitment to public services have been redefined in accordance with the changing dimensions of our political culture and the nexus of survival develops which eats into the vitals of a responsible permanent bureaucracy as envisioned in the constitution of India. Thus, a peculiar mindset is ruling today's bureaucracy. Bureaucracy is largely exemplified by bloated egos, exceeding sense of self-importance and is adept in capturing their master's brains due to their closeness and knowledge of the system. Thus, a caucus like situation prevails in the corridors of power when the permanent members of bureaucracy are not fair and thus take over all real authority in decision making. In the process misuse the power shredding to pieces the intents of article 311 and 313 of the constitution when they give primacy to their own agenda than the public interest and neutrality. One of the reasons for the poor performance of the government is the incompetence of its civil servants and the arrogant way they arrogate all power and wisdom to them and in the process behave like demi-gods to their subordinates and common people but crawl like a pigmy before their political bosses.

This ailing disease does not get highlighted as no one bothers and most of the clever people in the system compromise their positions and those who do not kowtow are hunted in packs. This is very well prevalent within the ramparts of all civil services when the good-intentioned people are side-lined by their own servicemen who are hand in gloves with Lutyens's coterie.

I had throughout my career always been a fearless, people-centric, professionally well-equipped and conscious civil servant with considerable professional and diverse administrative experience and with an impeccable character. A few years before my superannuation, I faced the most difficult period of my career with these elements as they mounted a full-throttle attack on me with the help of a few disgruntled elements in IFS, as well as, other cadres of the central government. The narration discussed below will show how the 'operation white-collar crimes' to defame an individual out of nothing are conducted in tandem by few power intoxicated pygmies occupying senior positions in the sacred portals of the government in the central secretariat. They create adverse opinion through character assassination and a brazen show of authority and misuse of power. This is done when our political masters are completely ignorant or feign ignorance or are part of it or are incompetent to handle as they only concentrate on exploiting the system for their selfish and political agenda. Once vendetta is initiated against a person the whole system runs after that person in a mafia-style.

As per the All India Services tenure rules for the Secretary level posts under the government of India, there is no limit of tenure and the incumbents get the posting till they retire from the service. I was, however, as a peculiar case only appointed for two years. As soon as I joined I represented and the Ministry send the proposal for modification. However, the Mandarins in PMO returned the proposal saying it should be submitted closer to ending the tenure. It was only in November 2012 that the proposal was again sent to ACC for extension of the tenure till retirement.

As this proposal of my tenure for an extension as DG ICFRE beyond 17th May 2012 was kept pending in the DoPT at the behest of the new Secretary, a volley of emails bombarded to PMO, DoPT, President office with the help of an Under Secretary against whom I had taken action during my tenure in the Planning Commission. These communications were not only baseless oft-repeated allegations but purely malicious. To prepare the ground a Director level officer belonging to Central Secretariat Service who was promoted 'insitu' to the level of Joint Secretary was deputed to visit ICFRE ostensibly to sort out the pension issue of the ICFRE personnel raised by me with the Ministry and by the Forest Scientists Association (FOSA) of ICRFRE through their Memorandum and discussions with the Secretary in which they also protested about the deliberate emails being generated to defame the DG ICFRE. The Secretary deputed this particular officer on 12th April 2013 in response to the representation of FOSA to sort out the problems raised by them. In the meanwhile, just before this visit, one interview was slated for the promotion of one lady scientist of Tropical Forest Research Institute (TFRI) Jabalpur on the direction of the Central Administrative Tribunal (CAT) Jabalpur, to consider her promotion on merit under the flexible complementing scheme applicable for the scientists. This Director level officer contacted the DDG Recruitment Board Mr Omkar Singh over a phone call and said that Ministry demands that this particular scientist must not be promoted. The DDG came running to me before the start of the interview and informed me about the phone call. I had to call him back and snub him over for such gross impropriety in trying to run after a lady scientist and took up the matter through a letter to the Secretary. However, the Secretary and the Minister's office were deftly using this officer to get a report against me on the basis of engineered mails. So he visited ICFRE and instead of discussing pension issues he won over the then Secretary ICFRE in a drinking session over dinner promising him that Minister and Secretary have conveyed that they will grant him an extension for 2 more years and asked him to join them in creating records against me. It was a golden opportunity for this officer for taking revenge on me for two things. First, I refused his inclusion in a foreign trip of a delegation as it was solely meant for the scientists and secondly, I complained to Secretary for taking action against him for telephoning the Deputy Director-General Recruitment Board on the eve of the interview Board meeting for promotion of scientists to higher grade under the flexibility complimenting scheme for scientists.

It is these kinds of ugly happening in the country's highest offices that I have decided to write a book to expose the hidden dirty belly of the central secretariat, the last pillar of governance so that our intelligentsia and the informed public can root for reforms otherwise our democracy is being slowly taken over by such a bunch of crook masterminds.

When I found a well-orchestrated campaign is being managed in a very coordinated manner as if VK Bahuguna as DG ICFRE has become a national security threat as minutes to minutes coordinated monitoring was being done between Cabinet Secretariat, DoPT, MoEF and keeping PMO in the loop to see that I am repatriated back. Sensing this and getting fed up repeatedly replying to these completely baseless tendentious allegations I filed a case in the Allahabad Bench of Central Administrative Tribunal (CAT) on 6th May 2013 against the DoPT for sitting on my extension proposal without any basis. The CAT issued an order that I will continue as DG ICFRE till 18th July 2013 the next date of hearing fixed. The Secretary ICFRE who helped draft my case informed the Ministry on the same day that I had filed the case in CAT. The Ministry swiftly wrote a letter to DoPT asking them to keep the proposal of extension in abeyance. The

Secretary ICFRE fled the ICFRE campus soon leaving a leave application for a month and went to the Ministry to help the Secretary in his conspiracy.

The aim of DoPT and the Ministry was to withhold the proposal till 17th May 2013 which was supposed to be my last day in office but after I filed the case in CAT on 6th My 2013 the Ministry wrote the letter on 6th itself as the Secretary was stunned of getting the news of stay by the CAT till 18th July 2013 and immediately the entire lobby of his friends swung into action. The Under Secretary who was being used against me was prompted to write a letter to CAT Members alleging that I have bribed them. The then DoPT Secretary took up the matter with his batch mate who was the Administrative Member of Allahabad CAT and convinced him to vacate the stay without even advancing the date of hearing. However, suddenly on 4th June 2013 on Sunday the Administrative Member of the CAT discreetly opened the office and without hearing vacated the stay at around 8 PM and my advocate at Allahabad was surprised over this illegal way of vacating the stay when I phoned him at 1115 PM. On the same day by 11 PM, I was relieved of the charge of DG ICFRE and the DG Forest was given an additional charge of ICFRE. In the annals of the history of CATs and Judiciary, this decision will be remembered as a landmark for raping the Indian judicial system in nexus with a few individuals in the bureaucracy thereby making a mockery of justice and fair play.

I had after filing the case in CAT on 6th May 2013 decided to leave but before that wanted that these bogus charges are cleared through a high-level inquiry. I, therefore, wrote a letter to the then Principal Secretary of the Prime Minister intimating him that I am not interested in remaining in my present position and requested him to constitute a committee consisting of senior scientists, an IAS officer outside MoEF and a senior IFS officers to enquire into these baseless allegations and also give me a personal hearing so that an enquiry is ordered into how records were created and how the government machinery is being brazenly used to target an officer of the rank of Secretary and defaming him in the eyes of public out of malice. I wrote that after the inquiry by the team is over I will leave.

The then President of IFS Association Central Unit Mr AN Prasad also wrote a letter to the PMO on some other issues and when he knew about it, he included the issue raised by me in my letter to the PMO. In his letter he stated that even after vigilance cleared my case and the ACC was informed the Ministry without giving any reason withdrew the proposal of extension. He in his letter protested such illegal activities and demanded an inquiry to bring out the facts. Before this, in March 2013, Mr TKA Nair Advisor of the Prime Minister visited ICFRE and wrote a encouraging message in the book we released about ICFRE's work for the upliftment of Tribal people. Interestingly the Secretary after the visit of Advisor to PM swung into action and poisoned the Minister that I am trying to create a department and taking ICFRE outside the Ministry. PMO instead of taking note of my letter and the letter of the IFS association the chorus against me rather increased man fold; thus, proving that the PMO was patronizing these elements against me.

I present the letters written by the IFS Association (Central Unit) and by me and the purpose of reproducing these two letters is to show how the top civil servants in Prime Minister's office were working in a blatantly partisan manner as no action was taken on these letters. This is the crux of the problem in India's governance today when some people occupying top positions becomes bias and misuse their positions there is no scope for justice in any form from the highest level of government at all as courts also frown upon such cases totally and do not act. So, the net result is the win of untruth over truth and the untruth become a sacrosanct truth in public eyes.

"To,
Shri Pulok Chatterjee
The Principal Secretary to the
Hon'ble Prime Minister of India
South Block
NEW DELHI

Sub: Issues relating to Indian forest Service officers – regarding

Sir,
On behalf of the IFS Association (Central Unit), I am writing thisletterto bring to your kind notice the discrimination meted out to the Indian forest service officers vis-a-vis other All India service officers. On several occasions we have raised the issue of parity in pay promotion and other facilities for our service members working on deputation in Government of India and its autonomous bodies. One of the glaring disparities is of not giving in-situ promotion to our officers despite fulfilling all the requirements whereas the same is granted to IAS and IPS officers in a routine manner. All IFS officers working in central government are eligible for in-situ promotion to next level, some even to two levels but till date not a single in-situ promotion has been granted to any officer. The other issue relates to tenure in the Apex scale. Sir, we have only two cadre posts in the Apex scale in Govt of India. One of our officer Dr V K Bahuguna was selected for the post of Director General, Indian Council of Forestry Research & Education (ICFRE) in the Apex scale through open competition by a special Search committee headed by Dr M S Swaminathan. As per the DoPT norms the deputation tenure of All India Service Officer in the autonomous bodies at the Secretary level posts is till the age of superannuation. However, in case Dr V K Bahuguna, as against the DoPT norms he was appointed only for a period of two years with effect from 20ᵗʰ May 2011.
Ministry of Environment & Forests accordingly sent a proposal for extension of his tenure as Director General, with full details of his performance, ACR grading and vigilance clearance on 04.12.2012.However, DoPT against

all norms of CVC guidelines sought a report on a complaint filed by a person who is not connected with the activities of the ICFRE.

Ministry of Environment & Forests vide its letter dated 26.04.2013 intimated DoPT that all the complaints were examined by vigilance and had been closed as they were found false. Surprisingly MOEF again based on some complaint wrote to DOPT on 6.05.2013 to keep the proposal in abeyance.

Sir, the Association will not support any case where inquiry establishes the charges levelled in the compliant. In the case of Dr Bahuguna, inquiry done by MOEF's vigilance has found the complaints false; hence there is no justification for writing to DOPT after ten days to keep the proposal in abeyance. This is against the laid down norms of the CVC and DOPT. We, therefore, request your kind intervention on both the issues so that an equal and fair treatment is given to IFS officers. We request to kindly direct the concerned officials to examine and process the proposal of grant of in-situ promotion to all such officers to whom it is due. In case of Dr Bahuguna, we would request to order an independent inquiry by a team consisting of Secretary level IAS officer, a retired IFS officer and an eminent Scientist from outside MoEF to ascertain the truth.

Yours faithfully

(A N Prasad)
New-Delhi, May 2013
President, IFS Association (Central Unit)"

"To,
Shri Pulok Chatterjee
The Principal Secretary to the
Hon'ble Prime Minister of India
South Block
NEW DELHI

Sub: Request for Justice on the proposal for extension
of Dr VK Bahuguna, DG ICFRE

Sir,
I am writing this letter due to grave injustice and unprecedented harassment meted out to the undersigned by a group of people through and their nexus in the Ministry of Environment & Forests and other offices. These are people against whom I had undertaken administrative actions for serious malpractices. I feel a serious miscarriage of justice is going to happen if I do not seek the indulgence of PMO as the final authority on ACC matters. I was selected by a Search Committee headed by an eminent scientist Dr. M.S. Swaminathan for the post of Director General, Indian Council of Forestry Research & Education in the Apex scale of Rs.80000/- fixed. However, as against the DoPT norms I was appointed only for a period of two years with effect from 20th May 2011.My tenure is coming to an end on 19th of May 2013.As per the DoPT norms the deputation tenure of All India Service Officer in the autonomous bodies at the Secretary level posts shall be till the age of superannuation. In accordance to this the Ministry of Environment & Forests had sent a proposal for extension of my tenure as Director General, Indian Council of Forestry Research & Education with full details of my performance, ACR grading and vigilance clearance on 04.12.2012. However, DoPT against all norms of CVC guidelines sought a report on the complaints of TJS Chawala who was Under Secretary under me in the National Rainfed Area Authority (NRAA) and against whom disciplinary action was taken and one officer of ICFRE who was holding the post of Dy. Director General (Research), ICFRE whose Ph.D. degree was withdrawn after a reference from UGC after due enquiry and against

whom a charge sheet was submitted to MoEF for financial impropriety. Recently On 6th May 2013 Ministry based on a blatantly false report had conveyed to DoPT that my case for extension may be kept in abeyance. This was done against the Ministry's letter on 26.04.2013 intimating the DoPT that all the false complaints were enquired into by vigilance as I had to fight the nexus and ultimately the Ministry agreed and send a reply to DoPT on 26.04.2013 asking it to proceed with the proposal of extension. It is Mr. Surjit Singh who has been acting as a super boss of ICFRE had submitted a bias and false report to Secretary, MoEF, who in turn processed it and this latest communication to DoPT. I have come to know that he had alleged that I received the Queen's award 2000 without Government permission. This is total lie and ludicrous and all records must be in the Ministry and I also supplied CVO all travel documents. There are other charges also in which he had written total lie. I had to salvage my image and hence I filed a case in CAT and got a stay till 18th July the next date of hearing. There is not a single complaint from ICFRE it is the outsiders who are writing letters.

During my two years tenure this organisation has regained not only its international stature but had become a very vibrant and people centric organisation. Those who have visited the organization have written and appreciated the new directions. This included Advisor to the Prime Minister Shri T.K.A. Nair who had praised the work on vanishing Naxalism in 10 villages in Jharkhand and livelihood of Tribals under FRA 2006 and linkages with Panchayats. Mr Nair himself sat with the Panchayats members for 30 minutes. Planning Commission Members and Parliament Standing Committee Members have all praised the new dimension.

Sir now, I am not keen to stay in this position if the Minister does not want me to continue. However, going rather unceremoniously based on false allegations of TJS Chawala and Surjit will be a great injustice to truth. The people who bring changes in the system must be protected from the rogue elements otherwise nothing will change in the administration. I am suffering because I want to deliver to the public and I am honest and upright. I will request to kindly constitute a committee consisting of a senior scientist, an IAS officer outside MoEF and a senior IFS officers to enquire into these baseless allegations and also give me a personal hearing so that an enquiry is ordered as how records were created and how the govt. machinery is used to achieve hidden agenda. After getting my honour back I will leave. Hope you will accept my request.

Yours faithfully

May 2013

(Dr. V.K. Bahuguna)"

After the dismissal of my writ in the CAT in a surreptitious manner, I filed a writ in the Uttarakhand High Court against the CAT order only to seek the truth but I had already made up my mind and planned my journey back to Tripura. The High Court initially fined the Secretary Ministry of Environment and Forests and ICFRE Rs 5000 each for filing an incorrect and false reply. However, on the technical ground that I can only represent against the CAT on the initial cause of the application in CAT (which was on delays by DoPT in clearing proposal on my tenure) and hence dismissed the writ on 15th July. During the debate, my advocate argued the case mostly relates to false affidavit by the Ministry, the Chief Justice opined during discussions to file another case if we like. In the meanwhile, on 10th July I got a call from the Chief Secretary Government of Tripura that the Chief Minister wants me to join the State immediately. On 11th July I got a call from Mr Jitendra Chaudhury the Forest, tribal affairs and rural development Minister Government of Tripura and conveyed that I should not waste my energy as an important assignment befitting my seniority as an All India Service officer is being considered for me. I immediately on 11th July 2013 booked my tickets for 18th July for Agartala without caring for the decision of the High Court slated for 15th July.

After my departure, the Ministry asked the DG Forests who was in additional Charge to create false records against me so that action can be initiated against me. On 17th July after reaching Delhi I came to know that the Chief Minister is in Delhi and I met him and requested him to make me Principal Chief Conservators of Forests (PCCF) Tripura at least for a few days for historical reasons but he refused saying I have got my name scrolled in the incumbency board of government of India on the top post at ICFRE.

I thus joined the State on 18th July 2013 and was handed over my appointment letter at the airport itself by the State protocol officer as Principal Secretary in the Apex Scale to look after the Planning, Coordination and Economics Department and kept in the pecking order as per my Pay Scale and seniority. Later on, after a month, I was allotted the Forest Department and Planning department went back to Chief Secretary. A month later, I was allocated the Agriculture and Animal husbandry Departments also which I retained even after I was re-employed and until I resigned in April 2015.

Soon after my joining, one officer who was brought to the Ministry by the then Minister as Additional Director-General of Forests from Mizoram on the understanding that he will have to serve under one 1980 batch IFS officer who was appointed DGF in regular Apex Scale for 3 months in November 2012 after the retirement of Dr PJ Dilip Kumar. This particular officer from Mizoram was, however, appointed DGF later on after the retirement of Mr Jude Sekar as DG Forests and DG ICFRE.

The new DGF was also appointed DG ICFRE and asked to create records against me while in additional charge as DG ICFRE. This officer on joining DGF and DG ICFRE in tandem with one Director level officer of Establishment Division(ED) of MoEF assisting the Secretary in his agenda (who was smarting after returning from a US tour as a prize for launching no hold bar attack on me and demoralising the officers and scientists of ICFRE) with the help of Secretary ICFRE who was given two years extension to create records against me and who was double crossing me as well.

The first thing they ordered was a special audit by the Comptroller and Auditor General (CAG) on ICFRE's work but they found that there was no bungling in my time nor any misuse of funds but found a lot of discrepancies before my time. They then kept ordering another six audits by CAG on one pretext or the other but could not find anything. Exasperated as they were they then checked the records of the ICFRE delegation's visit to Rome to attend the World Forest Week from 24th to 25th September 2012 during Committee of Forestry Organizations (COFO) organized by the Food and Agriculture Organization (FAO) a United Nation body, where, on World Forest Week on 24th September 2912 as DG ICFRE, I chaired a session and led a delegation of senior officers. They gleefully discovered that in a receipt of taxi availed by the delegation for returning to the Hotel from the FAO dinner meeting there was an advertisement of a dance bar on the taxi receipt. The receipt though had the name of the Taxi service but the DG Forests and the Director ED mischievously claimed it as if we had gone to the dance bar and spread the rumour all around to defame me and the delegation. They then also decided to dig up other tours and arbitrarily decided that in each tour one DA was taken extra and hence asked me to refund the amount. I stoutly refused to refund as there was no discrepancy and quoted the rule position and filed a case in the Guwahati branch of CAT along with all proof. The CAT stayed the order. I will discuss this case in the Chapter on Judiciary but one thing I may State here the CAT in both the cases initially acted and decided properly but after the first order on stay then the lobbying started to bias the administrative members. Finding nothing in ICFRE the Ministry seized all files of recruitments of scientists and staff to invent some material against me in these files. Ironically, this DG Forests was rewarded by the Ministry official by selecting him as the Expert Member of the National Green Tribunal. So gullible climbers crawl their way to top posts and the result is poor governance.

After five months and after creating some fictitious narration and jumbling them up in November 2013, I received a show-cause notice from the Ministry of Environment and Forest for alleged irregularity like telephone bills, underpayment of electricity charges, purchase of mobile phones, the appointment of scientists, spending money on the repairs of DG residence and naming of DG's residence as Council House etc. The DG ICFRE is not at all remotely concerned with these. I replied to the notice in January 2014 refuting all the cooked-up charges and even providing evidence how I curtailed the expenditure on office work and phones and also provided how the previous DGs of ICFRE were having extremely expansive bills on these items (their mobile bills were in the range of Rs 22,000 per month as against mine of Rs 5000 that too with one disputed bill of China visit).

After elections in May 2014, the BJP under the leadership of Prime Minister Shri Narendra Modi came to power and I wrote a letter to his Principal Secretary about my harassment and crimes being committed from the high offices and sought time from him as well as the Forest Minister Mr Prakash Javadekar. I met both of them but both did not give any ear to my complaints as Principal Secretary to PM supported the Secretary who was his cadre mate in IAS and the intensity of harassment became even more in the changed regime.

After this, in yet another interesting case of creating fudged records in the files, the DGF and Director ED created a false narration in the file of the Established division that I had transferred one Under Secretary Mr Dhirendra Kumar from Jabalpur Institute to Allahabad Centreof FRI after I demitted office in the backdate. I wrote about this to Mr Prakash Javadekar as well as to his predecessor Mr Veerappa Moilly with the proof of date of his transfer on 23rd May 2013 as printed on the fax send from ICFRE to Jabalpur but no action was taken by them. It shows that anybody's character can be ruined by civil servants by creating false records and false fudging narratives to Ministers with impunity. The question is none is bothered and these scamsters become the close advisors of Ministers. Is it not Ironical in the governance of world's biggest democratic country?

In July 2014, closer to my retirement in September 2014, the Tripura Chief Minister called me and asked me to continue in Tripura for next few years beyond retirement and an order was issued to re-appoint me w.e.f 1st September 2014 for one year initially on the same post I was holding in the State Secretariat. The news spread in the Ministry and the Director ED immediately wrote to the Tripura government that due to telephone bills and other recoveries my pension proposal should be withheld. This communication was issued again when the new Secretary joined the Ministry in September 2014. Thanks to the Chief Minister of Tripura Mr Manik Sarkar who after close scrutiny of the letters and the contents therein found them totally without any credible proof and asked the Chief

Secretary to find facts and act as per the rule and do not give credence to spurious communications.

In the meanwhile, I was not enjoying my re-employment and was contemplating resigning. I resigned from the post-retirement job on 30th March 2015 (after meeting the Chief Minister in the afternoon same day) due to some differences with two Ministers in Forests and Agriculture Departments (mainly when the Chief Minister did not take action against the PCCF of the Forest Department who was found indulging in corruption and harassing one young IFS officer who was working as DFO North Tripura and who was not obliging the PCCF and the new Forest Minister in issuing Transit passes for the transport of timber outside Tripura. There were other serious complaints against him for harassing other honest officers. In one such case, a senior officer of the 1985 batch belonging to the weaker section was implicated falsely in a sexual harassment case by the PCCF and a certain officer of the Chief Minister (CM) Office wanted him to be fixed in tandem with PCCF. But I did not oblige and recommended closer of the case with irrefutable arguments. Incidentally, this officer had to suffer a lot but was cleared on the intervention of the Ministry of Environment and Forests. The then aides of CM and the some of these corrupt forest officers became cosy with each other on this issue and one day CM abruptly transferred me as Director-General of State Institute of Public Administration I however, did not join and immediately resigned. Later on, even after being persuaded by emissaries to take back my resignations, I did not take back my resignation and ultimately left Tripura on 25th April 2015. I met the Chief Minister on 30th March and thanked him for having reposed his faith on me.

One of the reasons for the defeat of CPM in the assembly election in 2017 was the deterioration of objectivity and neutrality in decision making in the CM's office otherwise Mr Manik Sarkar was a very efficient, honest and popular Chief Minister who finished terrorism in Tripura and created a ground for rapid development of infrastructure in the State. He used to praise the then NDA Home Minister Shri LK Advani for helping Tripura in many ways in containing terrorism and cross border crimes. But later on, he became a prisoner of his personality and a pawn in the hands of his loved bureaucrats and alienated himself from his party workers and people. I saw in him a big change during my last posting in Tripura within 22 months primarily due to poor advisors.

Going back again to the communication on my pension proposal from the Ministry. The Ministry then wrote to Accountant General (AG) Tripura to stop my pension proposal. The Accountant General wrote back in October 2014 asking for substantial detailed proof. The AG Tripura did not get any response from the Environment Ministry for more than four months and reminders; after which my pension proposal was cleared. Once the Ministry officials knew that my pension proposal has been cleared and I have applied for the post of Member National Green Tribunal (NGT) in May 2015, they again became incensed because during Karnataka Supreme Court ordered Environmental Impact Assessment I had noticed several cases of granting environmental clearances against the advice of open hearings by the District authorities as the Bellary Collector during December 2011informed our team that as soon as the public hearing reports were decided the parties would go straight to Delhi and get the clearance in next 24 hours. It speaks volumes about the way this wing of MoEF was functioning at that time. So the mandarins decided to hurriedly block my entry in the NGT and simultaneously asked others to apply. To prevent my possible selection just before the interview they issued me a charge sheet with no supporting documents on 20th May 2015 to torpedo my case. They were, however, clever enough to call me for the interview and then rejected me on the obvious ground of being charge-sheeted as the inquiry is pending and once again rewarded the then outgoing DG Forests instead who created all the false records against me while holding charge as DG ICFRE. The fight for dignity and my experience with Delhi CAT and the Central Vigilance Commission inquiry and being given clean chit is being discussed in another chapter.

In nutshell, the readers of the nation should judge how the honest and upright civil servants can function when the governance in the top institutions is so much degraded and top civil servants brazenly committing white collar crimes in the grab of their positions. Such cases must be happening in other Ministries and offices as well and the system is turning rotten and the smell of these rotten eggs is spoiling the air in the corridors of powers and ambience of democracy. It is a tiny minority that is committing such crimes but can we allow such elements to flourish in the high portals of our democratic governance. Ignoring this disease will be suicidal in the long term for the survival of rule of law in India and the image of civil services. The political executive's inaction is giving impetus to such people and they are mushrooming in all departments.

Having narrated the above experience with civil servants in the Central Secretariat, I would like to mention that in this Ministry I also have experience of working with excellent IAS apart from a few names I have mentioned in my acknowledgement. Another IAS officer who had solidly contributed in the Ministry of Environment and Forests is Mr Vinod Vaish who as Additional Secretary helped creation of Forest Development Agencies as the federation of JFM Committees. Mr Shasi Sekhar Additional Secretary acted impartially as Financial Advisor and clearly disliked the politics played in the Ministry. Among Secretaries Dr Pardipto Ghosh and, Dr TT Chatterji brought some fresh air and professionalism during their tenure. In the state of Tripura, I have seen some of the best IAS officers as Chief Secretaries in late SR Shankaran, Mr NP Nawani, IP Gupta, Mr M Damodaran, Mr RK Mathur and Mr SK Panda. Among others were Mr Praveen Srivastava and Mr Anil Mishra. These officers were classical civil servants who served their cadres well but were equally open to the welfare of people and officers of other services and departments.

Among the old initial recruits of IFS who occupied the post of DG Forests (then known as Inspector General of Forests and Additional Secretary) I remember the elan with professional knowledge, commitment and unmatched boldness was only shown by Mr BP Srivastava and Mr Hari Singh. Yet another officer was Mr CL Bhatia who was a very successful dynamic officer to have served the government of India. Among seniors late Mr Shyam Sunder, the former PCCF of Karnataka was perhaps one of the best foresters and civil servant of the last century along with Mr Hari Singh, Padam Shri KM Tewari, and Mr HS Pawar, late Kailas Shankhla, Mr Parmeswarappa and late Saroj Rai Chaudhury and Dr DN Tewari. Closer to mid nineties and thereafter several outstanding IFS professionals served in the Ministry but could not succeed much in their leadership except Mr AK Mukherji and up to some extent Mr MK Sharma and Mr JC Kala among those who held the post of DG Forests. Dr PJ Dilip Kumar was one of the best well equipped professional brain of his generation to become DG Forests in the government of India but perhaps sadly missed an opportunity to create the Department of Forest and Wildlife when his IIT Mumbai colleague Mr Jairam Ramesh became the Environment Minister and brought him to the Ministry considering his integrity and knowledge and wanted to make him Secretary and bring reforms. Only Dr DN Tewari had shown the versatile leadership among all the foresters not only as DG ICFRE but both inside the profession as well as outside as an institution builder of remarkable capacity. Mr RC Ghosh of West Bengal cadre was one of the best forest officers after Mr SK Seth who set milestones in FRI mid sixties and early eighties. Some officers of post 1966 era after the creation of IFS namely Mr RL Singh of UP cadre, late JB Lal and Mr Ram Prasad, and late Padam Shri PK Sen of Bihar cadre were some of the names I know who have contributed a great deal to forestry profession. Today there are a large number of outstanding IFS officers serving in the country with aplomb and to name a few will be an injustice to others.

Among the old FRI Scientists who brought good names to FRI were Dr PK Sen Sharma, Dr Pratap Singh, Dr ML Kapoor, and Dr MN Jha to name a few I remember off hand. Among the new generation of Scientists Mr Sudhir Kumar now DDG Extension in ICFRE has shown great potential in creating expertise on mining. Another remarkably competent people oriented scientist of extraordinary talent Dr Pawan Kaushik whom I was expecting to contribute to forest based livelihood and whom I picked up over others to head the Agartala Centre died of covid-19 on 7th June 2021. Had he been alive he would have contributed a lot at senior levels.

Encounter with Judiciary

07

For the last few decades, the judiciary has been a saviour of the democratic rights of the people especially through the concept of Public Interest Litigation (PIL) and forced the executive for course correction. However, we also need to discuss if any reforms are needed in the functioning of the Judiciary. As stated earlier, in the preceding pages, this writer is examining these aspects purely from the points of view of improving the system of natural justice in a welfare State based on his own experience of over 37 years in the administration both under the Central as well as State Governments. In this Chapter, I would like to dwell upon particularly the efficacy of the Central Administrative Tribunals (CATs) having first-hand experience as a litigant as well as an administrator in various capacities.

My first encounter with the Judiciary as litigant was when I filed a writ in the Allahabad Branch of Central Administrative Tribunal (CAT) on 6th May 2011 against the Department of Personnel and Training (DoPT) and the Ministry of Environment and Forests (MoEF). The CATs were created in 1985 under Article 323-A of the constitution because of the huge pendency of service-related cases in the High Courts. However, this decision seemed to have proved counterproductive today as there is huge pendency in all branches of CATs and rarely the high-profile case get quick justice. A poor lowly clerk if he had to go to CAT to get justice had to finish his savings and even borrow a loan as the date after date's delays the justice because routinely on most of the occasions the government does not give replies and keep dragging the matters for years on flimsy ground. There is neither accountability clause nor monitoring provisions in CAT's working both for the CATs as well as the government. The CATs remain moot spectators and sometimes willingly allow the government to drag on cases. The records would show that Secretaries and senior officers of the Ministries are becoming more and more obdurate against staff they want to harass if they find their batch/service mates are in the CATs. There is a need to make a thorough study on the efficacy of the tribunal system on various subjects and the number of tribunals needs to be restricted to only for a few matters which require less legal interpretation and are more regulatory.

When I returned from Tripura after superannuation and resigning from my post-retirement job under the State government of Tripura in the last week of April 2015, I got a hint from some sources in the Ministry of Environment, Forest and Climate Change (MoEF) that my application for the National Green Tribunal (NGT) may be withheld. On 20th May I received a charge sheet which will be remembered as the cruellest joke on accountability and fair play in the annals of Indian bureaucracy. All charges were based on the bogus allegations initiated by some Ministry officials and were enquired into properly by the vigilance division and the administrative department of the Ministry and were found baseless. Surprised by this charge sheet, I got in touch with one brilliant Supreme Court Advocate Dr Harsh Pathak who decided to fight my case in the main bench of CAT in Delhi. After going through the articles of charges he understood clearly that it is a malafide case born out of vengeance and with intent to deceive the system and to create road blocks for my selection in the NGT. However, he Stated that the Supreme Court ruling in matters of disciplinary cases says that the courts should not intervene till the inquiry is over except in case of a malicious decision to fix the officer deliberately. It was a fit case of malice as a bogus narrative built upon totally baseless and completely twisted facts and in complete violation of laid down procedures for inquiring the complaints against the senior officers working as Secretary to government and Secretary equivalent posts under the central government. A circular issued by the Department of Personnel and Training (DoPT) in 2010 stipulated that no action can be initiated on the complaint against officers of the Secretary and Secretary equivalent rank officers in the apex scale of Rs 80,000 (now revised to 225,000) unless the complaint is examined by a Committee Chaired by the Cabinet Secretary and three other Secretaries. This was done to protect the senior functionaries of the government in the rank of Secretaries and equivalent posts from frivolous allegations so that officers can take fearless and correct decisions.

As soon as we filed the case in the main branch of the CAT in Delhi in June 2015 the new Secretary and other officers in the Ministry became hyperactive in lobbying. I filed two cases in the CAT. In one case we challenged the charges as malicious, completely frivolous devoid of an iota of truth and; in the other case, that the charges levelled are *Abinitio* void as the normal procedure of the first examination by the Cabinet Secretary led Committee was not followed and hence the entire procedure is untenable. The Administrative Member of the CAT who was the batch mate of the then Secretary MoEF (who created all the problems for ICFRE and for me after he joined on the retirement of Dr TT Chatterji in November 2012), very surprisingly from the very beginning was not ready to understand the English language of the said DoPT circular which a class X student could very easily understand and interpret. The Judicial member was sitting silently and perhaps due to whatever reasons or lobbying they had already decided not to entertain my case and were not prepared to listen to my Advocate's arguments. The Ministry in its reply gave a very farcical explanation that for Secretary equivalent post a separate order is issued by the government which was a golden lie submitted with impunity under the oath. The Administrative Member called the shot in this case and was openly helping the Ministry with ebullience.

The situation changed a bit when another Judicial Member joined as Chairman of the CAT and took over my case. My Advocate vehemently raised the issue of violation of the guidelines again and stated that the charge sheet is full of perversity. Ultimately, during arguments, the Chairman CAT as Judicial Member in the bench had to admonish the Administrative Member for not understanding simple English. However, before ending the hearing the Chairman CAT told me and my advocate that he will give an order to the Commissioner of Inquiry of the Central Vigilance Commission (CVC) to complete it in the next 6 months in a 'time bound' manner and also to examine if the DoPT order is applicable in my case. He commented "even if CAT rejects the charge sheet on this technical ground, their intention is to harass you and the Cabinet Secretary led Committee may take years to decide and you will suffer. Better agree to this proposal of time-bound inquiry by Central Vigilance Commission (CVC)". We immediately agreed. The CAT issued the final order on 16th August 2016 directing the Commissioner of Inquiry to complete the order in four months and the Ministry to decide once the inquiry is complete within the next four months. The CAT further ordered the Commissioner of Inquiry to examine all other issues as raised in the application. The Commissioner of Inquiry Mr Mukesh Kumar started the inquiry immediately in September 2016 and I fully co-operated with the inquiry process. I submitted around 800 pages of defence documents. Mr AN Prasad my batch mate acted as my defence assistance and we completely demolished the charge sheet as a perverse attempt to damage the reputation of an honest senior officer and the Presenting officer a Director level officer failed to provide any records to substantiate the charges. The Commissioner of Inquiry completed the inquiry and submitted his report on 4th January 2017. During the inquiry thus none of the Charges was proved and, in his report, he mentioned that Ministry had violated the DoPT circular by not referring the complaints before the Cabinet Secretary led committee as stipulated. His report was sent to me by the Chief Vigilance Officer (CVO) for comments after about four months in May 2017 in clear violation of CAT orders. I agreed with the report of the inquiring officer fully on 8th May 2018 and informed the Ministry. In this regard, after conveying my agreement, I met the Joint Secretary vigilance MoEF. The JS vigilance an honest IAS officer was with me in the past in the Ministry and knew about my character. He opined that this case was a case of undue harassment reflection of the poor mentality of a few and Stated that everybody knows about my reputation and requested me not to file any defamation suit against the Ministry as the issue will linger on. To this, I smiled and did not say anything and requested him to make a decision immediately on the inquiry report. So while leaving the room I said my aim is not to quarrel but to fight for my honour and it has been vindicated by the CVC's Commissioner of inquiry. In between before the CVC inquiry, I also filed a case in Delhi High Court when the CAT did not grant a stay on my application. The High Court Judge admonished the government advocate by saying that you did not find anything other than these trivial charges like challenging the legitimate Telephone bills, purchase of mobile etc.

However, no action was taken by the Ministry for more than six months after I agreed with the report of CVC so, in November 2017, I had to file a contempt petition in the CAT as the Govt was supposed to decide the case within four months of the submission of the inquiry report. The CAT, however, strangely enough, gave the government more than two and a half months to decide and fix the date in February 2019. During this period, I could learn from the most reliable sources that after the Ministry sent the report of the inquiring officer for the second opinion to the CVC as per the procedure, the CVC however, sought clarification from the Ministry as to why such a senior officer was charge-sheeted that too after his retirement if the government was not having documents to support the charges and if documents were there then action should be taken against the Presenting officer who was a Director level officer in the Ministry and belonged to Indian Railway Personnel Service. Earlier an IAS officer was appointed by the Ministry as presenting officer but he cleverly excused to be a party to this case on some pretext after going through the articles of charges as probably he knew about the motive of the case and its real worth. The Ministry under the pressure of contempt notice ultimately informally convinced the CVC to help them get over from the mess and CVC ultimately intimated the Ministry exonerating me of all the charges. The Ministry, on 8th February 2018, issued the exoneration order and the Secretary of the Ministry submitted his unconditional apology before the CAT for all the misdoings of the Ministry in this case.

Thus, the fight for justice in this court ended and I won with an apology before the court by the Secretary. With this, the ugliest work of senior functionaries of the Central Secretariat came to an end. As a consolation and also to see that I do not act further to drag them to court I was nominated by the Ministry in the ICFRE Society the apex policy-making body of the ICFRE headed by the Minister of Environment, Forest and Climate Change. I was personally invited to the office of the Minister and told by his Private Secretary, an IAS officer of good intent Mr Hardik Shah that a loud message is being sent to the system as to what the government felt about this case by appointing me to the ICFRE apex body. I told him that just when the new government came to power in May 2014, I had met the Minister as well as the Prime Minister's Principal Secretary and told them about the matter but at that time they both did not take any action rather became a party to the harassment. This is the way the government is run and the perpetrators of such crimes get away and even flourish in the corridors of power. So, the irony is such that such officers who behave like venomous serpents to others are the 'Man Friday' of powerful politicians in the corridors of power and that is the tragedy of our governance in our nation.

Another encounter was with the Guwahati CAT where I filed a case against the recovery order of Rs 37,710 ordered without and basis by in-charge DG ICFRE on the verbal orders of the Ministry officials on 18th June 2014 almost one year after my departure from ICFRE and after six audit reports of Controller and Auditor General of India found no irregularity of any kind during my term on all these issues. I had led a delegation of senior officers to Food and Agriculture Organization (FAO) Rome from 24th September to 28th September 2012 to Chair a session on "strengthening the of Forestry in the land use decision making" in the World Forestry Week meeting. I also led a delegation of Scientists to Australia from 2nd March to 8th March 2013 at the invitation of the Australian government's Department of Mines for bilateral cooperation. We travelled as per the itinerary and route chalked out by the host country officials and approved by the Minister. The Secretary ICFRE booked the journey tickets for the delegation at the lowest cost. However, just to find fault the DG ICFRE who was smarting under the newfound bonhomie with the Minister and was in charge of creating false records against me created the false narration that our halt at Singapore and Hongkong were planned trip and hence DA and hotel charges should be disallowed. The CAT stayed this order but after that surprisingly the Administrative Member an IAS officer of UP cadre came to the rescue of his cadre mate the then Secretary as even after submission of relevant and pertinent valid documents tried to prevaricate repeatedly and did not take any action even after the final hearing on 23rd march 2015. However, strangely enough, CAT Guwahati despatched the order on 14th September 2015 (clearly visible in the signatures Deputy Registrar) but wrote 23rd March as the date of passing the order on the order sheet just to comply with rules. This order was received by me after 23rd September and complied with it and sent the representation as directed. It is this kind of white-collar crimes committed by the persons sitting on important positions that are dragging India from its path of progress and fair governance.

The point I would like to hammer here is that on many occasions the CATs are becoming an extension of such bureaucratic mafia of a few and their actions are brazenly against the natural justice akin to a guard on protection duty mollycoddling a thief. In any civilized society, such actions of the government and the institution of delivering justice will fall in the category of committing white-collar crimes. This rot needs to be stemmed. The Supreme Court and the Law Ministry should, therefore, jointly appoint a Committee to examine if the purpose of creation of these bodies were achieved. The famous sociologists Edwin Sutherland the most respected American criminologists of the 20th century described white-collar crimes in 1939 as "a crime committed by a person of respectability and high social status in the course of their occupation". His concept is historical which he introduced in his speech on 27 December 1939, to the American Sociological Association, titled *The White-Collar Criminal*). The white-collar crime, the concept takes on the prejudices that aristocrats can do no wrong (which was famously expressed in the ancient legal view that a king could do no wrong). So, in today's India the illegal actions of powerful people we see day in and day out is akin to this. There may be umpteen number of cases that can be cited to invoke the conscience of our legal fraternity to see if the country can review its legal framework and at least to simply it in many cases and make changes in several other fields so that it looks futuristic jurisprudence. The same is true of the top government offices of the Centre and States. A Supreme Court intervention like in Keswanand Bharti case in which the court ordered enunciation of the doctrine of Public Interest Litigation (a relaxation on the traditional rule of locus standi) by Justice PN Bhagwati opened the courts to socially disadvantaged sections of society and opened doors for course correction by it in the functioning of the Executive. A similar reform is needed in India to nail the people who occupy top post and commit white-collar crimes.

Have Tribunals justified their creation?

Democracy brought the concept of 'welfare State" in governance aiming at social security, rule of law and social justice for its citizens. This put tremendous pressures on the judiciary as the volume of the cases rises in a geometric proportion as the courts are overburdened. This had raised many administrative and quasi-judicial questions relating to disputes in the areas of industrial, labour, service matters, consumer welfare, taxes etc. To ensure expeditious justice delivery led to the setting up of Tribunals under Article 323A and 323 B of the constitution of India. The dictionary meaning of the Tribunal is "a seat or a bench upon which a Judge or Judges sit in a court". This is a broad definition and includes ordinary courts of law also. But in administrative law, this expression is limited to adjudicating authorities other than ordinary courts of law. It thus gives a wider connotation in terms of the delivery of justice in a welfare State. Thus, the Indian Judicial system is a mix of Courts, Tribunals and Regulators. The Tribunals are constituted as per the relevant statutory provisions for expeditious redressal of grievances and adjudications of disputes for the specific subjects. They are thus theoretically meant for a very potent judicial weapon in the hands of the citizens to get quick justice.

The Supreme Court had clarified about the status of the Tribunals; the Supreme Court in *Bharat Bank Ltd v.Employees of Bharat Bank Ltd. observed that "tribunals are adjudicating bodies, which decide controversies between the parties and exercises judicial powers as distinguished from purely administrative functions and thus possesses some of the trappings of a court, but not all'*.

This means that those who occupy the positions in the Tribunals must be qualified and have a sharp judicious mind. These days, the cases in Tribunals are increasing very fast due to various reasons mainly resulting in injustice, arbitrary and wrong decisions by the decision-making powers.

Therefore, in the judicial system today the knowledge gaps can be filled up easily by the members of the Bar as the Advocates are quite apt in law and its advocacy before the bench and full of material of what is needed in these quasi-judicial bodies for arguments. These bodies, therefore, need the people who have an incisive eye for discerning the facts early are fair, quick and judicious with high moral values and can act independently without bias so that natural justice is done to the litigants. The question is whether the people who are appointed to these bodies are legally qualified enough to deliver justice. And secondly, whether the objectives of the creation of these tribunals have succeeded in quick and rightful disposal of cases? Is there an alternative way to improve the functioning of these bodies? A neutral mechanism will find the conduct of Tribunal members in this case study not only as completely unworthy of such high positions but their conduct bordering on criminality going by the rule book of our constitution. God knows how many people are suffering these white-collar crimes at their hands.

A cursory look at the cases referred above and in other cases, in various CATs, it is crystal clear that except in few complex cases the disposal is quicker in High Courts than in CATs. Take for example the cases of the Indian Council of Forestry Research and Education an autonomous body under the Government of India. During the period from 2009 to 20014-15, the Council had spent more than Rs 50 lakh in litigation with employees in the various Courts of the Country. Out of this amount, 95% was spent on various CATs. The reason is obvious the High Courts have given the verdicts fast and the cases in CATs have been lingering. In high profile cases, there are abnormal delays as some Administrative Members take advantages of their previous avatars in the Government and carry their bias and judicial incapacity to the bench. Biased decisions in Tribunals have become a routine as they do not wish to grant justice so they first tire the litigant by first delaying it and ultimately deny even issuing the final orders after six months of the final hearing even as CAT rules stipulate that after hearing, the judgements cannot wait for more than a week. It is common knowledge that people go to CAT after they exhaust the official channels available but some CATs are again forcing the applicants to go to the authorities once again to avoid deciding in favour of the applicants due to extraneous reasons of bias and networking and after months of the hearing. In my high profile case Delhi CAT had made a mockery of the judicial system by refusing to understand the meaning of words deliberately of an Office Memorandum of the Government and at the same time kept the matter open for discussion so that neither the justice is done nor the applicant move to another court. It happened after I moved to the High court which ordered me to revert to the CAT.

Without prejudice to some of the best civil servants and Judges who excelled as Members of these Tribunals when these instruments were created now many are bringing bad names on these institutions of justice created to deliver quick justice. One of the reasons for this is the poor character and inherent bias shown by some of the Administrative Members who belong to mostly a single service i.e. IAS and tend to favour their friends in Government with whom some of them sit, dine and routinely meet in social gatherings and such Members are used to getting away with arbitrary and patently illegal decisions in the government and carry the same mindset to the sphere of the judiciary. It is this lack of accountability and the supervision by High Courts that things have come to this pass in CATs because there is no supervisory mechanism to oversee the performance of the Tribunals. The appointments in Tribunals are made by the Government in the Department of Personnel which is the cadre controlling authority of the IAS and there always is a queue and intense networking by IAS officers (months before retirement)/few Judges and Advocates seeking these post-retirement benefits. The political class consider them fortunate to have such fantastic experts at the top with them and endorses DoPT proposal. Yet another reason is the quality of judicial appointees. Many advocates whose practice is not very good are made Judicial Members and when they preside over the bench in the Tribunal they generally go by the opinion of the Administrative Member and virtually play second fiddle to them. Further, as Stated there is no supervisory and monitoring control over the Tribunals and thus are totally independent resulting in non-accountability which is reflected in many Tribunals like in Consumer Forums, CATs when the Members do not attend office in time and the people have to suffer. Many Government agencies take the CATs for granted prevaricate and procrastinate in filing replies by seeking repeated time in order to tire the litigants, create records and cases that linger on for months and years together. This beats the very purpose of the creation of these bodies.

The Government of India is taking up reforms in the judicial system of the country and pushing for the appointment of the Judicial Accountability Commission in the country. There should be a fair assessment of what the tribunals have achieved. They have failed in expeditious disposal of the cases the basic reason for which they were created. The worst thing is that their benches are run mostly by the retired Judges and retired bureaucrats and this introduces the arbitrariness in the concept itself. While the Tribunal system may be good for regulatory functions as they have to work within a set formatted framework but in other cases where jurisprudence is the primary concern, it should be again thought of if the High Courts are again transferred this function with creation of more posts of Judges. Alternatively, the Act should be amended and a time frame of three months as upper limits should be fixed to dispose a case along with stringent monitoring for capacity assessment and annually auditing the way judgments are made with administrative control of the High Courts.

If the tribunal system had to remain, a mechanism should be evolved for the appointment of Tribunal Members and fix accountability for their decisions. The Government should constitute a Recruitment Board, headed by a serving Judge of the Supreme Court with three other Judges as members to select all postings in all the Tribunals and the board should be housed in the Supreme Court. The Board should advertise the posts of judicial and administrative member and recommend the names to the government for the appointment. The Government should also reduce the age of retirement in the Tribunals to 62 years only for the non-judicial members and all those who are selected should have five years of service left before they apply for the post and in the event of their selection their services should be transferred to such Tribunals and they should retire from there. This will foster accountability and commitment as only interested persons will apply and they will still be in service and within the purview of conduct rules. Will the Government take a call on this?

When it comes to assessing the governance mostly the performance of the executive and its monolith bureaucracy is scrutinized by the media and experts. The sound, effective and independent judiciary is equally important for bringing a sense of happiness for people and for protecting their constitutional rights. The Judiciary was in the limelight when a letter was written by the former Chief Justice of India (CJI) Justice Ranjan Gogoi to the Prime Minister in 2019 on pending cases and requested for increasing the retirement age of judges across the judicial spectrum. Today more than 3.5 crore cases are pending in the courts in India and increasing every year almost at the rate of 9.7%. In the Supreme Court alone pending cases as of July 2019 were 58,669 while in hearing there were 20914. For admission alone, 37,775 cases were listed. The issue of increasing the retirement age of judges may have merit whatsoever, but judiciary must ponder if pendency is the only issue for the Indian judiciary to deal with. The real issue, however, is an absence of quick, affordable and accessible justice for a fast section of our people

The moot question in today's scenario is why the judiciary is perceived to have failed on the issue of providing quick access to justice to a commoner in the remote countryside, urban ghettos and middle class. The cost of getting justice is very high not only for the poor but also for the well-to-do upper-middle-class families. Justice is painfully cumbersome and time-consuming and the powerful people get away with their misdeeds in many cases. The judiciary, therefore, needs reforms to provide timely affordable justice and change its age-old British style functioning. One Supreme court Judge who recently retired in May 2020 echoed the agony of poor people who find it difficult to get justice in the apex court.

The Judiciary must, therefore, evolve a protocol so that judges decide the cases within a time limit and develop a mechanism to quickly deal with the intricacies of cases. Another issue is of charging reasonable fees by the advocates and providing judicial assistance. It will bring more professionalism and effectiveness. For the Tribunals etc no retired person should be made eligible and only serving judges should be appointed.

Tussle for an Acronym

08

The following account is on the acronym, IFS, being used by the two Groups A services – the Indian Forest Service and the Indian Foreign Service. Of late for the past few years, the Department of Personnel and Training (DoPT) had in most of their orders has started using IFoS for the Forest Service. It has started at the Lal Bahadur Shastri National Academy of Administration where both the Forest and Foreign Service officers are together during their foundation course and to distinguish, they started this practice. Now the mandarins of DoPT who are a law unto themselves and guard the fortress of IAS have slowly started to apportion IFoS to the forest service. This article was published in 'Pioneer' and a little different version in the 'Magazine Bureaucracy Today' in 2016. It is an interesting reading on the way how things imposed by the dominant group in the bureaucracy in a coordinated manner on their less powerful siblings.

For the last 30 years or so the acronym IFS is being used in Government correspondences for both Indian Forest Service and the Indian Foreign Service. The Forests Service is an All India Service like IAS and IPS whereas Foreign Service is a Group A Central Service like IRS etc. Recently, however, an amusing correspondence between the External Affairs Ministry, the Department of Personnel & Training and Environment & Forest Ministry are going on as Foreign Service considers itself as older than Forest service and hence had objected to Forest Service using this acronym and wants to arrogate itself the sole use of this acronym.

In this regard, it will be interesting to remember an incident that happened with one of my batch mates while we were on probation at the Indian Forest College, now known as Indira Gandhi National Forest Academy. Once the former Prime Minister late Chaudhury Charan Singh while meeting this Forest Service Probationer from his constituency in June asked him how many forests he had seen so far in his training and what is their condition. The probationer was surprised and gathered the courage as to how the PM asked him straight about the forests as soon as he entered his room. He gathered the courage while leaving the room and asked him how he knew that he is in the forest service. The PM said, "After seeing your visiting card and after noticing your dress I could guess that you are an Indian Forest Service officer because a Foreign Service officer would have come to meet me in full suit tie with sweating in his face in this scorching summer". This story can be linked humorously with the way two cadres position themselves before civil society. Recently the officers of foreign service have raised a hornets' nest by writing the department of personnel that the acronym IFS should only be written for the Indian Foreign Service as the service is older than Indian Forest Service who are also using the acronym IFS. The department of personnel had in turn written to the Ministry of Environment, Forests and Climate Change for their views. Indian diplomats are known for the 'fuddy-duddy' style of language and have created a funny situation for the government to appropriate the name IFS for their service. There is a big difference between the natures of both these services. The Indian Forest Service is an All India Service whereas the Indian Foreign Service is a Central Group 'A' Service. As such, there is no need for the diplomats to usurp the acronym IFS as their clientele are different.

The acronym IFS is in use for both the services for a long time regularly by the central as well as State governments and it can be easily deciphered by seeing the context of the use for which service it is being used. The fact is that the Indian Foreign Service most of the time is communicating with foreign governments and with other Ministries in the Centreand States and while corresponding with other offices the need for use of this acronym is not common. On the other hand, this acronym for the Indian Forest Service is used mostly by the State government and largely by the common people in the districts, sub-divisional towns and in about 170,000 villages near the forests. The department of personnel of late has been writing IFoS for the forest service in its communications and sometime, IFS also. Now consider the funny picture of phonetics it will generate all over the country with different style of pronunciations. What the majority of people in India in districts and sub-divisional towns/villages will pronounce this word IFoS. It will be very funny phonetic of "Ifoosh" officer Mr such and such did such thing to another "Ifoosh" officer. The whole character of the service will change in the funny acronym.

Now let us examine this from the perspective of correct historical perspectives and of course common sense. The Indian Foreign Service was created in 1946 by the then Prime Minister late Jawaharlal Nehru by largely handpicking officers without any competitive examination and many of the people of princely States were rehabilitated in the service. A few years later it was made part of the IAS examination and for many years it was the preferred service of the top rankers. The Indian Forest Service was constituted in 1866 after the creation of the forest department in 1865 under the British Government of India and it was then known as Imperial Forest Service and the acronym IFS was used for this service since then. The officers were trained in Britain till Indian Forest College was set up. The Imperial Forest Service was for European only until the recruitment of Indian started and it became the Indian Forest Service in 1920 with the recruitment of 4 Indians. At that time there was no Foreign Service as the Foreign affairs were directly under the control of the British crown and British Indian Government. The subject Forest was transferred from federal list to State list after the enactment of the Government of India Act 1935 and the recruitment for Indian Forest Service was discontinued after 1932 until it was revived in 1966. But what is noteworthy to mention is the fact that Indian Forest Service Officers who were recruited in 1932 continued to serve till the early sixties and the IFS acronym was used by and for them. So historically the acronym belongs to the Forest Service. The Indian Forest Service Association had raised the issue and demanded that the acronym for their services should be retained as the acronym IFoS would create a big confusion all over India.

This Ministry of Environment, Forest and Climate Change had given a detailed justification for using the acronym IFS for the Indian Forest Service citing historical facts of uninterrupted use of this acronym for the forest service officers since 1866. The Ministry had argued that the Foreign Service should use the acronym IFoS or IFS on the same pattern, Indian Postal Service is using IPoS and IPS as All India Service is using it and on a similar pattern, all three services should use the three-letter acronym.

This writer would suggest that the name Indian Foreign Service is contradictory in itself and is an oxymoron considering the use of the word name Indian as well as Foreign. The better name of the service should be

Indian Diplomatic Service or **Indian External Affairs Service** to make it more meaningful for the diplomats like Forest Service sounds for the foresters. Till such time both the services could use this acronym as the areas of operation of both the services are totally different and so is the context in which it is used in the government correspondences. It is not an issue worth quibbling after all the days of Victorian English are over and people can easily decipher the context of the use of the IFS acronym even if it is used for both the services as acronyms have not yet been patented nor any law allows it.

There has been no action by the DoPT on the request of the Ministry of Environment as well as the IFS Association and the matter has been silently buried. However, to keep the matter alive intermittently the DoPT uses in some of its notification IFS for the forest service. Gradually the forest officers have accepted it as '*fait accompli*' which could have been otherwise settled for both the services if not in favour of forest service which has been using it since British time.

This article was also included in my previous book which is compilation of my article but I find that it is more relevant to be made part of this book as well. The way the DoPT and the bureaucracy had treated the historical claims of Indian Forest Service on the acronym well supported by the Ministry of Environment, Forests and Climate Chang, reflect the bias and self righteous mindset of the people who are responsible for ensuring fairness. The DoPT could have allowed both the Indian Forest Service as well as Indian Foreign Service to use it in general correspondences. At a time when the world is in the midst of severe ecological threat we need to attract the youth to forests service. The political leadership need to step up efforts to upscale the career value of those who work in the field of environment and forest.

Comedy of Errors

09

'Comedy of Errors' is one of the shortest slapsticks play by William Shakespeare. Slapstick is a style of humour involving exaggerated physical activity that exceeds the boundaries of normal physical comedy. The phrase is used to describe a situation that is so full of mistakes and problems that it seems irritatingly funny yet entertaining. The narration here is not less than an act of comedy of errors by the government officials. It also resembles the story 'Tragedy of Errors' by Henry James in which, with mistaken identity a man was killed (who was having an illicit relationship with a lady by the boatman hired by her to kill her husband so that she can be with her boyfriend). I am giving these examples so that the readers can have a hearty laugh as well as see how the wrong decisions in the system of governance can cause immense harassment to the public.

In 2003, when I was posted as Inspector-General of Forests in the Ministry of Environment and Forests, Mr BS Sajwan who was Secretary Forest and Conservator of Forests in the Union Territory (UT) of Dadar Nagar Haveli, Diu and Daman came to the Ministry and met me and discussed the matter regarding declaration of the private lands as Protected Forests by the UT administration in 1988 which has resulted in great hardship for the common man. In the meanwhile, we were also seized of the matter as the local Member of Parliament had also written a letter to Mr TR Baalu the Environment and Forest Minister. The issue was the declaration of 30 meters of land, mostly private lands, on both side of the Kotar (locally known as rainwater drains) as Protected Forests (PF) under Section 29 of the Indian Forest Act 1927 vide a notification issued by the UT administration on 25th February 1988. We both were wondering that it should not have happened so, as land which is owned by the government can only be legally declared as PF.

The provisions of Section 29 thus are: *"the State Government may, by notification in the Official Gazette, declare the provisions of this Chapter applicable to any forest-land or waste-land which, is not included in a reserved forest but which is the property of Government, or over which the Government has proprietary rights, or to the whole or any part of the forest produce of which the Government is entitled"*.

Mr Sajwan (who later on became a Member of the National Green Tribunal) also said that even the Additional Director-General of Forests (ADG) Forest Conservation had visited the site a few months ago on this matter but no action has been taken by the Ministry so far. I was wondering if the action was taken under section 35 of the Act (under which there is a provision prohibiting a few things on any forestland irrespective of the ownership but here also the land should be a forest land to invoke this section) instead of 29. I told Mr Sajwan that I will see the file and will act on this and in any case, the letter of the MP will have to be replied to as such communications as per procedure is treated as VIP reference.

After Mr Sajwan left, I called for the file and studied the matter. After going through the papers in the file, it became clear to me that the UT administration did notify parts of private lands contiguous to government lands along the Kotar as PF under section 29 of the Indian Forest Act 1927. The decision of the then Conservator of Forests and the Administrator was to increase the greenery but while doing so they glossed over the fact that it was an ultra vires action as private lands cannot be legally declared as PF land as per the provision of the Act. While going through the file I found that the trial Court and District and session Court of UT had given relief to some local petitioners whose land was declared as PF. However, here comes the intransigence attitude of the senior government functionaries who are responsible for interpreting and implementing the law for better public service. Knowing full well that they have transgressed the law by locking the private lands of thousands of people as PF land they approached the various Courts including Bombay High Court against the decision of the lower court. The Bombay High Court in its order dated 21st January 1998, in case No 197 of 1997 (Union of India v/s Jitendra Singh Mohan Singh Parmar and others) though agreed that the intentions are good to declare PF but decided that the petitioner's land cannot be declared as PF. It, however, did not quash the entire notification but only granted relief to the petitioner. There were thousands of other victims having small portions of their land declared as PF. The UT administration had again gone for appeal against the Bombay High court judgement.

I discussed this matter with the DG Forests and informed him about this mistake of the Administration. He approved my plan to visit Silvasa and discuss the matter with the local people and the administration. So, I telephoned Mr Sajwan and submitted my travel plan to him. I landed up in Silvasa on the appointed date and went to the office of Secretary Forest and Conservator of Forests. There we held a meeting with his officers, scrutinized all the relevant papers on the status of the land and the procedure followed while declaring the PF. We also met a few affected people in the CF office. It is an interesting story to know how our key officers follow the rules without application of mind and become the slave of some papers. One young man who had just done his MBA and wanted to develop a shopping complex on his land and his father spent a considerable amount in developing his land. However, the forest department told him that before he starts the work, he will have to seek forestry clearance from the Bhopal Regional office of the Ministry of Environment and Forests because after declaring the land as PF it is mandatory to obtain clearance under the Forest Conservation Act 1980. He applied for forestry clearance and the proposal was sent to the Regional Chief Conservator of Forests (RCCF) Bhopal. The RCCF Bhopal asked the applicant to pay the Net Present Value (NPV) of the forestland. This was a sizeable amount. The young man told me in presence of the officers that his father is very angry for spending so much money on this land without ascertaining the facts and had expelled him from his home making him a vagabond. He was about to break into tears and wanted the government of India to help him. There were other people also who demanded revocation of the PF. The next day we held a public hearing in the office of the Collector where a large number of people came were agitated on taking over their land. The Administrator was not available as he was out but the Collector and Secretary Revenue and Forests were present and endorsed the public demand. I also came to know from the records that the due procedure was not followed by the administration in declaring the lands as PF.

The provision of subsection 3 of section 29 which interalia reads thus *"No such notification shall be made unless the nature and extent of the rights of Government and of private persons in or over the forest-land or waste-land comprised therein have been inquired into and recorded at a survey or settlement, or in such other manner as the State Government thinks sufficient. Every such record shall be presumed to be correct until the contrary is proved: Provided that, if, in the case of any forest-land or wasteland, the State Government thinks that such inquiry and record are necessary, but that they will occupy such length of time as in the meantime to endanger the rights of Government, the State Government may, pending such inquiry and record, declare such land to be a protected forest, but so as not to abridge or affect any existing rights of individuals or communities."*

The UT administration did not follow the statutory requirement as per 29(3) and all of a sudden declared the land as PF. After meeting the public and the UT administration I got convinced that though the intention of the forest department may have been in the interest of conservation, it was done without application of mind, and in a nutshell, a large number of private lands were included in the notification as PF land due to the sweeping and arbitrary inclusion of all kinds of lands within 30 meter on both sides of Kotar (rainwater drains) without even caring for sending a notice of settling their rights. It had thus caused immense hardships to the people. What can be a better Indian scenario of a Shakespearian story than this done by the very educated people who were at the helm of affairs by virtue of their knowledge and merit? It was purely a stupid decision by all means.

At the end of my trip to Silvasa, I was convinced that this patently wrong decision and it cannot be condoned with a specious argument that it was done with good intention. It is a case of unruly committed people who did not bother about the fall out of their misplaced zeal to achieve their objectives. But a mistake is a mistake and a wrong after all cannot be sustained for long. In their overzealousness good people can do wrong it doesn't make them less good. But it also doesn't make the wrong less wrong. So, in return, I decided to propose rescinding the notification and redoing it only for the government land. I discussed with the DG Forests and put up a detailed note suggesting withdrawal of this notification with the advice that the UT administration can issue a fresh notification as per the provisions of Section 29 and after duly settling the rights on such forest and wastelands lands owned by the government. When the file reached the Secretary, he was flabbergasted and had a hearty laugh on the matter but wanted me to first write to the UT Administration and take his concurrence on the proposed advice to the UT administration more so as the UT administration had also gone to the Supreme Court against the judgement of Bombay High Court. I conveyed the decision of the Ministry to the UT Administrator and sought his concurrence. A prompt reply came from the Administration of the UT agreeing for withdrawing the notification and I despatched the letter requesting to rescind the 25th February 1988 notification. It vindicated the stand taken by Mr Sajwan to give justice to the people of the UT even though the UT administration was trying to move to the Supreme Court. The administration took action as per our advice and the entire population owning lands near Kotar were given their land back. I only hoped that the young man who met me in Silvasa to tell his agony of his father expelled him from home got his home back. Had the Bombay High Court struck down the notification itself rather than giving relief to individual litigant, the people would have got justice long back. However, the obstinate attitude of the administration prolonged the agony of people and only when fair-minded officers joined hands the people got their land back in a just manner.

As a saying goes, the court cases proved that the love of justice in most men is nothing more than the fear of suffering injustice. This action of ours proved what Mahatma Gandhi had said "Truth never damages a cause that is just."

Saga of India's Foresters

10

The Indian Forest Service (IFS) was revived in 1966 when under the All India Service Act 1951 the government of India thought it necessary to create this service so that there is uniformity in approach in protection, conservation and regeneration of forest resources through common recruitment and training. The objective was to develop a shared vision and a sense of *Esprit de Corps* among the forestry professionals at the senior level. The credit for the revival of the Indian Forest Service goes to Late Sri Hari Singh who was the Inspector General of Forests (IGF) at that time and the then Prime Minister late Mrs Indira Gandhi who was an avowed nature lover. It was her foresight and love for nature that today we have an excellent legal and environmental framework in the country and the country must be indebted to her for this and especially for the farsighted decision of enactment of the Forest Conservation Act 1980 and the Wildlife Protection Act 1972. She discussed a great deal with Chipko movement leader late Sunder Lal Bahuguna who had also influenced her policies on forest conservation. If these ACTs would not have come, the State governments under political compulsions by now would have bartered away vast chunks of the forests in the name of the settlement of people and development. The United Progressive Alliance (UPA) government in the Centreled by her daughter-in-law Sonia Gandhi's Congress party, under pressure from allies for meeting political ends, diluted the Forest Conservation Act by enacting Forest Right Act in 2006 under which so far 52 lakh hectares have been vested and the process is still on. It has become a political issue for the competing political parties. It is true that there were a few unsettled claims; I have as IGF collected data from all States during 2003 on the disputed settlement claims but the total disputed claims were not more than 3.5 lakh hectares in all over India and a total of around 13 lakh hectares of forests were reported under illegal occupation which the forest departments claimed as encroachments. Now the Act has become an open-ended Act and in the vortex of politics. In reality, Indira Gandhi was an early Environmentalist.

It will be worthwhile to mention here that Mr Hari Singh (who was quite junior considering the fact that many officers were senior to him in the position of CCF in States) was the Chief Conservator of Forests (CCF)

Gujarat when all the CCFs of States gathered in a meeting in Delhi and passed a resolution unanimously that Mr Hari Singh should be appointed as IGF and many senior foresters willingly had foregone their chances because Mr Hari Singh was having sufficient tenure as an IGF and he being a dynamic officer, most of the CCFs believed that he can carry the task of the revival of the IFS to its logical end. This incident may be only one of its kinds in the annals of Indian civil services where today we witness just the opposite when officers are at each other's throat to occupy the top posts and the present generation of the IFS is no exception to this tendency. The present and future generation shall ever remain grateful to those foresters who forgave their chances to be IGF and it is an example to be emulated by all in the bureaucracy. Mr Hari Singh was Inspector-General of Forests from 1964 to 1969 and accomplished the task of establishing the only All India Service created post-independence. This veteran visionary forester died in the year 2003.

The British laid the foundation of the Indian Forest Department in 1864 when they appointed Dietrich Brandis as the first Inspector General of Forests, and thereafter they slowly developed the legal and institutional framework for the governance of forests by bringing in Indian Forest Act in 1865, which they modified in 1878 and finally enacted the Indian Forest Act 1927 which is still the legal framework all over India with certain State-specific Acts based on it for the governance of forests. The British announced the 1894 Forest Policy which was based on the JA Voelker Report in 1893 on the improvement of Indian agriculture. The policy placed forest resources under State control with revenue generation as a major objective, along with importance given to furthering greater agriculture.

To scientifically manage the forests the British on the advice of Brandis created the Imperial Forest Service (IFS) in 1867. The officers recruited from 1867 to 1885 were trained at Hanover in Germany, and Nancy in France, and from 1885 to 1905 at Cooper's Hill, London an Engineering College. From 1905 to 1926, the University of Oxford, University of Cambridge, and University of Edinburgh trained the officers of Imperial Forest Service officers. Later on, in 1920 it was decided to train the IFS officers in India at the Imperial Forest Research Institute (FRI) Dehradun, which was set up in 1906 at Chandbagh (now houses Doon School) Dehradun to conduct research on Silviculture, Mensuration, Management and Utilization and train the subordinate foresters. The FRI trained the IFS officers from 1926 till 1932. As the opposition of 'diarchy' under the Government of India Act, 1919, grew from all sections of Indian political diaspora after the first-round table conference the British government was toying with some idea to transfer some subjects like Forests to the Provincial governments and thus due to lack of demand the IFS training was stopped in 1932. The new conservative government in 1933 appointed a Joint select Committee of British Parliament under Lord Linlithgow which after around 18 months deliberations recommended a new federal set up amidst stiff opposition from the then conservative Back Benchers like Winston Churchill. Consequently, the Government of India Act 1935 was passed by the British Parliament in which the subject Forests was transferred to Province. The Indian Forest College was established in 1938 to train the officers of Superior State Forest Service from various Provinces till the revival of the Indian Forest Service in 1966.

The newly established IFS of 1966 was nowhere near the old IFS in terms of pay scales and consequently the status. The newly created service had to struggle to come to terms with the unprecedented opposition and step brotherly treatment from the well-entrenched bureaucracy. This writer once met Late Hari Singh in 1985 (who is credited with the creation of the service) in a seminar in Delhi on wastelands development. When the Secretary of the Agriculture Ministry in his inaugural address remarked that the foresters have destroyed the forests in league with contractors rendering a large chunk of forests as degraded wasteland, a few of us attending this seminar during the tea break went to and asked Mr Hari Singh and Mr KM Tewari the former President of FRI about the damning Statement on the foresters by the Secretary Mr Mukherji. Mr Hari Singh blamed it on the lack of boldness among the initial recruits who could have taken action on the unfinished agenda after his retirement. He said there was a strong lobby of bureaucrats which was opposed to the creation of the service, providing it better scales like other All India Services and he had to compromise on some initial irritants and was single-handedly focused on seeing the revival of the service first. He was successful due to his proximity with Prime Minister Indira Gandhi who also advised him to first create the service and then take up the issues later on. Mr KM Tewari along with us went to Mr Mukherji the Agriculture Secretary to counter his sarcastic remarks in the inaugural session. Mr Tewari blasted him badly saying you people are always making these vague and patently incorrect Statements because you know nothing about the forest management and making such baseless Statements with a simple intention to defame the good work of the foresters of the country. The Secretary immediately was pushed on the defensive and agreed and said he made the Statement because this is the general view in the society. In the next session, the Secretary retraced his Statement. Mr KM Tewari was a very bold professional who made a name for himself was awarded 'Padam Shri' for his contribution to promoting social forestry in UP. I have quoted this discussion because it reflects the situation in which the IFS officers had to travel in their journey as members of an All India Service and part of Indian bureaucracy after the revival of IFS in 1966. A tendency to ignore its creation among the well-entrenched bureaucracy!

On the positive side after more than 50 years of its creation, all the different wings of State forest departments have achieved spectacular results in conserving the forests, wildlife and the bio-diversity of the country despite such a large and ever-growing population which puts more and more pressure on the forests as more than 40 crore people (including more than 10 crore tribal people) living in 170,000 fringe villages in and around 32 million hectares of the forests. The service offers variety in job and is an excellent profession to be in and a well-trained forester is a composite expert with fine administrative skills. The achievements of the government of India in meeting the targets for the climate change Paris deal on mitigation and planting of trees is nothing but outstanding due to the hard work of the field officers and subordinate forest staff.

The performance of any service, however, depends upon the measurable parameters to speak for and the overall public perception. The public perception depends upon the importance attached to it by the political masters and general public. Indian society of today's democracy is 'law and order' centric because we are yet to achieve a status of an integrated society due to diversity of languages, culture and rising conflicts due to economic disparities. The only show of semblance of authority is a guarantee of social acceptance. The forest service lacked bold and cohesive leadership and hence has intrinsic career value infirmities which accord it a low value compared to its counterpart All India Services as the general perception of the public towards the importance of forests is poor. It also lost its pre-colonial trappings at the district level. During colonial times the infrastructure was quite well for a forester to live in the forests for a long time. The Conservators of Forests had a well equipped ration vehicle for their long tours and the DFOs were having elephants and horses and daily runners as assistance between the forests and the office with beautiful forest rest houses. It gave the forests service a unique status. In UP and many other States the Conservators of Forests used to have flags on their cars. Today the administration in any field needs a sound infrastructure of men and material which also raises the stakes for the service in the eyes of the society. In case of IAS and IPS the seniors as well as the government in the name of law and order rightfully provides them with good number of vehicles, houses and other infrastructures. The young IFS officers as well as the DFOs in the districts have bare minimum vehicles and that too of not commensurate to the status of an AIS officer like in other services. The young IFS fresh from academy get demoralized and many become lethargic officers with less motivation. The good British time Bungalows of forest officers on many occasions were taken over and given to other officers. The seniors of the service who were in the helm of affairs have failed to provide strong leadership or became prisoners of circumstances on this fundamental requirement of present time to give a strong professional and infrastructural support at the district level. Gradually the bureaucracy deliberately choked the forest service of good infrastructure at all level and the forest officers meekly surrendered. The public image of an officer in the field is directly proportional to the performance of the department. The anti-social elements specially the poachers and smugglers monitor these things very well. Even the CAMPA funds have put restriction on spending money on infrastructure for the forest department citing a court decision. One of the needs of the hour is to forge a unity of purpose among the AIS officers in the fields to tackle the emerging developmental and problems like Naxalism and the State government must create some institutional mechanism for this.

As Stated some of the infirmities are self-afflicted when we did not create a sound and efficient organizational structure with suitable infrastructure for the present time at the district and sub-divisional level. It is hoped that the mandarins of central and State governments will act now on the recent orders of Supreme Court on 8th January 2021 in T. N. Godavarman Thirumulpad Vs Union of India & Other, on providing good support for the field formulations. The Apex Court took serious view of the situation and said that the forest officers and staff would be in no position to protect the environment and the forests which are normally vast tracts of uninhabited land and of which poachers take undue advantage for carrying out their nefarious activities. "It is difficult to imagine how any law can be enforced by the forest officers and staff who are poorly unarmed against poachers who are likely to be heavily armed," the bench of Chief Justice S. A. Bobde, Justice A. S. Bopanna and Justice V. Ramasubramanian said.

Mr Hari Singh's focus after the creation of the service was more on creating the State cadres of the service through 'initial recruitment' from State forest service which was fraught with State-specific complications and many court cases as it was based on a certain fixed formula. By the time he completed the cadre constitution he had no time left for completing the other initial hiccups he encountered during constitution of the service and he retired before the implementation of third pay commission report. Later on, the focus of initial recruits shifted on creating more and more vacancies in the cadre for creating scope for the remaining State service officers and for those who missed the bus to be elevated in IFS. The deleterious effect of this was the splitting of divisional forest offices and the creation of more than one divisional forest officers at the district level. This lopsided expansion was done irrationally and it dented the image of the service at the field levels and relegating it to a position not commensurate with the status of an All India Service.

The forest service controls 23 per cent of the landmass of the country and if we judge the overall performance of the service in conserving and preserving the forest resources since independence, it is outstanding by any measurable parameters. First, after the independence, it got all the poor category forests of princely States and ex Jamidari forests. The way field formulations have been committed to their work is very clearly shown by the 'State of Forest Report' brought out biannually by the Forest Survey of India for the last more than 25 years. The Project Tiger, Project Elephants and the management of National Parks and Sanctuaries is a shining example of how to conserve the wildlife over 15 million ha of protected area network. The introduction of people's participation through the Joint Forest Management (JFM) in the nineties of the last century, for management and rehabilitation of degraded forests, is a first of its kind for sharing the responsibility of managing government resources. More than 25% of the recorded forests are being managed today jointly with the local people. After 1990, the central Government did further empower the JFM through its 2000 and 2002 guidelines bringing good forest area also in its ambit. However, now the JFM is stagnating and need to be further strengthened through second and third-generation reforms. In developing technologies for agro and farm forestry our scarcely funded research organizations have done a very satisfactory job.

Having said this, if one roams around in the corridors of powers in Delhi the IFS as a service is everyone's whipping boy be it the Prime Minister's office or the Ministry of Environment or Tribal Affairs or Planning Commission (Niti Ayog now) etc. One of the main reasons for this is the totally uncalled for inter-service rivalry between the IAS and IFS and the mindset of bureaucracy and Ministers to deny the service its legitimate role and space at the higher policy-making levels. Take for example, the report of National Commission of Agriculture (NCA) report 1976 which laid down recommendations for better forest management. If the government had implemented the NCA's recommendations the forestry sector would have contributed a great deal in nation gross domestic products. Similarly the National Forest Commission set up in 2002 by the then Prime Minister Atal Bihari Vajpayee submitted its report in the year 2006 is gathering dust in the archives of Ministry of Environment and Forests. Even the National Forest Policy recommendations were not implemented in full. There may be several such incidents in other sphere of governance and the nation must raise an issue of accountability on constitution of such commissions and committees and then junking them with bureaucratic disdain.

The present generation of the IFS to a certain extent should share the blame for the pitiable condition of its officers in the Environment, Forest and Climate Change Ministry. We must equally share the blame with IAS for the perceived poor performance of the forestry and environment sector. Today, there are three types of officers in the country among the IFS and this is true to all other civil services too including IAS in their service context. First, true professionals a minuscule group who are sincere, committed and honest and bold enough to oppose wrong dictates and have the guts to fight. They end up either side-lined or do their work silently for fear of being harassed. The second group is similar to the first group in professional competence except that they are selfish and they compromise and join hands with the powerful people and enjoy the perks and make themselves comfortable no matter what happens to their service or profession. The third group is of poor professionals who are corrupt and have no qualms about what they do and simply damage their image and of their cadre. This scenario is a reflection of today's society and the IFS is no exception.

The large numbers of officers of IFS are, therefore, in the grip of self-centred anxiety about their career. The direct impact of this is in the quality of leadership IFS officers exhibits. These days if one gets into a position of authority in the State or Centregovernment, he or she caters only for his or her group and close friends in the service and exhibit a disdainful attitude towards other fellow officers and the seniors. It is this nature of a few officers of the service that is quite noticeable by the people outside the service in the system and that determines their overall treatment of the service. The sense of camaraderie for which the old foresters were famous, is now seen only in group camaraderie which is self-defeating, both in the short term as well as the long-term performance of the service. If such things happen in an organised service having an

All India character, the service officers on many occasions behaves as conglomerate of a hotchpotch. I had vividly noticed it in the way some of the officers who used to run around me killed some of the people-oriented initiatives, I had taken in ICFRE like demolishing the extension counter created for the tribal handicrafts which was to bring good name to the institution, foresters and scientists. The second was deliberately underplaying the monumental work of revisiting the forest types of India just to prove their loyalty to officers outside the service. It also reflects the poor professional focus by senior forest officers on scientific and technical matters in the State forest departments. If we do not know the status of changes in our forests, how can we combat the climatic changes and degradation in our ecology? This monumental work done by a team of 1800 experts from ICFRE and the State forest department was acclaimed widely in the international forums because the world looks to India to guide on the status of changes in the forests of India.

The way the Ministry of Environment is run by the bureaucracy and Ministers is a glaring case of degradation of values that has occurred among the governing institutions. My experience in this Ministry for more than seventeen years at various levels as well as in the Agriculture and Planning Commission at senior levels makes it amply clear that the institutions of All India Services and Central Group A and B services needs a thorough overhauling. The IAS officers in this Ministry take blatantly partisan decisions to ensure their dominance in all policy matters and behave in mafia-style and the IFS officers have given in to this systematic demolition of the morale of the forest officers and a few are willing partners in the game. In my personal experience, it appears to me that these officers create silent ginger groups in the Centre and States to monitor the behaviour of bold officers, and committed to their profession and then target them in their career.

The pressure on forests for developmental purposes makes an average forest officer vulnerable for criticism and IAS join hand with politicians to run down the service and promote pliability and incompetence among officers. After the creation of the Forest Conservation Act 1980, the forest officers are perceived to have become quite powerful hindrances in the system. This situation was irritating the bureaucrats and the political powers and added some time by the intransigence attitude of the few forest officers in the field in defining the violation of the Act led to the development of a nexus between the social activists and all those who see the forest department as an irritant.

The situation of governance may be similar in States and other ministries of the government. In this regard, I would also like to give an example of how the bureaucracy of the Agriculture Ministry reacted to the appointment of Mr JS Samra, a hard-working agriculture scientist, as the Chief Executive Officer of the National Rainfed Area Authority (NRAA) created by the then Prime Minister Dr Manmohan Singh as a policy-making body for increasing the productivity of Agriculture and other natural resources in a holistic and integrated manner. They tried to choke it for funds and staff and ultimately Mr Montek Singh Ahluwalia, the Deputy Chairman of the Planning Commission who was the mentor of Dr Samra shifted it from Agriculture Ministry to Planning Commission but there also the problem continued, especially, with the Financial Division where the Financial Advisor tried to stop many proposals but here the situation was not so bad compared to the Agriculture Ministry. The Department of Personnel tried very hard to prevent the fixation of Dr Samra's pension in the Apex Scale at the Secretary's pay when he retired from his parent department the Indian Council of Agricultural Research (ICAR). Despite the clear instruction of PMO where he has the support on the day of his retirement from ICAR his pension in the forenoon was obdurately fixed at the level of his scale in ICAR but the last-minute intervention by the Prime Minister's Principal Secretary the decision was reversed in the afternoon and his pension was fixed in the Apex Scale at the level of Secretary to the government of India, the post he was holding. After the retirement of Dr Samra, the NRAA has been taken back in Agriculture Ministry and is being headed by an IAS officer of Secretary Level.

Thus, the IFS though after a revival in 1966, has increased the intelligence level in the profession however, as a professional cadre at the national level it is losing its sheen as a large number of its officials have adopted an expediency dominated approach crucifying the profession at the altar of personal gains. The culture of sycophancy, corruption and undesirable networking for personal gains is quite widespread in the service in the States. This phenomenon is not unique for the forest service's but is the trend among all the services, however, its deleterious effects are more pronounced for the IFS as it lacks proximity to the Ministers who are the Centre of powers hence the capacity to influence the policy formulation is lowest among the All India Services. Because of this, it is easy to play with the interests of the profession and the sector at large.

The forest officers must remember that the overall performance of the forest departments in the country considering the measurable parameters are not bad at all but then why the service is not able to shed the negative propaganda about its role in the close circuit of powers? One such example is the creation of the Forest Right Act 2006, the housing of the National Bamboo Mission and National Medicinal Plant Board outside the Ministry of Environment and Forests. In a nutshell, the revival of the service in 1966 has partially met the objectives for which it was created. A large number of its officers though for past few years have been deployed in the Central Secretariat in different departments and also being posted in various departments of the States and the officers are giving outstanding performances in their works this assessment of the author is only with respect to the forest and environmental conservation at the top policy-making levels. While comparing with two other All India Service one of the biggest reasons for poor perception about the service is the structure of the service at the district level. During the British period, the area of many DFOs was spread in more than one district but after independence and revival of the service, the lopsided expansion had resulted in the creation of more than one DFO in a district. Further, the feeder service to the IFS, the Provincial Forest Service or the State Forest Service (SFS) had no independent position in the department and in most of the State, SFS officers are simply attached to the DFO offices. I had corrected this in Tripura by convincing the Chief Minister when I was posted as Principal Secretary Forests and revamped the structure of the Forest Department. In Tripura, we had created the office of District Forest Officers at par with DM and SP for better administration and coordination with them. We created the Sub-divisional forest offices to be headed by the SFS officers with the powers of Drawing and Dispersing Officers and made Range offices co-terminus with Blocks. This system was created in 2015 and is working smoothly. It has improved the delivery system at the critical point of interface with the people as well as coordination with other departments at the district level. The point of success is a better utilization of manpower. This has certainly enhanced the overall prestige of the department in the eyes of people.

In the case of IAS as such, there is generally no scale to measure the effectiveness of service as it is rated largely the way it can keep its political masters happy and satisfied because they are the ultimate source of power. Even at the district level, the performance of the District Magistrate is rated more on how they satisfy the political masters and not much on maintenance of revenue records and law and order. The IAS officer's biggest advantage is they are closest to the seat of power and integral part of the final decision-making apparatus. In this, they are protected by the institution of Chief Secretary and Cabinet Secretary the ultimate advisors to the rulers in Stats and Centre. The institution of District Magistrate has been given tremendous powers and freedom which the good and well-meaning IAS officers use to streamline the functioning of the government scheme and hence are successful in their job. This exposure of IAS officers makes some of the better administrators and hence they bring good name to their service. There is, however, an inherent bias for the protection of their colleagues as the survival of the service depends upon supporting each other through their total grip on the system of governance. Fairness and accountability have no meaning to these institutions today because their selection depends upon the sweet will of the Chief Ministers and Prime Ministers. The job of an IAS also gets support from the general public and local press as they are always giving something or the other to people and sitting on judgements on the activities of others. Due to the nature of the job and the way our socio-political culture and system functions in India, the career value of an IAS is much better than the other services. They become the blue-eyed boys of the political powers and reward them profusely.

In the case of IPS, it is the reduction in crime rate and the State of law and order which can determine the image and prestige of the service. The IPS has the added advantage of their direct access to the Chief Ministers in the State through DG Police and Prime Minister in the Centre through the Director Intelligence Bureau and Director Central Bureau of Investigation. The IPS has also the added advantage of a senior Minister as the Home Minister at the Centre and in the States. With the expansion of the economy and more and more money circulating in the market, the increasing gap in income disparity leads to more and more crime syndicate growing with political patronage in the districts makes an IPS officer more important as well as vulnerable. The IPS as a service has, therefore, consolidated its position quite well during the last decades and one of the reasons is that police now invariably touch the lives of every citizen in one form or the other.

The IFS service lacks direct access to the Chief Ministers and Prime Ministers and most of the time very junior lightweight politicians become the Forests and Environment Ministers in the Centre and State. These Ministers have no serious commitment to achieve the objectives of the Department they control and are more interested in granting clearances and removing roadblocks in forestry and environmental clearances. So, the forest officers have no natural allies in the government. This leaves the service and its officers vulnerable as they have to control land-based resources which are eyed by one and all – from poor villagers, smugglers, sand and stone mafia to rich miners to development administrators – as land is a scarce resource in India and all common and wastelands have been either encroached or distributed.

It is also true that on many occasions a few forest officers also create unnecessary roadblocks in developmental projects on minor issues in the name of forest laws. So, whosoever is angry in furtherance of their motives targets the forest officers. This has created several enemies for the forestry profession both inside the bureaucracy as well as outside who target them in tandem as anti-people and anti-development in an era of modernisation no one listens to a forester. The fact is Indian environment sector has received only lip service from the institutions of governance except for the judiciary which has come to its rescue time and again. Indian society as a whole thus lacks a balanced approach in dealing with environmental matters.

However, on many occasions, it is futile to blame others if you are not sure where your feet stand and IFS officers in the Ministry as well as the PCCFs in the States must not allow the junior functionaries to play with the cadre officers careers on flimsy ground. For example, take a simple case of correspondence on promotion that came to my notice recently for the State of Tamil Nadu. The promotions to different posts in the States are held based upon vacancies in the cadre strength as per the Gazette notification issued by the DoPT, but in one, the State government officials in the name of an innocuous circular from the government of India tries to postpone the promotions by writing to the Ministry of Environment, Forest and Climate Change seeking confirmation about the post at different levels. In the case of promotion of IAS and IPS officers it is not done and only poor IFS officers are singled out to delay their legitimate rights. This circular of DoPT is not at all given any importance of the States as in case of IAS they have created innumerable posts in Apex scale and promote the officers batch wise whereas the rules says that not more than an equal of ex-cadre posts can be created against the cadre posts. However, officials in State secretariat enjoy sadistic pleasure by forcing the officers to run around in the corridors of powers when their promotions are due. States know full well how much the cadre strength is there as it is clearly stipulated in the gazette notification and very much readily available with the States. Then the low-level functionaries like the section officers and Under Secretaries in the IFS division of the Ministry start playing with these kinds of letters waiting for some officers to come to meet them. On 13th January 2021, the Additional Chief Secretary of the State writes to the Secretary of the Environment Ministry seeking concurrence on the number of vacancies at different levels from PCCF to DCF selection grade level. In this letter, the State lists the vacancies as per the gazette notification. On 22nd January 2021, the Under Secretary of the Environment Ministry writes back to the State government and gives concurrence on the number of vacancies in all post from DCF selection grade to APCCF but mischievously omitted the PCCF's post. The State has three clear vacancies at the level of PCCF. One of the retired officers from Tamil Nadu contacted me if I can help find some contacts in the IFS Division as one of the 1989 batch officers is camping in Delhi who was on the verge of promotion to PCCF level. Only on the intervention of the Director-General of Forests (DGF) Mr Sanjay Kumar the Under Secretary sends another letter confirming the vacancies at the PCCF level. This simple incident summarises the audacious arbitrariness in our governing system which shows how even the lower rank people sitting in sensitive posts misuse their positions blatantly and how the IFS officers posted in the Ministry tolerate/overlook such mistakes or mischief by an Under Secretary in the Government. It shows that the officers have become self centred or have accepted such things as a routine. The young officers get disappointed and de-motivated and thus rendering the service profile without energetic elan' (enthusiasm and liveliness).

The outstanding work done by the forest officers in the field in conserving the forests and the bio-diversity, and performing well in other Ministries at the Centre and States is not recognized at the national level. One of the reasons is the calibrated campaign against the IFS in the higher echelons as branding it anti-people with the aims that in their own fields they are not trusted for top policy making posts. There is no justification for not trusting the DG Forests as Secretary of the Ministry of Forest and Wildlife and for that matter Ministry of Environment, Forests and Climate Change. Similarly there is no justification why ICFRE shall not be like ICAR, CSIR and ICMR and be declared as a Department. Unless this mindset persists it would be difficult to groom good officers and the service will continue to be languishing because the efficacy of any cadre is measured by how well it does in its own field and as long as the IFS officers are not recognised as top policymakers in the Ministry of Environment, the image of the service shall remain questionable. This situation is having a cascading impact on the morale of young officers across the country who in desperation seeks mentors outside the service.

Though for past many years in various departments of the government of India IFS officers at the level of Director, Joint Secretary, and Additional Secretary and even at the Special Secretary level are being appointed and are doing good work but their image and position in the Ministry of

Environment makes the overall impression about the effectiveness of the service. It is this impression among the politicians along with the imaginary fear and propaganda that forest officers will be acting as road blockers in the decision-making process and therefore, the post of Secretary Forests is not given to an IFS officer. However, as group of professionals, the forest officers are considered stubborn and powerful as they control a vast resource covering 23% of the landmass of the country and the behaviours of the people who are in the government depend upon the perception and bias they carry about this service about its performance real or imaginary.

On future improvements of sector there is a demand also from some quarters to create a Forest Research Service on the lines of Agriculture Research Service of ACAR so that the task of technology development can be transferred to this service both in the centre as well as states. The focus on technology task development is very poor in states. There is however another view that IFS should promote specialized knowledge gathering exposure through better cadre management but refrain from splitting up the subjects to too much micro lanes of disciplines except in some research posts. We have developed an excellent pool of officers in wildlife who with their prolong stay in the wildlife posts delivered excellent results to name a few among the recent generations like Mr RN Mehrotra, Dr Rajesh Gopal, Mr SP Yadav and Mr Ramesh Pande; similarly we have professionals like Hemanth Kumar of 1989 batch and Mr Prasad Rao of 2010 batch showing the sparks of old foresters in all round professional abilities both managerial as well as technical innovating thinking. Today there is a need to have better resources managers and officers like Mr MK Jeevrajika, Mr Vinay Luthra, AN Prasad, AK Goyal, Mr Ashok Pai, Mr Bala Prasad, Mr Arvind Kumar, Mr Bharat Lal, Mr Ganeriwala, Mr Rajiv Gupta, Mr Subhash Chandra, Anuraj Bajpayee, Dr AK Joshi, HS Sohal, SK Chaddha and SK Sethi and so many other in Delhi Central Secretariat etc who have proven records as resources administrators at the higher levels comparable to the best in the country in national organizations outside the forestry sector. Mr Promode Kant of Tamil cadre has developed a niche for himself as an FAO expert. These are several other examples of success which are not personally known to me of hand due to better exposure, career planning and grooming.

In a nutshell, the present IFS cadre needs to evolve a sound professional ethics and leadership of quality. The officers should not fall victim to bureaucratic politics of control otherwise effectiveness of the service in managing the sanctity of forest lands will always be challenged by the vested interests. The performance of the service also lends to suggest that overall reform in the civil services is essentially needed. The forest service needs to better plan the career management of the officers to create a composite pool of expertise to handle the emerging needs.

Rigmarole of 'Netadom'

11

The bureaucracy in the country is everyone's whipping boy and rightly so because in India they are the real source of pain or pleasure for the common citizens. The question comes into mind why this happens when bureaucrats are only supposed to carry out the policies and programmes of the government run by the elected public representatives. After the country became independent in 1947 and promulgated the Indian constitution in 1950 the power came to our elected political leaders through the democratic institutions. The permanent structure in the executive is the bureaucracy which is supposed to implement the people's welfare policies of the government in power faithfully and in accordance with the established rules and conventions. Indian bureaucracy soon after freedom under the stellar leadership of Sardar Vallabhbhai Patel had brought integration and stability to the Indian union and also strengthened the federal structure of the constitution and the democracy. The freedom movement produced leaders of character and conviction whose first love was to serve the nation and achieve the targets of independence. They were committed to certain lofty ideals and but for these great leaders, Indian democracy would not have taken the shape as it has today a firmly grounded largest democracy in the world. However, over the years there has been a gradual decline in the character and quality as well as moral standards of the political leaders and India's bureaucracy was no exception to this trend.

Over the years the fissiparous tendencies based on nepotism, casteism and regionalism overtook the sentiments of love for the country and the quality of many of our political leaders started falling sharply. The dynastic politics of congress spurred similar family-based, caste-based regional fiefdoms all over India. It started with the first general election of Parliament after the constitution was promulgated when the tickets were given based on the caste configuration in the constituencies. The creation of linguistic States by the State Reorganization Commission in 1956 further promoted the sectarian mindset in the general public and the local politicians and gradually the inward-looking parochial feelings started shaping the contours of polity in the hinterlands. The creation of linguistic States is one of the blunders by the then political leadership which prevented the synthesis of various cultures of India in the governance modules of the country. The All

India Services though with all their shortcomings and criticism excelled in building up and protecting the federal setup of the country as enshrined in the constitution.

When the constitution was adopted as a temporary measure under Article 15(4) and 16(4) of the Constitution enabled the State and Central Governments to reserve seats in government services for the members of the SC and ST for an initial period of 10 years. Article 334 provides that reservation of seats for Scheduled Castes and Scheduled Tribes in the Lok Sabha and the State Vidhan Sabhas (and the representation of the Anglo-Indian Community in the Lok Sabha and the State Vidhan Sabhas by nomination). These measures were intended to be temporary only for 10 years because the Fundamental Rights, among others, ensure equality before the law and equal protection of law; prohibits discrimination against any citizen on grounds of religion, race, caste, sex or place of birth, and guarantee equality of opportunity to all citizens in matters relating to employment. However, these provisions on account of electoral politics and also due to continued disadvantageous and discriminatory social status of the Scheduled caste and Scheduled Tribe communities have not only assumed permanency through the constitutional amendments extending the reservation for further ten years, each time the period of extension come to an end but now are even applied in promotions which have created a big schism in the society. The initial reservation policy is flawed on two counts. First, it did not make any Statement to create infrastructure for up-gradation of their skills with the objective to broad base the choice so that the disadvantaged sections among them can be given a level playing field with better-equipped families. Yet another flaw of reservation policy was the inclusion of some tribes or castes that were neither disadvantageous nor deserved to be included and today are cornering the reserved posts disproportionately.

The post-emergency emergence of regional caste-based leaders in India after the Late Jai Prakash Narayan led the agitation in 1975, brought into fore the backward caste leadership and the electoral politics got deeply entrenched in caste politics. Already after 1967 General elections both in North as well as in Tamil Nadu and other States in the South there was consolidation of backward caste votes and; in 1980 when Mrs Indira Gandhi stormed back to power (after the Janata Party a conglomerate hotchpotch of opposing ideologies and egoistic ambitions of a few leaders fell and mid-term elections held) set up the Mandal Commission to propose reservations for the socially and educationally backward classes. The Mandal Commission in its report equated the caste system with social and educational backwardness and recommended that 27 per cent of posts under the Central and States governments should be reserved for the other backward castes. The Mandal Commission report hence became the fulcrum of political mobilization. The opposition targeted the then Prime Minister Rajiv Gandhi over the Bofor scam. Mr Viswanath Pratap Singh who was portraying himself as an honest man in the government and the one who is not being allowed to take action against the corruption by Prime Minister Rajiv Gandhi defected from the Congress and came to become Prime Minister in 1989 with the support of BJP and implemented amidst fierce bloody agitation reservations for the backward castes. For few months it put the entire country on fire when several people mostly poor upper-caste students immolated them opposing the way reservation was made and the way other backward classes were defined. The defining social and educational backwardness of the people to caste was a purely political gimmick that permanently divided the Indian society as many poor people among the upper caste felt it as patently partisan and against the spirit of the constitution.

In order to mollify the upper castes the NDA government led by the Prime Minister Mr Narendra Modi had announced 10 percent reservations in the government jobs for the economically weaker sections of the upper castes. The caste based violent reservation demands are growing in many States like Rajasthan and Haryana and it does not augur well for the progress of the country as well as harmony among the different sections of the society.

There is, however, a consensus in the society for considering caste-based discrimination for the Scheduled caste which has to tolerate the heinous practice of untouchability perpetrated by upper caste people on them and the Indian people have largely accepted the extension of reservation in jobs for them. However, now many people are arguing that a new group of people who have benefitted from the reservations for Scheduled caste and Scheduled Tribe has emerged as a powerful pressure group and is cornering the benefits leaving a large section among the SC and ST deprived because they have no way to compete with them as government policy has no programme to build up their capacity as mere reservation in an educational institution does not matter if there is no hand-holding. The government must create special residential schools for the deprived sections among them to make them capable to compete with the better of candidates in their category. Some people of disadvantaged sections among SCs and STs in many States have been demanding introduction of creamy layer concept in SC and ST reservation also so that the deprived sections among them could be benefited. However, it need to be handled carefully till such time the mentality of dominant classes does not change towards the weaker sections though the younger educated generations has largely overcoming this barrier quite fast.

The political class in yet another great folly of vote bank politics started reservations of jobs in promotions which was neither the intention of the constitution-makers nor it was desirable from the point of efficiency of government functioning. In the process of reservation, the merits take a back seat and there is vehement opposition for reservation is promotions which should be strictly based on merit and seniority. It gobbled up the core of Article 14 of the constitution on fundamental right of equality. The warring groups have locked horns and the case is still sub-judice which has held up promotions in many States. The provision in the constitution for reservation is meant to uplift the disadvantaged section of the society by giving them representation in the government jobs and not in the hierarchy of the government posts. Today many politicians in private conversations believe that reservation in promotion a wrong decision yet they have no guts to oppose it fearing loss of votes. For the past ten years or so the courts including the Supreme Court of India are debating over the constitutional validity of this. This has divided the workforce at the cost of administrative efficiency. One possible solution to this is to give *'insitu'* promotion by delinking it with the hierarchy if at all it has to be retained. This suggestion of granting '*insitu*' promotion should be given a serious thought by the government in the interest of merit.

The expediency dominated approach determines the way our political rulers behave and the tendency is giving many people of dubious character to become political leaders if they can mobilize people on sectarian ground. The vote bank politics of dividing the people on caste, religion and region prevents and popular government to take correct decisions on matters of national importance like population control and uniform civil code. For many people the politics has become a profession now and a way to generate wealth. The classical case of vote bank politics was seen when the Congress-led UPA government of Prime Minister Manmohan Singh divided Andhra Pradesh and created Telangana. So many people in today's politics have amassed huge wealth through illegal way and this is providing a path for the hooligans to enter politics. Now the way politicians and regional outfits are coming up in small towns, cities and villages the constitutional makers would be shedding tear in their graves. Many hoodlums have gained power and recognition all over and are responsible for the collapse of rule of law, corruption and division in the society which we citizens see day in and day out. The increasing presence of such elements in politics is the greatest threat to the democracy and stability of India.

The Supreme Court intervention in the famous SR Bommai versus Union of India in 1994 had laid down the principles of imposing Article 356 in the State and dismissals of Chief Ministers and the court's powers to review imposition of President Rule. This decision though had put a break on the arbitrary dismissals of State governments on the whims and fancies of Central government, it has however, also created a piquant situation for the country when the State politicians do not run the administration in true spirit of constitution and indulge in violence against opponents, run oppressive governance and misuse the resources blatantly. The constitutional though has theoretical remedy for conduct of public servants but there is no sound and clear political way to do it.

This deterioration in political culture also affected the Indian bureaucracy. The people started seeing the rut of corruption, insensitivity, poor performance and red-tapism in government departments and this naturally led to criticizing the way civil servants performed and critics sarcastically opined the word 'Babudom' for their way of functioning. India's Babudom due to their access to political class not only became the eyes and ears of politicians in power but also the depository of wisdom and knowledge and groomed politicians in power into a self-seeking group which ultimately becomes a mutually benefitting club of a few in power in which both got benefitted at the cost of fair governance and people's welfare.

Assessment of Public Servants

12

The objective of writing this book is to bring to the public domain the need for a rethink on the way our country should be governed and to do that, it is necessary to assess the status of our public servants in the governance of this country and to see if our public servants are working efficiently and honestly in bringing progress and happiness to the nation. The narrations in this book are not against any service or group as such or our political class. The purpose is to pinpoint how the individuals make or mar the reputation of their cadre or service or class. In a democratic system, ideally, the politicians who win power to govern are accountable to people who elected them as they have to face the public after a fixed time frame during elections and hence the non-performers are voted out of power. In the case of civil servants, their role is to faithfully and within rule help the political masters in implementing public welfare schemes and they are accountable to the system of governance. The civil servants maintain continuity in the governing system and are an important link during the transfer of power after the new people's representatives assume power. In this section, we will assess and discuss where our rulers stand in these parameters. Let us discuss the positives and negatives of these actors of governance.

Political Executives: A lot has already been said in previous pages about our political class. On positive side for more than 74 years after Independence, the electoral democracy in the country have taken fairly deep roots notwithstanding occasional hiccups and time and again it has been proved that the power of the people is supreme in India and attempts to impose dictatorship or malfeasance in governance is met with a firm hand during elections and such leaders and political parties are voted out. The aspiration of growth and prosperity as a nation of more than 139 crore people been achieved in different fields of nation's life with varying degree of success be it in defence of the country or the internal law and order or the rural development or environmental conservation or natural resources management etc.

Considering the varied geographic, demographic, socio-economic and cultural profiles of the people of the country the system of governance in India need to be continuously monitored because, in a vibrant society, change is a must and inevitable sign of progress. The political leaders during the freedom struggle were born out of struggle and were an utterly devoted bunch of people to nationalism and were thus deeply committed and a fearless lot. It was their intellect, vision for a united India and selfless leadership that laid the foundation of democracy and rule of law in this country.

However, no society and its political leaders can live on the laurels of their past leaders and their achievements. Over the years the short-sighted electoral polity in India had given rise to numerous divisive tendencies on caste, region and religious lines and the emergence of such leaders and political forces whose survival depends on raking up and mobilizing people on these factors. This is happening at the cost of severely damaging our nation's inherent strong cultural umbilical cord from Kashmir to Kanyakumari which had united the people through thousands of years and survived even during hundreds of years of foreign rule. This is a serious threat to national integration and good governance. For example, the lack of foresight among the political class is all-pervasive and crony capitalism and nepotism has dented the meritocracy which is considered the cornerstone of good governance.

When the political leaders divide the public on issues like this, the type of democracy we get is not sustainable in the long term as more and more political leaders discover more and more divisive agenda. The promises on freebies during elections for catering to vote bank politics like free electricity and water made by the politicians is a clear case of promoting rampant economic hara-kiri and is a corruption of the highest order. No one can be authorised to loot the exchequer for garnering the votes. Such undesirable incidences are increasing and are converting Indian democracy into electoral democracy.

The second issue of concern is the criminalization of politics and the emergence of criminals as powerful satraps and political force in many parts of the country. Earlier these elements were engaged by caste-based political leaders for booth capturing but gradually they became political leaders and gaining social acceptance once they win any election. Once such elements enter the governing institutions the lawful governance becomes the casualty. The fast-rising moral and financial corruption in the country is yet another issue that is adversely impacting sound decision-making and is making it difficult for honest citizens to get justice and at the top of the list are our political masters. Many sub-standard project executions and natural disasters are manmade and at the root of this is the corruption of our political leaders.

Now the elections are won by those who have the money power as honest citizens cannot afford to fight even the election of a village Panchayats or Municipal Corporation/ urban body what to say of State assembly or the parliament as crores are spent in village Pradhan's elections. Tickets are issued on payment of cash and a huge amount of money is spent during electioneering and voters are bribed openly. Once these leaders get the power, they use the system to get back their cash and amass huge assets and a vicious cycle of corruption is evident all over the country. The increasing violence during an election is because of this deteriorating political culture in the country.

The politics of the country gives easy entry to anyone and is gradually becoming a good profession to enter politics and earn easy money and since there is no age or educational bar anyone can enter politics. This situation in our governance has given rise to a culture of politics which this writer calls 'Netacracy or Netadom' (Rule of upstart political leaders) and is responsible for several ills in the society and administration today. For a long time, the people have been blaming the bureaucracy for all ills in governance but now the politics of 'Netadom' is equally responsible if not more. This disease must be cured through the overall reform process in our governance system and culture if the democratic fibre of our nation has to survive with dignity and prestige in the eyes of our citizens and the world. The question is what Netacracy or Netadom is all about? The answer is the implementation of the orders of political masters which does not stand the scrutiny of merit within the rules and when the bureaucracy is used to implement those dictates of the political masters. Netacracy or Netadom is directly hitting at the concept of neutrality of civil services and promoting inefficiency, corruption and pliability among the bureaucrats of all shades.

It is a well-known fact that a certain amount of political interference is essential to set right the wrongs of a few in the system or to provide hand-holding for the poor and marginal sections of the society but when it is rampant and arbitrary than it becomes the rule of Neta (political leader) and not of law and hence Netadom which ultimately spurs the Babudom because when the bureaucrats satisfy their masters, then they also become reassured about their powers and position and red tapes, misuse of powers, corruption, injustice percolates downwards and even small clerks start harassing the common citizens. It is this Netacracy that spoils the bureaucracy as well as other wings of government the legislature and the judiciary. It is because of the failures in our governance institutions that the judiciary intervenes and tries to set things to correct trajectory. Many problems in nation-building like population control could not be enforced due to political reasons and are one of the big drags in our goal to achieve progress and prosperity.

One of the reasons many intellectuals attributed to the present ills in India's politics, is the granting of the universal adult franchise at the time of independence and the formation of the constitution. Even in Britain, women were given universal suffrage only in 1918. It is said that two important members of the constitutional assembly C Rajagopalachari and Sardar Vallabhbhai Patel during discussions in the constitutional assembly recommended that we should not opt for a blanket adult franchise for the time being. They argued for educating the people first to make them worthy of discharging their duties as citizens by an honest and sensible vote. In the 1935 Act which created provincial governments the voting rights were given to only 10 per cent of the people. The voting under the 1935 Act took place under the scheme of separate electorates, based on class and economic status, the character of the electorate, on the property and formal literacy-based qualifications. The voting rights of women were linked to the status of their husbands. It deprived 90 per cent of the people to cast their vote. The constitutional assembly at that time decided that it will be a mockery of getting independence if the entire population is not granted the voting right. It thus granted the voting right to 100 per cent of the people and allowed the people to decide their destiny.

Israeli scholar, Ornit Shani, who is a scholar on modern Indian history has authored a book *"How India Became Democratic: Citizenship and the Making of the Universal Franchise in which she described how the constitutional assembly decided to make a transformational constitution that ensured continuity with the good provisions of governance enshrined in the government of India Act 1935 and yet it broke off from the colonial approach of restricted voting rights and empowered the people fully to decide their destiny"*.

Did we break from the tradition of the colonial past in our new constitution or we created a new class of rulers? Many people argue that our constitution is largely based on the 1935 government of India Act with some cosmetic changes but the granting of the universal adult franchise was really a revolutionary step that laid the true foundation of participatory democracy in India. Had the country introduced universal franchise gradually perhaps many of the present ills could have been averted but there was no guarantee that it would have helped because of a lot of divisions in our society and the way powerful people cling to power by any means. I made a passing reference to the debate in the constitutional assembly on the universal franchise just to stress the need of educating the citizens and if possible, we could have laid down some qualifications for fighting the election to State assemblies and the parliament.

In November 1949, when the Constitutional assembly was giving final touches to the new constitution H.N. Kunzru, the veteran freedom fighter and parliamentarian was quite uncomfortable with the Constitution's adoption of universal adult franchise. Mr Kunzru was nominated for the highest Indian civilian award, the Bharat Ratna, in 1968 but he declined, citing his opposition to such honours in a Republic, which he had first voiced during the Constituent Assembly debates. He was, however, honoured on a postage stamp of India in 1987. He was not sure if *'sudden expansion of the franchise that will be brought about by adult franchise will be helpful to the development of democratic ideas and that sense of discrimination and restraint on which the successful exercise of democracy depends'*.

He preferred a more gradual expansion of the franchise. He felt that this would have given enough time for *'political parties and individual candidates to meet the electors and educate them'*. According to him with the full adoption of universal franchise in one go, educating the voters will be a difficult task. It is thus clear that several learned members though ultimately went with the majority view expressed that 100 per cent of voting rights needed a deep thought. Today, in hindsight, I think that the gradual process would have strengthened the democracy in India by producing matured leadership.

However, the counter view is also true that it could have turned into a fiefdom of a few and I fully support the sagacity of the founding fathers of the constitution about granting a universal franchise. We must, however, always remain prepared for the changes in the system because without a change there cannot be worthwhile progress and therefore, change is a must and inevitable.

Civil Services: Whosoever may be the Prime Minister or the Chief Minister in around 80 to 90 per cent of cases it is the bureaucrats who decide and exercise the real powers and based on their perception and attitude a particular case is decided or a scheme is implemented. In classical good governance accountability, transparency, honesty and neutrality are the hallmark of good governance. It is also a fact, however, if a well-meaning bureaucrat is at the helm of affairs, it is the best situation in delivering quick remedy for the people especially at the district level and there are instances of plenty of such officers available in the country but this number though is gradually shrinking.

However, the Indian bureaucracy is a very varied and large group of several services with completely divided loyalties and are inherently biased and do not blink an eye in harming the members of other groups and lording over the general public as they know nothing will happen to them as their colleague swiftly comes to their rescue. A large number of them have mastered the art of hoodwinking the politicians and people at large with superb fineness and in the process take self-serving decisions which are tantamount to committing white-collar crimes. Another quality of the bureaucracy is procrastination and complete insensitivity to the problems faced by the people. There is no value of timely action on the disposal of papers no matter how serious the matter is. Further, the bureaucracy with alacrity creates more and more bureaucracy and proliferates everywhere with more and more bottlenecks for decision making and openings for wrong and self-serving decisions and actions. It brings so many loops to entangle the Ministers to whom they are subservient that it is difficult for them to understand that they have been done in to sign on the dotted line. Several poor Ministers both in the Centre and States think it is better to join the bureaucrat rather than the people who elected them. The net result is poor delivery of services to people. Because of this, the bureaucracy is criticized everywhere in the world and Indian bureaucrats of all shades in all the services are on the top of the list of hate mail.

Thus in the performance of every civil service both facets the positives as well as negatives exist. A lot has been said about the way civil services function in this country in the preceding chapters and it should be discussed only in the context of future reforms and also the fact that civil services will always be there as a solid pillar of governance. While doing so we need to understand and recognize; the benefits of the creation of organized services are due to their systematic and organised way of taking decisions. Their training brings a sense of professionalism while discharging their duties keeping in minds the needs and aspiration of the people from their profession. Their success depends upon how faithfully they carry out their duties in the public interest. However, it is experienced that while taking decisions they give precedence to their service interests over the larger public and professional interests and hence acquires inherent bias in the decision-making process. This behaviour of the members of different services is at the root of the failure of our civil servants apart from the general slide in the character and moral values of the officers. The bureaucracy sees the benefits and disadvantages of toeing the lines of their political bosses. The art is to cultivate the boss and then assume unbridled control over the system. In short, as stated earlier we need urgent reforms in public services take remove arbitrariness in public life and make the political class and the civil servant accountable for their performance. The assessment of the performance of their All India Service has been discussed in some details in the Chapter dealing with Indian Forest Service. However, in brief, I would like to summarise;

Civil Services of all cadres have played key roles in stabilizing the democracy and ensuring the unity and integrity of the country.

As we progressed in our path of democratic governance due to falling standards of quality and integrity of our political class led to the gradual deterioration in the performance and attitude of civil servants. The services are made of individuals and gradually a kind of typed personality of the service is developed which is reflected in the day to day conducts and attitude of its officers. Barring a few the general impressions in the public is such that the civil servants have become indifferent to the pain and agony of the common people and have no respect for transparency and accountability.

A time has come when the country should give serious thought to reform the cadres of civil services to make them accountable, transparent, neutral, people-centric and service-oriented rather than the patronizing and arrogant self-centric.

The criticism of any service in this book is not against the service but against the individuals who in the name of their service have been indulging in activities that undermined the image of their service. Until a few decades ago the IAS officers were looked at with respect by other departments as their sense of justice and fair play was better as compared to other line departments' officers. Similarly, the old IFS officers were professionally very sound, effective, committed to public welfare and used to behave as father figures to their juniors and though they were tough taskmasters but used to make their junior comfortable and looked after their welfare. This is no more seen today and though the levels of intellect in the forest service have increased much is desired today professionally as well as on their commitment to the welfare of people as the services are deficient in leadership. The situation is more or less the same in other services too.

We must also give credit to some of the finest social and political leaders, Bureaucrats, Soldiers, Technocrats, Doctors, Scientists and faceless hard-working people Indian produced in all the fields that we have achieved so much despite hugely rising population and the conflicting demands. We need to, however, take a lesson from these people and also from the failings of our system so that we march and emerge as a strong and powerful nation in the world. We have the cultural background, inner resilience and intelligence to overcome our failings to lead the world. We must change the old systems and ways of doing things in running the country. We must increase the ratio of good people in the polity, as well as in the bureaucracy and other fields of the nation's social and cultural life and find ways and means to do it.

For a Better Tomorrow

13

The preceding chapters bring out the fact that for healthy governance the country requires the undertaking of thoughtful reforms by the policymakers, social reformers and the public in general. The constitution of India brings out the contours of the governance and the aspiration of the people to shape their destiny. It has a vision for inclusive growth, freedom of incorporating changes because it is flexible enough to enable the country to adopt any social and economic system the people's representatives may choose to adopt in the Constitution and the organs of government.

The wish of the people is final in the democracy and there is a dire need of undertaking varying degree of reforms in three wings of government i.e., Executive, Legislatures and the Judiciary in India. The constitutional governance anywhere in the world has to be a dynamic process and must reflect the wishes and aspirations of a changing society. To ensure stability and progress in society a good constitution would continuously strive to meet the challenges of changing times. Indian constitution has that resilience and flexibility, as soon after the enactment of its promulgation in 1950, the first constitutional amendment was passed in May 1951 on the Fundamental Rights. Since then, 104 constitutional amendments have been made making it one of the most flexible and dynamic constitutions in the world. However, in the Keshvanand Bharati case (write petition (civil) 135 of 1970 the Supreme Court in a landmark decision ruled that the basic structure of the constitution cannot be changed by the Parliament through the process of amendments in the constitution. It stated that some principle in the framework of the constitution is inviolable and cannot be touched by the Parliament. A 13-member constitutional bench in a divided (7-6) verdict curtailed the powers of the Parliament. This verdict had laid a principle that the people's representatives cannot be trusted completely on amending the basic features of the constitution. It is a debatable issue if this one majority verdict is for all the time to come or it can be changed any time in the future, though it has put on hold an aggressive political agenda to tinker with core values of the constitution.

There has always been criticism of the functioning of our democratic set up particularly the way constitutional values are undermined and the way our politicians and bureaucracy have failed to meet the aspirations of the society. To propose changes in the machinery of the Government of India so far two Administrative Reform Commissions (ARCs) were appointed by the Government. The first ARC was set up, on 5th January 1966 under the Chairmanship of Morarji Desai. The mandate of the commission was to suggest changes in the government machinery to achieve the highest standards of efficiency and integrity and for making public administration an instrument for the social and economic development of the country. The Second ARC was set up on 5th August 2005 under the Chairmanship of Mr Veerapa Moily to examine the present system and propose a future set-up for an efficient public administrative structure. The reports of both the reform commissions were never implemented honestly as *status quoist* did not allow the commission to recommend any substantial reforms and dealt with the issues rather superficially. In fact, it has become a norm whenever there is a demand for change and there is severe criticism of some aspects of governance at the national level either some committee or commission is set up which ignites hopes in the mind of the people but after so much of resources are used by these committees and commissions their reports are seldom implemented as the *status quoist* are so deeply entrenched in the system that they never allowed any worthwhile changes to occur. Take the case of Forest and Environment Conservation in the country which is being closely monitored by the Supreme Court of India after the 1996 'Godavaram case'. The then Prime Minister Atal Bihari Vajpayee, in 2003, set up the National Forest Commission (NFC) under the Chairmanship of former Chief Justice of India Justice BN Kirpal to assess the status of forest conservation in India and suggest measures to ensure sustainable forest management policies. The commission suggested far-reaching measures to tone up the forest management in the country. None of the recommendations of this commission was accepted by the government of India. Only the Pay Commission reports are faithfully accepted nearly in *toto* by the government of India.

The previous NDA government (during 1999 to 2004) led by Prime Minister Atal Bihari Vajpayee on 22nd February 2000 also set up an 11-member National Commission to review the working of Constitution (NCRWC) under the Chairmanship of retired Chief Justice of India

Justice MN Venkatachaliah and to suggest amendments in it to reflect the aspiration of the changing society.

The mandate of the 11-member Commission was to examine, in the light of the experience of the past fifty years, how best the Constitution can respond to the changing needs of an efficient, smooth and effective system of governance and socio-economic development of modern India within the framework of parliamentary democracy, and to recommend changes, if any, that are required in the provisions of the Constitution without interfering with its 'basic structure' or 'basic features'. The Commission after three years submitted its 1979 pages report on 31st March 2002. This bulky report has never been considered nor circulated for public comments and was buried deep down. One of its members PA Sangma resigned from the Commission when his proposal to bar the foreign-born Indian nationals from holding high constitutional posts was not accepted by the other members.

For better people-centric governance, India needs reforms in all three wings of the government. Here I will discuss separately i.e., public representatives, civil services and judiciary. This is in addition to several direct or indirect suggestions already given in previous specific chapters relating to each segment.

Political Reforms

The following constitutional reforms need to be considered for electing public representatives in State assemblies and the Parliament. The future progress of our country will depend on how our political leaders in government can control the burgeoning population growth.

There is no provision of Referendum in our constitution and hence no one talks about it. A referendum is a sort of direct democracy and on some occasion, it may be needed in deciding national issues by the government and the Parliament with direct participation of the people. Many times, political parties discussed conducting a referendum on granting of Statehood to Delhi and the bifurcation of undivided Andhra Pradesh, but it could not be done as there is no provision of conducting a referendum in our constitution. This was also raised in the Constitutional Assembly on 17th September 1949 by Mr Brajeswar Singh raising the need for a referendum and said *"Sir, I am in favour of a referendum, because referendum has many advantages. A referendum is democratic as it is only an appeal to the people, and no democratic government can have any objection to resorting to a referendum in order to resolve a deadlock when there is a conflict between Parliament and provincial governments. Secondly, I am in favour of a referendum because it cures patent defects in party governments. People think that it is too radical a weapon and that conservative people like ourselves ought not to use it without proper consideration and thought. It is conservative since it ensures the maintenance of any law or institution which the majority of the electors effectively wish to, preserve. Therefore it cannot be a radical weapon. Thirdly, Sir, a referendum is a clear recognition of the sovereignty of the people. Fourthly, it would be a strong weapon for curbing the absolutism of a party possessed of a parliamentary majority."* However, Dr Ambedkar opposed it as it would be an elaborate and difficult proposition to hold it and because of this, it was dropped. In the futuristic scenario, it would be appropriate if we amend the constitution and incorporate a provision of holding a referendum on any issue of national importance if the Parliament passes a resolution with a two-third majority and half of the State Assemblies ratify it. The results of the referendum would only be applicable if at least 60 per cent of people agree to the proposal. It would bring direct democracy to our doors on certain matters.

The population growth is unsettling the economic and social gains of development. The country's constitutional provision for delimitation of constituencies is based on population growth and the net result is it punishes those States who do not take action for controlling the population growth and reward the States that perform well in population check. This is going to prove a powder keg for the politicians to manage the resentment it will bring among the masses. Therefore, the first and foremost thing we need to do is to amend the Delimitation Act which allows delimitation of the boundaries of the constituencies of the State assemblies and the Lok Sabha based on the Census. The delimitation must be based on site-specific conditions and should include the geographical features and many other site-specific parameters.

Around 10 per cent of seats in Lok Sabha and State assemblies may be increased and nominated based on the proportional representative basis to make the house more representative. To increase the representation of women the political parties must be legally bound to give 25% tickets to women or have a system of dual membership in 15% of constituencies on a rotational basis. There is, therefore, a need for larger comprehensive reforms in the electoral system.

The biggest challenge before the country is to check the money power and cash flow during elections and the criminalization of politics. Though there is no free hand to the candidates to spend as much as they like on their elections. During electioneering, a huge amount of money is spent and despite postings of observers by the Election Commission, the candidates find a lot of ways to circumvent the restrictions. For honest politicians, it is next to impossible to contest elections and gradually the turf is getting captured by many anti-social elements who have money and muscle powers. This is the root cause of criminalization of the politics and is the second biggest threat to democracy after population growth. These days due to the advent of several Television Channels and social media platforms for mobilizations of the voter, there is, therefore, no need for allowing a big gap between the day of filing nominations and the day of polling. The literacy rate has jumped to now 77% and therefore, the gap between the last date of filing the nomination and the date of voting should not be more than 8 to 10 days. The fund flow needs to be made transparent through better monitoring and curtailing the time of electioneering.

The Representation of Peoples' Act 1951 deals with the qualifications and disqualifications for contesting elections. The law prescribes that the total election expenditure shall not exceed the maximum limit prescribed under Rule 90 of the Conduct of Election Rules, 1961. It would also amount to a corrupt practice under sec 123 (6) of R. P. Act, 1951 and will result in the candidate's disqualification. However, it is noticed that there is no way to check the exponential growth in the income of people's representatives. There are other adequate safeguards in this act but legal lacuna needs to be plugged to prevent the entry of criminals into the assemblies and parliament. The Hon'ble Supreme Court of India, 10 July 2013, had tried to some extent intervened and tried to plug in the deficiency in our legal process in its judgment of the Lily Thomas v. Union of India case (along with Lok Prahari v. Union of India), decided that any Member of Parliament (MP), Member of the Legislative Assembly (MLA) or Member of a Legislative Council (MLC) who is sentenced for a crime and granted at least two years of imprisonment, loses membership of the House with immediate effect had. The earlier position, wherein sentenced members clung to their seats until the point that they exhausted all judicial solution in the lower, State and Supreme Court of India. Further, Section 8(4) of the Representation of the People Act, which permitted elected representatives three months to appeal their conviction, was proclaimed unconstitutional by the bench of Justice A. K. Patnaik and Justice SJ. Mukhopadhaya. The Prevention of Corruption Act 1988 should be amended to provide for confiscation of the property disproportionate to the known source of income.

The criminalization of politics needs to be debated in detail and the political parties should be made accountable for giving tickets to criminals. One of the suggestions is to bring the political parties under section 2(h) of the Right of Information Act, 2005. If it is done, the political parties would be bound to be transparent in every process of election. The voter of the country has the right to know how and where from the money is coming and how it is spent during elections as those who will be elected will be ruling them and hence to bring the political parties within RTI Act 2005 is justified fully along with third-party evaluation of cash flow.

The political parties at the time of registration must give a declaration signed by all their office bearers that they shall bear true faith and allegiance to the constitutional values and shall not be inciting the people on caste, creed, religion, and on other sectarian matters. The election commission should be authorised to take punitive action on the violation of the constitutional values and deregister such political entities and debar them for at least 10 years from fighting elections.

The covid-19 pandemic had taught us a bitter lesson that the country had neglected the Health infrastructure. The Health is not expressly recognized as a fundamental right under the Part III of the Constitution. It should be recognized as a fundamental right so as to emphasize flow of funds and infrastructure. Presently most of the rural poor are dependent on local healers. In education sector also we need to up-grade the quality of infrastructure at par with private schools. Through the Constitution (Eighty Sixth Amendment) Act, in 2002 provision of free and compulsory education to children was added as fundamental right in Article 21-A

The political parties, both ruling as well as opposition, must be made responsible for smooth functioning of Parliament and State Assemblies and a code of conduct must be put in place and the violation of the code of conduct shall render the elected representative to be considered to lose his membership for rest of the term.

The presiding officers shall take action on a violation of the code of conduct. The tolerance to unruly behaviours of MPs and MLAs by the Chair as is seen these days in the name of democratic protests cannot and should not be permitted as the sanctity of Parliament and State Assemblies must be maintained at any cost. It is necessary to define the norms and limits of protest in the Parliament and State Assemblies.

Though the Election Commission has been doing fairly well in conducting the election it nevertheless, some time faces unfair criticism. However, there is need to unify the electoral process in the country as presently State governments also appoint State election commissioners for local body elections which also faces criticism. To ensure better monitoring of electoral processes in the country the Election Commission should be have an independent status under the overall supervision of the Judiciary. The feasibility of constituting a separate All India or Central Group A Service for the purpose of conducting all types of elections should be seriously debated and considered. The responsibility of all elections in the country from village level to Parliament shall be of this service from the local village level to Parliament etc. It would make the election process more transparent. Otherwise, some tangible reforms in manpower management in the present system should be considered.

In order to bring more talent and experts in the process of governance in each State, a 20 to 60 member's legislative council should be established depending upon the size of the State. In these councils, persons of proven imminence from different walks of life like education, environment, medical, law and justice, art and culture, social workers, science and technology and other groups should be nominated and elected. The ratio of nominated and elected members should be 50 per cent each and the term of the council should be for six years with a maximum limit of 2 terms.

There should be a minimum qualification for contesting the election for the State legislative assemblies and the parliament.

At present, there is an upper limit of 15% of the total legislatures on the number of Ministers that can be appointed in the Cabinets. This is causing administrative malfunctioning and delays as the number of departments both under the Centre as well as in States have increased. It is also causing pressure on the Chief Ministers and the Ministers. The 15% limit should be increased to 25% for the smooth functioning of the administration.

The Member of Parliament Local Area Development (MPLAD) and Member of Legislative Local Area Development (MLALAD) funds should be linked to the annual budget based on pre-approved projects to be implemented by the line departments under the supervision of the MP or the MLA. But honestly, there is no need for such projects when we have a system in place for planning the developmental activities. Ideally, it should be done away with as it is also breeding huge corruption and crony capitalism.

There is therefore a paramount need to revisit our system of governance after more than 70 years of enactment of the constitution and more than 100 amendments in it. The reports of the National Commission to Review the Working of Constitution, the two Administrative Reform Commissions, National Forest Commission and various other Commissions need to be studied and acted upon along with these suggestions which are illustrative only.

The country's *crème della crème* both in the civil society as well as in the government must think if we need to shift to a mix of Parliamentary as well as Presidential form of governance considering the need for involvement of larger expertise in governance at the top levels of executive and to provide stability in the polity of the country. The country must think if it will be plausible to have a referendum to shift to a more cohesive and stable form of Presidential form of governance. In the Presidential system, the President, as well as the Governors of the States, will be directly elected and responsible for their policy and promise. No one will be eligible for re-election after two terms. However, an India specific mix of both Parliamentary as well as Presidential form needs to be evolved.

One of the most glaring experiences of arbitrary and arrogant use of power for selfish or partisan ends in our democracy is such that whenever anyone occupies the post of Prime Minister and the Chief Minister for more than two terms. We must learn a lesson from other countries and at least bring an immediate constitutional amendment to restrict the terms of the Prime Minister and the Chief Ministers to not more than 10years.

Civil Services: As I have dealt with in previous chapters in case studies based on my first-hand experience during my 37 years of service in diverse fields both under the Centre and State, the civil servants are and will always be key to the sound delivery of the schemes and programmes to the citizens of the country. Let me again reiterate and make it very clear that my aim of bringing out the deficiencies in our governance in the public domain is not to run down the contribution and importance of any service. The IAS as a top civil service has immensely contributed and is still the favourite of the young people but it is self-serving and resists changes that affect it or that are not liked by it on the sectarian ground or imaginary fears of losing control. The Police, Forest, Revenue, Railways, Accounts or the Foreign Service etc all have good and bad people and it is true also to any other field and most of the officers in these services have also made outstanding contributions. We must, however, recognize that there has been a considerable downslide in all the organized services in the country. It is a fact that all organized services in order to win the confidence of the people must change both in attitude toward the public and their job and put up larger public interest above their narrow sectarian approach. It is the character, aptitude and attitude of persons apart from the competence who joins these services that determine their quality and public perceptions and will continue to determine their relevance in future also. The case studies narrated in this book in preceding chapters should be taken by the public, political class and the bureaucracy itself at large as feedback to redeem itself and not as a reflection of personal frustration. The purpose is to force people to self-realization so that we improve the present system of governance. Today we must remember that civil servants have acquired enormous clout and the '*defacto*' power they have must be used for the good of the people of the country.

Unlike reforms in political setup, it is easier to remodel the civil services if the political class shows determination and will to change the system for better governance. The civil services of the future must have a deep commitment to the welfare of the people and their recruitment, and their promotion and longevity of career should be linked to their performance. They should have an impeccable character and desire to serve the people honestly, fairly and neutrally while assisting the political masters in their work. The education system plays a far greater role in the moral and character building of the citizens who will be holding responsible positions in the government and civil society. Indians aspiring to be leaders in different fields need to reorient their educational system to character building.

1. The first priority should be to inculcate the cultural ethos among the young minds joining the educational institutions and radical reforms are needed to achieve this in our education system.

2. The first thing to do is to restructure the Union Public Service Commission and make it responsible for monitoring the performance of civil services and bringing in transparency and efficiency in the bureaucracy. It can no longer be used as a place for post-retirement sinecure for the bureaucrats.

3. The civil services both the All India Services as well as Central Services recruitment for at least 50 percent need to be done on the pattern of recruitment of armed forces on the line of National Defence Academy (NDA) and Indian Military Academy (IMA). Like in NDA the UPSC should recruit the youngsters after the 12th standard for the entire gamut of organized civil services. They should graduate in the

Academy in different subjects relevant to public service including the specialised subjects and later on trained for the particular service and then posted in their respective fields. A certain percentage of the posts should be allowed to be recruited after graduation from Universities like in the present system to bring in variety and allow those who missed the chance and also to bring in private sector professionals who have more than 10 to 12 years of domain experience. The teaching subjects in four-year graduation shall be varied so as to bring out the best-groomed civil servants who are capable of handling the diverse fields of administration and who are well versed with the problems in their chosen field and are immensely motivated to perform. Based on their performance they should be allotted to a particular cadre or branch of the civil service and later on trained in that specialised field for a specific period.

4. After a certain period, say about 15 to 20 years, most of the senior posts in the central and States governments after a particular level should be opened for all the civil servants who had proven records of performance by the creation of a senior administrative pool of officers. This pool can be drawn after a written examination as well as an interview by the designated authority but this should only carry 50 per cent weight and the balance 50 per cent from their past service performance. This will bring diverse talent available in the country in governance and end the hegemony of one single group. The responsibility for recruitment and selection shall be of the UPSC and the State PSCs. This pool could be formalised in the form of senior management service to bring in uniformity.

5. The civil services discipline and conduct rules should be revised and civil servants must be made accountable for their action and it should be overseen by a 'civil services bureau' to be established for this purpose. This bureau should also be mandated to weed out the inefficient and corrupt civil servants. The misuse of powers by civil servants must be severely punished and remits of corruption redefined beyond financial corruption to include unusual delays, deliberate irresponsible and arbitrary acts of misuse of authority. In this regards

the officers who do commendable works must be rewarded and those who do not perform must be weeded out.

6. In a time when the Prime Minister is inducting fresh blood front the open market to strengthen the bureaucracy by bringing experts through lateral entry; it would be prudent to think why the departments of Space, Atomic Energy, Telecommunication, Railways have been excelling in their performance. The reason is not far to seek as the professionals have been asked to head the departments. A time has come to reassess our priority in a systematic manner and see beyond IAS generalist and create an equitable pool of man power.

7. For better coordination government should think of creating Indian Medical and Health All India Service. For better conservation of the Environment the Indian Forest Service should be renamed as Indian Environment and Forest Service and be made fully accountable and responsible for managing the sector.

Judiciary: The role of the judiciary is to give quick justice and ensure rule of law in the country. The judiciary had done extremely well in correcting the lackadaisical approach and inactions of the executives in so many cases and each day the judicial reach is increasing. It has original powers in enforcing rule of law and its decisions become the law. However, it also suffers from delays and in India presently more than 5 crore cases are pending in different courts. Justice delayed is justice denied and the judiciary must come forward to correct it. Some of the issues which need to be considered for reforms are as under:

1. The appointment of High Court Judges is too much in favour of Advocates in the Bar. The career judicial officers' quota is only 25 per cent. It should be examined if the quota of career judges should be increased to 50 per cent to bring in more professionalism. If this is done then there is no need to create an All India Judicial Service. The appointment of judges of High Courts and Supreme Courts should be made more transparent and broad-based.

2. The Supreme Court and the High Courts should frame guidelines for timely disposal of the cases by fixing maximum limits of dates

for adjournment of cases. The advocates and the Judges both are well versed with law and pronouncing judgement in most cases should not be a problem. It is seen that on minor issues the cases are allowed to be dragged for years. Except in heinous crimes the hearing process must be time-bound and should complete in less than six months to one year. The judicial accountability for the timely disposal of cases rests with both the advocates and the judges. The long-drawn cases drain the litigants of money and energy and the advocates waste their time, the cases pile up and the Judges become overburdened.

3. The Supreme Court need to assess whether a common citizen or even senior officers can fight the case in Supreme and High Courts because of the exorbitant fees of the advocates and the time taken to decide the cases. Voluntary guidelines for the range of fees need to be fixed by the Bar Council or Associations according to the status of an advocate.

4. One of the reforms in the judiciary in the eighties was the creation of Tribunals under Article 323 A, to reduce the workload of High Courts and to remove delays in deciding the cases. It also envisaged bringing experts into the judicial process. However, this experiment has not been a complete success and instead complicated the decision making rather it created one more level of the judiciary as High Court still are the appellate authority. Take the example of Central Administrative Tribunals (CAT) created in 1985 and the Consumer Forums. Most of these institutions have become post-retirement sinecure for the bureaucrats, advocates and Judges. The selection to these posts should be done by the independent body and those who wish to apply for these posts must have at least three to five years period of service left for retirement and with an impeccable record. It will make these bodies more professional, accountable and committed. A time limit of three months should be fixed for deciding a case in Tribunals as most of these are based on records. There is no monitoring and supervision for the quality of work of these Tribunals which is why the arbitrary and bias decision making go unrecognized and the litigants suffer. This results in poor decisions and it further lengthens the judicial process. One High Court Judge should be named as the Administrative head

for monitoring and supervising the Tribunals under their jurisdiction and there should be provision of annual audit of cases. Alternatively, these Tribunals should be scrapped and the number of High Court Judges increased with the creation of a pool of experts who can be hired if any need of expert is needed from time to time.

5. It is suggested that the Supreme Court of India, Bar Council of India and the Government of India must take these suggestions as feedback and consider a few reforms in the judiciary.

6. There is a need to gradually promote implementation of a common civil code in the country to ensure a same level playing field to all the citizens while preserving their own certain codified customs.

Looking Back – A Few Titbits 14

After a career spanning around 37 years, I had formally retired from the Indian Forest Service (IFS) on 31st August 2014 while serving in the cadre. It was an excellent feeling to have retired from your cadre and a place I loved much and treated as my second home. The initial five years in Tripura build up my character as an officer of my type. I had planned to chart out a new life as a freelance writer and analyst and also to run a Trust namely" Foundation for Integrated Resource Management" now renamed as (Centre for Resource Management and Environment). The Trust was promoted by me to take up the contemporary issues pertaining to the environment, governance and livelihood of poor people involving professionals and social scientists/workers. I had thought of making a federation of the grass-root level communities dependent on forest and other natural resources for their livelihood, art and artefact which I established as "Jan Vikas Manch" in Uttarakhand in 2015 soon after quitting my post-retirement job. I have always been neutral in assessing things and positive in my outlook to things and always support the good things I come across in my writings. On the suggestions of my friends and well wishers that in my each article there are positive suggestions for improvements, I had published the compilation of my articles for last five years "Making Indian Governance to work- a citizen's dream for his country" in May 2021 so that the article are not buried in the papers archives but made available for the larger audience.

Now looking back in terms of my journey in service, while I was preparing for a new life, the Chief Minister of Tripura Shri Manik Sarkar one day in July 2014 called me to his Chamber and asked me to continue work in the same capacity in the Secretariat for another few years to complete his agenda. As such, I was re-appointed on a contract basis for one year in the same capacity and I continued to serve Tripura. It had also ruffled few feathers in the Secretariat and the Forest Department. However, I resigned from my job in April 2015 when I felt that I am not enjoying the reappointment granted to me and left Tripura.

In these 37 years of service, I have seen almost the whole of India's forests, tribal and rural life, Indian culture and traditions; and rich industrialists & mining barons, politicians, fellow officers of different services and social workers of all hues. This exposure had enriched my vision in my professional life which is now a treasure to be proud of as it forms my core values towards life. It is reflected in my personality. My exposure to the world during my visits abroad further enriched my rational way of thinking while absorbing the best in their culture. Of special significance is my one-year Masters Course in Resource Management at the University of Edinburgh which transformed a forester in me into a balanced resource manager in the service of people and nature. It inculcated in me a sense to strike a balanced approach towards conflicting claims and a habit of asking questions to find out of box solutions. If I feel difficult to decide things I take recourse to my common sense. On firming up my views about the people and the world I was deeply influenced by the values nurtured by my father and the stories I heard about my grandfather's philanthropically disposed of character even when he had to suffer while helping the poor. The quality of straight and fearless disposition on issues, fighting for core values, no complexes, in any good or bad settings, honesty, commitment to work and love for my country were the gifts I received from my parents.

The professional life has given me immense insight for quick understanding of public needs, how to co-evolve with conflicting demands without breaking rules (though stretching a bit is always good to ensure public good and knowing well what is not prohibited in rules) and above all to be in harmony with the natural ecosystem and its components like trees, wild animals, flowers and rivers which provide us with our basic needs of life. I have always treated humans to be a very crucial part of the ecosystem and no ecosystem can be managed without humans. I had a fascination for the forests service as my grandfather worked for the King's forests in Uttarakhand as a forest officer. At the same time, I was conscious of the difficulties forest fringe communities experienced at the hands of foresters.

When I was allocated Tripura cadre, I was a little apprehensive of our careers and future life and when boarded the Indian Airlines Fokker Friendship aircraft on 18th July 1981, the fear of flight in the career also engulfed me when the plane was passing through monsoon turbulence fearing the bumpy ride in the job in a landlocked State like Tripura. Things started changing gradually as I found slowly that the place is no different from Dehradun in many ways and the State is culturally colourful and 18 tribes and Bengali communities mix very well, people are nice and live in harmony with nature. In a casual meeting with the late H.N. Bahuguna in Delhi in November 1981, he told me that I have got an opportunity to work in a State where one of the great leaders in Indian politics is the Chief Minister. He further said it also allows me to serve in eastern India from where the Bahuguna clan had migrated to the hills of Uttarakhand around 500 years ago or so.

I would like to narrate a few anecdotes which shaped the philosophy of my career. During initial 'on the job training' period Mr R.N Chakraborty Conservator of Forests, known as a hard taskmaster, handed me a 97-point action programme to be completed in the next 6 months. He wanted to grind the young IFS officers in the fieldwork in the forests and in dealing with other departments in the district. While following one of his programmes, once crossing a river in Pecherthal range for checking the stand marking of trees in Sidhongcherra 1981 plantation and some inquiries, I had almost lost my life as I slipped from the four-piece temporary Bamboo bridge while hurrying to latch on the protruding branch of a tree at the other end to get to that end but the strength of the branch of the tree and quick reflexes saved me. I stayed in the Pecherthal forest rest house which was one of the good rest houses in Tripura at that time but a lot of "tick-tick" sound by lizards during the night made me curious as in North India lizards make no such sound (soon I realized that these are friends, as they help control the mosquitoes and other insect pests in the room), I ate bread and banana with water and duck's egg for breakfast and dinner, and took lunch in forests with staff, travelled in trucks as well as on foot several kilometres to catch on the work. I could realize how forest field staff works in difficult circumstances in the interior areas when I saw some smugglers cutting Teak trees. I also noticed how some staff play truant with their duties. When our staff caught the Tribals carrying teak wood as head loads to sell as firewood for their livelihood, it was the dilemma of raising plantations of valuable species'. At the same time, I felt sorry for the poor head loaders who had to eke out a living by felling trees raising a question mark on the development programmes of the government especially on the failure of tribal and rural development activities. During on-the-job training at Kailashahar, I had a nice company in the district with other friends from IAS, IPS and officers from the judiciary. I also remember one Doctor Mr Abi, who after retirement worked as a consultant in a World Health Organization project who used to entertain us with his jokes.

I would like to narrate an interesting episode that helped me to develop my clear vision. In 1981, during the Durga Puja holidays in October, I held the charge of Kailashahar Division as the regular DFO had gone home to Kolkata. A young unemployed youth was given a contract based on the government policy announced by the then Chief Minister, Mr Nripen Chakraborty, to help educated unemployed youths to earn a livelihood, a work order (on a government-approved estimate) to construct a ring well in 'Jarultali' beat office was issued. One day the young man came to me and said that for the last three months the beat officer Mr Alkas Mian is not writing the Measurement Book (MB) and hence the payment for Rs 9600 for this work has been held up. I told him to wait and tell the DFO on his return. He informed me that he had twice met the DFO but no action is being taken either by the Range Officer or the Beat officer. The Head Clerk Mr Haripada Deb of the DFO office a seasoned and well-experienced hand came to me and told me that this is Chief Minister's pet project and if he knows about this type of delays, it will be very bad for the department. I had already had the experience of Chief Minister's anger last time when he visited Kailashahar and took the meeting of District level officers and flew into a rage against the DFO for disobeying the government policy on timber transit passes from forest land allotted to the landless migrants and tribal people. I had joined the Division just a few days ago on the job training when the DFO took me to that meeting. In the case of allotted lands, the government had waived off the royalty and asked the forest department to allow the trees as per Jote land provisions (Jote land is the term used for the private land owned by the people). However, the Conservator of Forests (CF) took a view that it cannot be allowed as per the newly created Forest Conservation Act 1980 and advised the DFO not to give a permit for felling the trees from these lands. He, however, did not give any written order. He was in the habit of giving such verbal orders often. When the Chief Minister (CM) came he was approached by his party leaders along with a large number of affected people and complained against the DFO. During the meeting in the end, he called the DFO and asked him to sit beside him and asked him why he is not obeying the government order on this. The DFO in a very plain manner told the CM that his Conservator of Forests had asked he should not issue the permit from these lands as these were allotted without the concurrence of the forest department. The CM asked him to issue the order immediately as per the Cabinet decision. The DFO however, remained adamant and refused to do so. On this the CM suddenly became extremely angry and told him "who is powerful CF/DFO or CM, who is running the government. I will ruin your career". The vitriolic attack on him continued for another 5 minutes and the CM's face was red with extreme rage and his body trembling. He had a squint eye and as I was sitting on the backbench, I thought he is directing his anger to me also. However, when the meeting ended, he asked all others, except the DFO to go. He told the DFO Dr PN Ray, "I had to show my anger as I am running the government and responsible for the people and had to be angry at your stubborn intransigence as you could have said that you will do it and inform the CF that CM had ordered". He though complimented him for his commitment. He patted him and asked us to go and be people-friendly. The way the CM behaved it is was a sign of a great leader which Mr Nripen Chakraborty indeed was. The CM had sent a message to the agitating public and at the same time watered down his anger and handled the officers also well in the end as officers out of grievances play with other government programmes. He was great communist leaders of national stature and I started adoring him. No sooner the CM left the CF again telephoned the DFO to allow the permit as per government order, obviously CM must have blasted him too. This was the biggest lesson I learnt which would put me in good condition in deciding about difficult matters. In fact, till 1985 no one in State governments really bothered about the Forest Conservation Act 1980 too much but such Protection Forests lands were allotted either just when the Forest Conservation Act

1980 was enacted or before that during 1979-80 when the CPM came to power in 1979.

Given my experience with CMs visit, I agreed to the advice of the Head Clerk and immediately asked the Range Officer and the Forester as well as the youth to proceed with the inspection the next day. I visited the site, though the entire State was in Puja Holidays. During the field visit, the forester insisted that only 7 iron rings were laid against the 9 stipulated for the purpose, but the contractor insisted that he had constructed the ring well with all 9 rings. After a lot of discussions, I said that the next morning the ring well would be demolished to verify the number of rings and if 9 rings are seen then the forester will reconstruct the ring well from his own money and will also face a departmental enquiry. Mr Alkas Mian as well as the contractor instantly agreed but I could read some tension hovering over the face of the forester soon after we started to leave the place. I ordered the contractor to reach the DFO's office the next day and then proceeded to the Jarultali Beat office at 11 am along with Range Officer, labours and implements to break the ring well to ascertain the truth. As soon as we reached the place, I found the contractor confident enough as I was about to order breaking up of the ring well I could sense that the forester is shaky and trembling. He suddenly fell on my feet and begged for mercy. The MB was quickly written and the contractor was paid for his bills within three days. These are some of the instances which change you forever; if you think that it was a game-changing event.

There was yet another incident that I would like to narrate. It shaped my learning process. One day, sometime in 1983 soon after I was posted as DFO Teliamura, the then Chief Minister Nripen Chakraborty visited the Taidu Rang office where he met local people in the forest Range office complex and one particular tribal person gave him a representation in writing which was in the Bengali language. The Chief Minister handed over the paper to me and told me to try to help this poor man. I returned to my office with the paper and asked my Head Clerk to read it as at that time I was not so fluent in the Bangla language. The application was related to permission for the felling of some trees on his land. I asked the Range officer (RO) for a report. After the report was submitted by the RO, I found that a portion of the land is disputed, according to the forest department; the trees were in fact a 'Gamar' timber tree plantation of the department. I decided to visit the spot and the revenue Tehsildar was requested to remain present with records. On scrutiny, I found that his jote land is surrounded by the forest department Protected Forests land. The forest department had in fact planted the trees but plantations were extended on his jote land (private land) also and about 40 trees of around 25 years old were standing on his land. I asked him to wait for a few days but he said he had to marry off his daughter soon and he had been protecting these trees from smugglers and extremists for a long time, tending them and had not used the land otherwise. I brooded over the matter for a few minutes and said I will allow you the first 20 trees immediately and the balance will be decided after we find how much the forest department had spent and under what circumstances the trees were planted. After returning to my office, I located the papers but nothing could be found but I calculated the planting cost. After some time, I concluded that we are already paying the farmers for the planting of trees on private lands under the social forestry programme and decided that though the trees were planted long back when this scheme was not there but today the trees are surviving on his land due to his efforts. I allowed him the permit for 30 trees and balance 10 trees which were standing on slope bordering forest land were retained for protection of soil. I requested him to protect these trees in the interest of his own land. He agreed and was so happy to get the permit. After that every 3-4 months he used to meet me and bring some home grown fruits and vegetables for me and would get angry if I insisted on payment. This continued for another 2 and half years till I went on Central deputation in May 1985. This encounter with this tribal person changed my personality as a public servant forever. I became primarily a people-centric public servant. Such small experiences in the formative years can shape and give direction to your decision-making ability for the entire career. This episode gave me an idea of starting a Van Premi Sangh (Friends of Trees organization) with one social worker of Mandai Range. Gradually I realized the importance of public involvement in the management of forests and how rules are to be interpreted in a balanced way. The rules are for the public welfare and designed in such a way that these are not used for selfish gains by the officers but can be stretched a bit to accommodate genuine public welfare without explicit violation of any provision of rules.

I have yet another incident while I was working as DG ICFRE I found a senior scientist in Jabalpur institute, indulging in extramarital affairs with a research associate. I ordered a secret enquiry; got the video of the time when they tried to check in a hotel and promptly suspended him. Later on, after he realized that he did a wrong and sought for pardon and his wife also vouched for his conduct, I reinstituted him, dropped the charges after issuing a terse warning and transferred him to another location. During my visit to the Institute after some months he met me and fell on my feet and thanked me for suspending him which was, in fact, a blessing in disguise otherwise, his family would have been ruined. He gifted me a watch which cost more than Rs 6000 in 2012 so that I would always remember him. I have always believed in enforcing the discipline strictly but keeping the reformist's face with human values top in my mind. I found that people behave in the manner, they are groomed and most of the people fall in line if treated intelligently and tactfully but without any prejudice. I always think that "*Desh* (country or place)", "*Kal* (timing)" and "*Paristhiti* (situation)" should determine the way a matter should be handled. The same situation in another place and situation will have to be tackled differently.

There was one curious incident of a different kind that happened with me when I was travelling in a Maruti Van on 21st May 1994 on three days casual leave specially granted by the then Chief Secretary (CS) Mr M Damodaran (who was also the Forest Secretary) to attend as a resource person in a national seminar organized at Shillong in Meghalaya on community forestry around 350 km from my office in Kumarghat by the Society for Promotion of Waste Lands Delhi. However, one Chief Conservator of Forests holding charge as PCCF who was on leave, at the eleventh hour denied me the permission to officially attend the conference. I spoke with the Chief Secretary about the need for permission as I was the resource person and the topic is of use to our State as well. The CS asked me to go on casual leave as I was travelling outside the State and write a letter to PCCF that CS has approved it. Next morning I started for Shillong with Mr Samarendra Das (Assistant Conservator of Forests attached to my office). While the car was cruising at a speed of 60 km/hr and was about 50 Km away from Shillong, due to heavy rains suddenly the vehicle swirled and turned turtle and landed on the edge of the road just a foot away from the deep gorge down below. We composed ourselves, came out by sliding the door. Just as I stepped out of the vehicle, I found an old man of around 75 years of age with a fair complexion and wearing a jacket of hessian cloth with several wrinkles on his face standing beside me putting over my head a colourful umbrella. We took shelter under this colourful umbrella for a few minutes and trying our composure to get back. He did not utter a word but just kept holding the umbrella. It was a providential escape that saved us from falling into the deep gorge. Had the vehicle gone down the hill, none of us would have survived. After a few minutes, two trucks came and stopped after seeing the accident and the truck drivers helped us to overturn the vehicle. The driver started the engine and the vehicle was fine except that its windscreen was damaged and some dents in the body. It all happened in a span of 5 to 10 minutes. As we looked to thank the old man but astonishingly, he was never to be found as we searched him and his umbrella for almost 15 minutes but the old man could not be spotted anywhere near neither there was any road nearby. After that, we left for Shillong. This incident has remained a mystery in my life as I could never know who this old man was with a colourful umbrella! I keep discussing this with Mr Samarendra Das even now. Few days before this incident, on the night of 4th May 1994, I survived a murderous attack by the cross-border smugglers in connivance with the then Conservator of Forests whose dubious role in illicit felling of timber in Jampui was being inquired into by a team headed by me. The smugglers broke open the door of one of the rooms situated on another side of the drawing-room and drank liquor and smoke more than 2 packets of cigarettes and then tried to enter my room around 2 am at the midnight after switching off the main switch. But for the casual work of the caretaker Mr Satendru who closed the door connecting two bedrooms to the drawing-room with the strong movable door fastening staple, prevented their entry to my bedroom. With a little bit of common sense after I woke up saved me as I feigned calling police over the police over phone and after they failed to enter my bedroom even through the skylight window of the bathroom. They left by climbing the gate. Later on, I loudly called for the night guard and the cashier whose quarter was beside the Forest Rest House. They came out along with the other staff residing inside the campus and saw the condition of the room. We found the miscreants had boozed and smoked inside and the articles of Almirah and cigarette butts were scattered all around in the room. The miscreants were some goons from Bangladesh. Later on, in the morning, the District Magistrate and SP came to visit with police sniffer dogs. The Dogs took the police up to the road leading to the border. I submitted the Jampui inquiry report and fixed liability on the then Conservator of forests amounting to around Rs 300 crore loss to the exchequer. The conservator of forests was charge-sheeted but later on, let off due to political reasons.

I would like to share my professional experience while working in various capacities under the State and Central Governments. Some of the actions taken had a tremendous impact on the lives of people. During my tenure in the Central Government, I had always kept the interests of the country, profession and the State uppermost in my mind and with a selfless zeal pursued the work. I stretched my neck in the year 2000 in the Ministry of Environment and Forests and threatened a foreign NGO to stop their operation in India for funding activists who were destabilizing the nascent JFM in the country and acting against the country at the hand of this NGO. I told them if they have some positive ideas on promoting community participation they can work with the government through professionally sound NGOs. Finally, the same NGO became a partner with the Government in networking with civil society members in strengthening peoples' participation in forest management as we created a network that was housed and manned by another NGO. It contributed a lot to promoting the JFM programme with civil society participation.

Similarly, when the Supreme Court appointed me the leader of the task force to carry out the Environmental Impact Assessment of mining in Karnataka during 2011, I steadfastly rejected the foreign-funded NGOs fanciful ideas of destabilizing mining in the country on specious arguments. I told them our job is not to stop mining in Karnataka but to see how we set standards for environmentally sustainable and scientifically programmed mining so that the country can progress and local livelihood is not affected and de-stabilized. The report was the basis of many Supreme Court orders on mining after the Central Empowered Committee examined the report of this task force. An interesting note I was handed over by the officials of the Federation of Indian Mineral Industries (FIMI) which they received from some sources that some NGOs working for Green landscape in Australia; received funds from American organizations to destabilize mining in Australia. A few of our NGOs are receiving funds to destabilize mining in India also but their job is made easy by a few corrupt and inefficient mining companies who only focus on profiteering with poor technology and destructive mining without any care for the environment. The State mining departments are also very inefficient and there is no real control over the mining of minor minerals like sand, stones and marvels in the country. The sand and stone mafias are the real challenge for the regulatory authorities today in India as their unscientific mechanized extraction of sand is a serious threat to our river systems, water and the agriculture.

I vigorously pursued the cause of allowing Rubber on forestland under the Forest Conservation Act, 1980 to permanently settle the Tribal shifting cultivators as far back as 1984. Rubber is the most viable and successful means of permanent settlement of tribal people even today and in view of the success of Tripura in rehabilitating the shifting cultivators, the Ministry of Environment and Forests with the help of Mr AN Prasad the then Deputy Inspector-General agreed to allow rubber trees to be planted in a phased manner on forest land over 9000 ha of forestland and released 1500 ha in 1997. The first thing that I did after joining back in Tripura in 2013 was to get Government approval for keeping the Rubber timber out of the purview of Transit Rules under section 42 of the Indian Forest Act 1927. I also convinced the then DG Forests to allow planting of Rubber on the land vested under Forest Rights Act 2006 for permanent settlement of shifting cultivators and a letter was issued on 17th August 2010 by the Ministry of Environment and Forests allowing around 3200 ha out of the balance 9000 ha area agreed by the Ministry.

I also seriously worked for the majority of the forestry and environmental clearances in Tripura for the power projects be it Monarchac, Ramchandraghat and all other projects. The then Principal Resident Commissioner Tripura Bhawan used to vigorously pursue with me to steer clear of many development projects from 2002 to 2004 and was rewarded by the Chief Minister later on by making him Chief Secretary. One of the significant contributions I made relates to convincing the DG Forests while I was Inspector General of Forests (IGF) looking after Forest Conservation to allow diversion of forestland for the Tripura State Rifles Battalions inside the forests. Initially, the apprehension was that once we allow such things to happen it would open a Pandora's Box and would also increase illicit felling of trees. I countered with the argument that if security forces are stationed in the interior areas the illicit felling at the behest of militants would come down and the State would be safer. In fact the militants were felling Teak trees and smuggling across the border and it was a big headache for us. Almost all the 7-8 proposals of TSR were cleared and within a few years time the State became rid of terrorism and is peaceful today as the extremists' hideouts were busted and the State areas sanitized completely.

I also devised the concept of one-time clearance for the International Border fencing under the Forest Conservation Act 1980 in consultations with the Home Ministry and was successful in convincing the then Forest Minister to agree to this proposal. This expedited the border fencing erection work along Indo-Bangla Border and significantly reduced cross border crimes.

The seeds of Forest Rights Act (FRA) 2006 were sown when the Ministry of Environment and Forests, the government of India, in November 2003 granted permission to the Kerala government to settle the tribals on vested forestland to set right any injustice done to them and in 5th February 2004, we had issued guidelines to settle the long-pending disputed traditional rights claims of the tribal people through a well-planned action under the Forest Conservation Act 1980. This notification opened the door for the enactment of the Forest Rights Act 2006. If the NDA government had returned to power the notification of 5th February would have been implemented as it was a better way of granting the rights as it was linked to funding for livelihood model development and would not have remained as open-ended even after 14 years of its enactment. The FRA is a good intervention but its implementation is faulty as it is promoting further encroachments on the forest lands; and had become a tool in the hands of a few people with vested interests. In 2018, I had given a presentation on this Act before the tribal welfare Secretary government of India along with some social worker so that these lands are made productive for tribal livelihoods and also requested him how the revenue, forest and tribal affairs departments are not able to ascertain the occupation of land so long. He agreed but said the government want it to be an open-ended Act. One of the reasons is the competitive politics between Christian missionaries and ultra-leftists who are always instigating innocent tribal people and branding mainstream India as exploiters. The Vanbasi Kalyan Ashram and some other organizations for the last 15 years have done really good work in the tribal areas by promoting their cultural and traditional values and have to a certain extent checked the nefarious influence of these groups. The government need to infuse money on these lands and on development of the tribal hamlets in collaboration with forest department.

I have been a witness to the poor infrastructure of forest department in all the States. As the central government Ministries were directed by the then Prime Minister in the year 2001 during the NDA regime to spend 10% of their outlay in the North-East but in the absence of projects, it was difficult to implement and grant funds. I took this opportunity and converted this weakness to strength and prepared a special project for the development of the infrastructure for the North-East. The Ministry sanctioned more than 100 crore Rupees during 2001-02 to North-Eastern States to upgrade buildings, computer networks, other infrastructure, and vehicles for the field staff. The long-felt demand of forest officers for a field officers hostel at Agartala and other State capitals was sanctioned. The infrastructure push gave a big boost in checking cross border crimes and smuggling of timber to Bangladesh as detection of offences also increased the revenue manifold. Tripura also got Rs 4.5 crore for the Hathipara Forest Academy and part of the building was taken over by me as DG ICFRE after signing an agreement with the Chief Secretary for opening an ICFRE research Centre in Agartala named as *'Centre for Forest-based livelihood and Extension'* at The Centre is working in the interest of farmers of the State with several initiatives for improving livelihoods, especially, by providing superior Bamboo planting material and agro-forestry models.Incidentally now this Centre is one of the best functioning centres of ICFRE as I have put a very young and brilliant scientist Dr Pawan Kaushik as its Director who created immense potential for the Bamboo based livelihoods for the people and became very popular among masses. Unfortunately, he succumbed to covid-19 on 7th June 2021.

During my previous tenure at ICFRE Dehradun (October 1995-June 1997), I sanctioned a landmark project for the extension of a technology developed by the FRI for utilization of Rubber timber after treatment (without treatment it is a waste but after treatment, it is as good as teak) by taking advantage of the World Bank Project. The technology was for the treatment of rubber for use as timber and it proved to be a boon for the people of Tripura and Mr DK Sharma the then GM executed it very well. Today, it is an industry worth several crores in Tripura and providing livelihood to so many thousands of people. The Rubber plantations after Tripura Forest Development and Plantation Corporation had successfully rehabilitated the Tribals are the backbone of tribal and non-tribal people's economy in the State now. The Rubber enterprise created by me won the Corporation prestigious Indian Express-EMPI Silver trophy in 2006. Rubber, timber and furniture have now become a household name in Tripura. There is not a single office and household in Tripura which does not have Rubber furniture. The Tripura Rubber Factory is one of its kinds in the country. More than 100 carpenters work daily in 'Unakoti Arts and Crafts' through a joint venture with the best of machines. There are two private enterprises providing jobs to many carpenters. The State-of-the-art door factory is using Rubber Boards. Under the JICA project, a Bamboo common facility Centre has been created for value addition of the Bamboo. A large number of families are dependent on the activities of the corporation.

For rehabilitation of Tribal shifting, cultivators got 3794 ha of Forestland diverted in 2006 for planting Rubber by TFDPC. As Chairman of the

State Rubber Mission, I prepared the vision document and implemented the same for the expansion of Rubber and today we find the production of Rubber to have increased manifold just as envisioned and has crossed the 85,000 hectares in the State.

I played a crucial role of negotiator for the first phase of both the Indo-German and JICA projects during 2006-2007 and was the first CEO of both the projects and successfully negotiated the JICA and Indo-German projects and as CEO during 2005 -2006 and planned the implementation of these projects. The key features of these projects were the integration of primary sector project with bio-diversity conservation and livelihood by involving all the departments like agriculture, horticulture, animal husbandry, fisheries, food processing and village industries and the forest department. These two projects are the watershed in the forest-people interface and have immensely benefited the people of the State as well as helped the development of infrastructure of the forest department.

As Principal Secretary Forest department I initiated the second JICA project during 2013-14 which was approved and ultimately started in 2019. The talks of making forest department with civil administration have been a subject of discussion among all concerned agencies except for proliferation of senior posts in the States nothing had been done for a long time. The administrative structure of the forest department was thus completely reorganized and forest sub-divisions have been created by replacing the existing Divisions. This has brought the department co-terminus with the Districts. By this restructuring, the administration has been taken closer to the people for ensuring better delivery. It was a long felt need and is a landmark reform agreed by Mr Manik Sarkar the Chief Minister who could visualise the benefits in the hierarchy of forest department and got the approval of his cabinet despite a lot of opposition from vested corners. I had visited Tripura in February 2020 and interacted with people in the villages and the officers of the forest department and it is working exceedingly well in delivering the services to people, efficient in the execution of works and checking the smuggling of timber, especially, cross border crime along Bangladesh border etc.

As the Chief Wildlife Warden for bringing Tripura in the map of National Parks in 2006-2007 recommended the creation of two National Parks for the two flagship species of the State and smoothly steered the declaration of the core area of Sipahijala wildlife sanctuary as *'Clouded leopard National Park'* and the core area of Trishna Wildlife Sanctuary as *'Bison National Park'.*

JFM has been given a big boost at the national level through my academic work at IIFM Bhopal and by formulating a policy framework for JFM as well as Sustainable Forest Management (SFM) while working as Inspector General of Forests (IGF). The first-generation reforms in JFM were initiated by two guidelines issued in the year 2000 and 2002. In the State, we issued guidelines for creating a large number of water bodies in forest areas under JFM with a full stake for the people for their livelihood while ensuring conservation and regeneration of the forest's resources. It had helped in a quantum jump in fish production in the State. As Agriculture Production Commissioner in 2013-14 while guiding the Krishi Vikas Yojna (Agriculture Development Scheme) of the government of India, I had tried to substantially increase the allocation of the Fisheries Department from this scheme. After the creation of Forest Development Agencies (FDA) as federations of the JFM Committees, the IFM Programme got a big boost and changed the fate of Aforestation programmes.

For better integrated natural resources management in the country, a convergence project was sanctioned from the National Rain Fed Area Authority for integration of forestry, agriculture, animal resources and fisheries sectors and other rural developmental activities for developing a new model of natural resources management in the country. There is a need to know the status of availability of natural resources in the country for better productivity of agriculture and allied sectors. From the NRAA we sanctioned six crore to FRI Dehradun for compiling the status of resources on Forests and adjoining non forest lands in 74 Districts of the country so that better rural development planning can be ensured.

In the Agriculture department in Tripura, we had taken three decisions which were very well received by the farmers. The first was a timely supply of seeds, fertilizers and other inputs by streamlining the administration at the grass-root level and procurements which resulted in an increase of rice productivity by 45,000 Mt in one year. Second, I scrapped the tendering system in providing subsidy to the farmers under which we got very poor feedback from farmers during my frequent tours and direct contacts with farmers and instead implemented the proposal of maximum discount on the Maximum Retail Price (MRP) on the Indian Standard Institute (ISI) certified machineries and the farmers got a chance to choose from a basket. There was no use forcing farmers to buy based on lowest tenders when the government is giving only subsidies. People were getting substandard Chinese pieces of equipment. Third, I released as many as 16 high yielding climate-resistant varieties of rice, fruits and vegetables, which were pending approval for long developed by the ICAR's Agartala Centre for rice, pulses and fruits. These were pending for more than five years. These varieties are doing well now with the farmers adopting them. The Agriculture and Veterinary Colleges were suffering from an acute shortage of faculty and the recruitment process for more than 50 faculty was completed and the colleges started functioning properly. A farmer's portal was created a first of its kind in the country to provide farmers technical assistance round the clock on agriculture, horticulture, animal resources and forestry matters.

In the Animal Resources Department, a unique programme of production of fodder for cattle was started in collaboration with Joint Forest Management Committees of the forest department which helped the farmers to get fodder and open grazing was reduced in the forests. In a major decision, we reduced the procurement of foreign breed cow semen and started promoting indigenous cows for the production of A2 milk by introducing the artificial insemination of Sahiwal semen. The State government also designated me as Agriculture Production Commissioner and intimated the Ministry of Agriculture about it. Sadly the portal has become non-functional now as reported by the website hosting it.

I had the privilege of shaping the contours of the JFM Programme in the country and piloting the idea of creation of Forest Development Agencies as the federation of JFM Committees for bringing out genuine participation of villagers in the forestry programmes through a Committee Ministry constituted. I also streamlined the Forestry clearances as IGF forest Conservation by amending the rules twice in 2003 and 2004. Through 5th February 2004 notification of the Ministry of Environment and Forests laid the background for the enactment of Forest Rights Act 2006 by the next government which came to power after the general election of 2004.

One of the most significant contribution I had made as IGF in the Ministry of Environment and Forests was to Chair a Committee which was constituted after the Supreme Court order of 30th October 2002 for creation of a Compensatory Afforestation Fund. The Committee also included Mr AN Prasad former DIGF and officers from Computer and Auditor General Office and |Finance Ministry and we recommended creation of Compensatory Afforestation Planning and Management Authority (CAMPA) which today is headed by an Additional Director-General of Forest level officer and manages a corpus of more than 75,000 crore. The CAMPA after lot of haggling has been created by an Act of Parliament.

I was conferred the *Queen's Award for Forestry 2000*by the Commonwealth Forestry Association for my contribution in policy formulation and spreading the community forestry and peoples' participation in the management of forest which had influenced the sector in the entire commonwealth. I was also conferred the *Great Son of India and Uttarakhand Ratan* awards by the India Intellectual Federation headed by former Governor and Union Minister Dr Bhism Narayan Singh. But of all the awards I received, what I cherish the most is the invitation to *Chair an important session on 'integrated land use planning' in the World Forestry Week* in which more than 140 Countries' senior national Forestry policymakers and with more than 45 Ministers heading the delegations of their countries. I felt good because the proceeding went on exceedingly well with very good discussions and my suggestions as Chair was well received in the end and I received an appreciation letter from the FAO. It was the success of Indian experiment that worked during the session. It was a proud moment because I was the only Indian to have been given this honour so far in the last five decades and to a professional who comes from Tripura a small State. After all,*E F Schumacher* had said long ago *"small is beautiful"*.

Though the State is small but being a landlocked border State with a 980 km international boundary with Bangladesh; has its own challenges and strategic importance. On recognition of my efforts; I admire most- when as Managing Director of Tripura Forest Development and Plantation the Corporation, '*the EMPI-Indian Express Silver*' Award was won by the corporation in 2006 for converting a loss-making government enterprise into a viable profit-making unit by introducing corporate culture and welfare of the workers. Among other awardees were the big corporate like Tata, Genepact etc. The Silver award was handed over to me by the then President Mr Abdul Kalam in Delhi in a glittering ceremony. Among all the glittering corporate honchos receiving the awards, Mr Kalam spoke only with me for a few minutes on the work done by the corporation for the poor people of Tripura as he previously visited the villages of tribal shifting cultivators permanently settled by the corporation.

From Horses Mouth – Reminicences of a Civil Servant

15

By:

Dr. M.H.SWAMINATH IFS Retd

(Former, Secretary Forests, Ecology and Environment,
Government of Karnataka
& Former, Director- General, Environmental Management and
Policy Research Institute(EMPRI) Government of Karnataka)

A Journey with civil servants of Indian bureaucracy was a most exiting journey of the life, on an uncharted path which was less traveled and strewn with thorns and pricking pebbles. The bumpy rides and jolts in every day's journey was an excruciating phenomenon. Though it was never a dull day, the journey was full of disappointments and dismay waiting to happen. However, the hopes and dreams for a better tomorrow kept the lamp flickering.

The journey was full of surprises and the show continued to be performed despite all odds against the civil servants. And it is worst if you are from an Indian Forest service as there are not many **'Mai-Baaps'** backing you.

Yet, it was a joy, to working under very troubling circumstances, especially during the decades of India's growth which were often worst time in the annals of India's great march towards fulfilling the aspirations of millions of people along with our own ambitions and dreams was worth its trouble.

Is Civil Service a Caucus Club?

It is a great experience to be part of Indian Civil service caucus. They are men from different planet distinct altogether from the Aam admi, oblivious to the world of reality. All India Service (AIS), Babus are made from different matter as they look and breath different from rest of the world.

The word 'Babu' was made official to describe AIS officers as "Babus" by Indian Prime Minister in his parliament speech by saying "Babus are not panacea "to solve all our problems. He must have made this observation after seeing their failure in fixing many of India's owes. However, they chose to just ignore the PM's comments and murmurs here and there on Twitter.

The AIS Cadre especially the IAS is also called as steel frame as it is very rigid in its beliefs, loyalty and commitment. In fact they strive very hard to protect every word written in the rulebook.

There was a lady IAS officer who was very bookish and interpreted every word literally to make a most atrocious decision on financial matters. In one meeting there was a discussion on fixing training cost to the villagers who are called for training. As the Finance Secretary she was so mean and rigid she was calculating food cost based on minimum calorie prescribed by World Health Organization (WHO). She never understood the practical aspects of field circumstances. After she left the meeting in a huff, another Secretary remarked, " if there is a rule to shoot somebody for some mistake, she will not think twice to question the rule but very obediently she will shoot the person". Like that, we have seen many officers who have always showed us rule book and never questioning the relevance or moral imperativeness. There are many such instances in the governance which did not justify the severe action needed to address very trivial issues.

Petty Mindedness!

I was in the Karnataka State government working as Assistant Director of Horticulture before joining Indian Forest service. After receiving the orders to join the training at Dehradun, I requested the Director of Horticulture to relieve me from service to enable me to join the IFS training. But surprisingly he wrote to government to recover the training cost from me as a penalty for leaving the State service. The matter went to another IAS officer who was Secretary Horticulture who also concurred with the Director of Horticulture, and sent the file to the Chief Minister office for final approval. Thanks to the visionary Chief Minister Sri Devraj Urs, who laughed at the recommendation to recover the penalty and gave his approval to relieve me without any conditions attached to it. The bureaucrats looked small and mean before such Statesmen like Sri Devraj Urs.

However, they are very unique and distinct class of people, who have served the nation with utmost rigidity holding the nation's destiny in their tight fist, with an unquestionable loyalty to the so called rule book.

Strict Disciplinarians

Perhaps the British rulers lasting legacy is the hierarchical structure and subordination. The subordinate were always taught to follow the protocols as prescribed and practiced within bureaucracy. Discipline was the fundamental principle of civil service. That was also the cardinal principle of administration.

When we joined service, we came across quite a few senior civil servants who were known for strict disciplines and would not tolerate any violations as such. We had a Chief Secretary who was very strict and did not tolerate any one breaking the protocol let alone the junior most Indian Forest service probationers. Our batch was due for senior scale promotion which is granted automatically on completion of four years and we were anxiously expecting promotions after completion of our two years of junior scale postings. There were vacancies available but the government was not processing the promotion files. Few of batch mates thought and decided that, we must go to our head quarters and meet the senior officers, who were handling the establishment section to know the reason for the delay in getting the promotion and also for requesting for an early promotion. We did not have any intention or desire to meet the Chief Secretary, let alone the Chief Conservator of Forest (CCF). We knew very well that they were unapproachable like Demigods.

But, to our bad luck, when we went to Department of Personal and Administrative Reform (DPAR) office to meet the Deputy Secretary who was handling the IFS Cadre promotion we requested for the permission to meet her and sent a chit with our names written and the purpose of our visit. Though it was visiting hour we did not get the permission to see her for a very long time. As the waiting became too long we were also becoming impatient and were losing hopes. Then, suddenly it occurred to us that we can take a chance to meet the chief Secretary directly, if he permits us. We went to his office and sent a chit and to our surprise, we got a nod to meet him instantaneously. As soon as Chief Secretary saw us, he looked annoyed and looked at us with a kind of disdain. He asked in a stern voice "whether we have taken permission from your head of the department to meet me"?

We were little scared, but managed to gather strength and told him that we have not taken the permission. He pretended that he was very angry and scolded us that we are too eager to get our promotion so quickly without working sufficiently long enough to deserve a promotion and have violated the protocol by meeting him directly. He told us to go and work and leave the promotion to their discretion. We were very sheepish and felt highly petulant and thought we have annoyed the God.

We were quite scared that he may take disciplinary action and rushed back to the field and prayed God to have mercy on us. After few days we were given promotion was a pleasant surprise.

We had these types of very hard core disciplined bureaucrats who never tolerated any violation of protocols. Bureaucracy thy name is protocol.

Files Worms!

Files are very holy to our bureaucrats. They will never ever allow the files to be shown any disrespect by violating its sacred principles and rituals.

The red tapism is another word for Indian bureaucracy as every decision is taken through the file system. Every file is very carefully tied with a red tape and making them untouchable and easily inaccessible to any. They love their files so much that they hold them to their chest; therefore, they are called hard core bureaucrats.

One of our senior IAS officers would describe the clearance of file by the officers as a very painful process as officers, love each file like their own children as they conceive, carry, and give birth after a prolonged period of gestation. He would conduct a meeting to dispose of every file with detailed discussion and noting.

It is quite amazing that, how the Indian bureaucracy has molded itself into a monolithic and evolving continuously as a highly secured, self perpetuating, and least accountable body. Papers containing carefully drafted notes, after passing through more than two dozen desks, with carefully designed and structured checks and balances; the procedures enables system to take a non partisan decisions that ensures no one's accountability. It is designed to be more of a collective responsibility meant to be confusing, and dragging to eliminate hurried decisions.

Masters of All

Babus start their career as not only the "Jack of all trade" and as the time passes in their job and they acquire the work experience they portray themselves as "Masters of All". I have seen many of our IAS colleagues becoming experts even in highly technical subjects in a very short time. One of our esteemed IAS officers is a Tiger Expert in a world, Tiger conservation network in Washington and another has become climate change expert after working in high carbon foot print projects. We also had one very senior IAS officer, who was appointed on every national committee of Wildlife Conservation.

"Know all is the trade mark of these false gods in civil services with bloated egos. They always look self- assured, confident and imposing on anything and ever thing around them. They assume supremacy and take over the complete charge of any situation and position.

Identity Trade Mark

Bureaucrats are easily identifiable objects as they have their own unique identity marks. Looking busy, serious lonely and looking lost.

Once I was waiting for my flight in Indira Gandhi International Air Port to catch my flight to Bengaluru. One guy came to me and smiled and asked "Are you going to Bengaluru"?

I said "yes "and told him that "it is departure lounge for Bangalore flight". So, It is not difficult to guess? He felt little embarrassed, and asked me whether I am an IAS officer. I told him, "yes you are partially right, but tell me how did you guess? He laughed and said; "Sir, it is very easy to identify an IAS officer in the airport as there will be always someone or the other who will be traveling in the evening flight; and they look serious and busy. And easily I can recognize them". They take command of the situation in any given place irrespective of their jurisdiction and behave like masters vested with enormity of responsibility.

All India Service officers are cartoonist delight. They fit into a character role in any one of Somerset Mom's comedy novel. They are beautifully represented in 'Yes Prime Minister' serial. They are born to say yes sir as depicted in that novel. Each one is Mr. Humphrey Appleby KBE, in every sense trying to please their bosses. Yes Minister, is a mantra that we all civil servants love to sing even in our dreams. I have attended many meetings chaired by the Chief Ministers and never even once I have heard any officer one saying no to anything.

One day a Chief Minister wanted to have free and frank discussion one to one discussion with all the secretaries. One entire day was set for the purpose. We were asked to speak for twenty minutes covering any developmental aspects. As soon as the discussion began, the secretaries were asked to comment and criticize the government. The meeting was called 'Chintan Mantan'. The secretaries went on sharing their vision of the development without criticizing the government as none of them were ready to speak the truth. I spoke about the need to adopt sustainable development model to conserve our natural resources through integrated rural development planning process. I pleaded for sparing the natural resources with least destruction. CM made a copious note and asked me to do what ever uttered by me without promising any support.

As meeting progressed there were no bombshells as expected. But one lady IAS officer who was secretary women and child welfare, made a passionate plea for women development and how the state has poor human development index in South India. Now, it is a history because of her criticism of government failing to provide protection to women from various types of harassment she was sent out of Bangalore for 4 years as a punishment to a post which was not important. All the secretaries who spoke on that day sang paeans by praising the Chief Minister, let alone doing constructive criticism. This is our culture in Babudom.

Enigmatic Personalities

Every member of the tribe (civil servants) is a good specimen for a psycho pathological analysis to understand and unearth the deep down mystery of their mind which is mostly post recruitment acquired trait. May be it is injected in the Academy which later develops into a typical trait.

Civil Servants have a kind of self imposed responsibility of carrying the entire world on their short and narrow shoulders. They always talk and lecture about principles, sacrifices and moralities, but seldom believe in the practice.

Compromise

The civil servants are very adaptive and change their views and principles according to the convenience. Soon they learn the art. The best use of principle is its sacrifice on the altar of expediency at appropriate opportunity.

Laughter Is the Best Medicine

This is not in their menu card. They cannot laugh. "Serious look" it is a necessary syndrome. They only get angry and shout at any one. Perhaps they have no genes for humor, nor possess funny bones. I have heard people telling they have no spines. But I cannot believe this they too have spines when it comes to admonishing their subordinate staff.!

Our training in Lal Bahadur Shastri National Academy Mussoorie is a starting point for civil servants to build their character and shape their ideals and chart their future path. When we went to the Academy for our foundation course we meet members from other services including central service, IAS and IPS and do share the rooms with them. This mixing of services helps in interacting and understanding probationers coming from different backgrounds. The civil service probationers particularly the IAS probationers do take little longer time to break the ice and mix with other services members. The vibes and warmth builds very slowly and doggedly. The experience is like "Romancing the stone". We had completed our training in Dehradun under very different environment and had no baggage or legacy of class or any ruling dispensation. When we came for our training for a foundation course we were excited to meet the members of other service members. There were two types or class of people trying to co-exist. Among the civil services it was a mixture of different services with different personalities and mental makeup with no affinity to merge or dissolve. The difference was more visible than what was yet to be unearthed we thought of playing a skit on civil services identification as a satire to describe some distinct unique features in them compared to other services probationers. It was well scripted with lot of punches in it and one of our IAS friends had agreed to play the role of IAS probationer. But we were not allowed to stage this skit by the faculty there. But nevertheless we enjoyed the script. It was a simple plot where in some trainees will come across a strange animal with some very unusual behavior which they had not seen earlier. The character of the animal is compared with many known mammals but was not possible to tell exactly after many tests. But one last test was to make it respond to a bottle of beer which was unpaid and free. The moment the probationar sees it he jumps over and grabs it. This was to show the probationers starving for alcohol drink in the Academy as it was prohibited in the campus.

Spine Less

Now a days we hear lot of people calling bureaucracy as spineless! Now I understand where and how they become spineless. They think they are carrying too much of burden on their lanky shoulders but it is a false notion. They suffer from or have many congenital diseases inherited along with the service like know all syndrome, holier than you grandiose disorder, and Demigod syndrome. All these disease are mostly acquired after they join the service. At the Academy these strange behavior manifest and becomes chronic when they go to home cadres. The Most horrible thing one can notice in the Academy is their ego-centric or megalomaniac behavior being nurtured very carefully by the Academy staff by giving them complete freedom to think and develop their Demigod type of behavior.

Many civil servants including IAS/ IPS and IFS probationers develop strange manners that are too early to their age and maturity. They stop laughing louder, lose sense of humor, learn to ignore people around you and walk with measured gait. In the district we have different types of interaction only at official interaction and hardly at personal level. However, there are some occasions where limited personal interaction is inevitable. In the districts the life is completely different as you are stranger in a new place with the power and Bungalow life styles commoners are not desirable for social gathering or community relationship. Therefore, one is forced to have some kind of limited interaction and in the process some good friendship develops.

I was posted in Dakshina Kannada district, where we had a very young and dynamic deputy commissioner popular with people doing good work. His previous posting was in the Chief Ministers office and that made him to command lot of respect in State Secretariat. He used to narrate a very interesting story about Mrs. Indira Gandhi when she was staying in Nandi Hill station near Bangaluru after she had lost power. She wanted to read some science books and had requested the Chief Minister to organize for them. The young deputy commissioner was deputed to organize it. He went and requested Mrs. Gandhi to suggest from the list of Books he had prepared by consulting Indian Institute professors. Madam Gandhi looked at the list and seems to have told him that she has read them long back. He was very charming and brilliant officer and naturally very dynamic but was bit publicity crazy. His wife had gone abroad for higher studies. He was young and handsome but cannot mix with commoners including district officers freely to avoid any controversies if not scandals if any. He would spend hours together with any lady visitors coming to his office and hardly spare or find any time for other people let alone for the district officers. My office was in the same building of the district magistrate office as was the practice that existing from British day administration. Couple of times I tried to call on him but it was impossible to meet him as he would be busy with some visitors or the other. However in one of those monthly meetings I could meet him and he requested me to take the press to the field for reporting the activities of the department. He wanted his district to be always in news for something or the other so that the Chief Minister and the district minister would appreciate his dynamism. In short he wanted to be in the daily news like a celebrity. It was some kind of addiction. As requested by him I organized a detailed field trip which was widely reported in the press.

Once, there was a heavy flood in the district causing huge damage to property and lives. He requested all the departments to help the poor and affected people through donations and contribution. I was very excited and responded quickly worked very hard to collect fairly good amount from wood merchant's and staff members. The money was to be handed over to some vague organization which was doing relief works in front of the district minister. The deputy commissioner asked me to accompany him to a nearby town where the lady minister was camping. As scheduled both of us met the minister who was staying in the guest house. She profusely thanked the deputy commissioner but praised me for having mobilized such a big amount besides providing the timber and bamboos to the flood victims and beneficiaries. Minister appreciation was not liked by the deputy commissioner and he wanted to get rid of me soon.

Tree Planting Program-a Failed Publicity Gimmick

The young and energetic deputy commissioner was very enthusiastic to do lot of planting in the district under National Rural Employment program through his block development officers. DC wanted to do something that will get the attention of media and public. He decided to do big massive tree planting program using NREP funds. The deputy commissioner gave targets to Taluk Development officers. But they were not able to produce seedlings therefore, he released some grants to raise seedlings for the program to the forest department. We did excellent work in a short time and supplied adequate good quality of seedlings to them. The block development officers had outsourced the work to contractors who instead of engaging laborers for the work used heavy machineries to dig pits and trenches. The funds were used for buying barbed wires and hiring machines instead of spending it on employment generation. Under the NREP guidelines it was mandatory to spend 25% of funds for plantation activities. The taluk development officers took up massive planting program using tractors and bulldozers to dig the pits and trenches. Once monsoon started they planted by taking seedlings from the forest department. The program was widely covered in the press. Yet another feather on this deputy commissioner cap.

After a few months the development commissioner was visiting the district and he wanted to see some developmental programs in the district. The development commissioner was a very astute administrator and during his inspection he was known for his critical analysis skills and would expect a quality work besides looking into cost aspect and its success rate to judge the quality of program implementation. The deputy commissioner was aware of the dangers of exposing his men to the risk of inspection and to avoid that he chalked out only forestry works to be shown to the commissioner under NREP programs. I later learnt that one of the purposes of his visit was NREP programs implementation in the district as the maximum work was taken up here. It was Sunday the deputy commissioner stayed back at his head quarter as he was to take care of children in his wife's absence (plausible excuse). I was asked to accompany the development commissioner and show him the forestry works. I took the development commissioner to visit different works done by forest department and showed him success of plantation works in various locations. I also showed him few other forestry works which were not related to NREP and found him highly impressed with the success of programs. At the end of the day I took him to one of the best plantation work to convince him how coastal afforestation could be effective in the prevention of sea erosion which was a very serious problem. The State government was spending very huge amount of money on this program but was not effective as the prevention measure was building massive wall of boulders in the coast line. The work did not have any desired results as felt by many fisher men living near the coastal area.

We took him to the coastal plantation and explained cost effectiveness and the success story of the plantation where fishermen folks were happy as they lived near the plantation site without any sea erosion threat. The development commissioner was very happy about the innovative work which was very effective and low cost option and made copious notes about it and encouraged to expand the program. It was very satisfying field visit and it was decided to end the inspection and as we were returning to the parking place and while getting into the car he saw a failed plantation plot visible but had a robust fencing with very few plants surviving and a display board with details of program. He asked me that why that plantation is so poor. He further asked me how in the same site one plantation is excellent and another is such a disaster. I was waiting for this question to be asked. I told him "Sir it is the program undertaken by deputy commissioner under his guidance". I explained how the work is executed through his block development officers who have no technical skills. Also politely I told him that the cost is at least two to three times higher than forest department's cost. Further explanations were sufficient to make up disappointed. The development commissioner was furious and held meeting with deputy commissioner and reprimanded him for doing such an unprofessional work. He went back to Bangaluru and issued a government circulars stating, any afforestation work on any site under any program shall be done by only forest department in the State.

Refusal to Transfer Revenue Forests to Forest Department

Dakshina Kannada is a Western Ghats district with more than 40% of total geographical area covered with forests and substantial land are falling under different land tenure with good tree growth under Revenue land records. Most of these areas were thickly wooded and fit to be declared as reserve forest. Despite many requests and official correspondence many deputy commissioners refused to transfer these revenue forest lands for conservation to the forest department. As a result most of these ecologically sensitive areas were encroached exposed to fires and destruction. Only in the public meetings and in front of press people they showed concern to the cause of forest conservation and in actual practice they did not transfer these lands. These forests without title are under encroachments and tree smuggling. It is sad that our IAS colleagues holding very responsible posts have refused to cooperate with forest department.

Ecologically Sensitive Forest Owned by a Timber Merchant

Dakshina Kannada which was part of the Madras presidency still had very large extent of well wooded Western Ghats areas of forest under private control. One such private forest located in ecologically sensitive area was owned by a timber merchant was very surprising despite vigorous implementation of land reforms Act restricting the size of holdings. It was found later that the private forests status was changed to the plantation status by manipulating the records. The land owner continued to exploit the forests without any hindrance. When it came to my knowledge seeking permission for timber extraction, I was surprised to see such a beautiful forest area in the midst of Western Ghats comprising of evergreen species of rich biodiversity value. The verification of records showed that it was private forests granted by the British officer to one Sri Hebbar for the hospitality he has received when he and his team members were marooned in a forest area due to flash floods. The ownership of forest area under private control went on changing through sales. I took up the matter with revenue department with a request to change its status as forest land due to its location and tree growth and to transfer the ownership to the forest department. The district administration did not act on the request and referred the matter to the lower level officers to handle. However, as the owner of the private was very powerful and rich he used his influence to stall the effort. I refused to grant him the felling permission on the grounds of ownership dispute and environmental considerations but he was tenacious enough to go to the court to get favorable orders to fell the trees. Meanwhile, thanks to an IAS probationer, who was probationary Tehsildar incidentally staying with me was a fresh unbiased young officer. He was convinced about the wrong classification took it on himself to set right the wrong doing and convened land grant committee meeting and passed resolution to cancel the ownership of the land. The resolution was passed by majority members opposing the transfer to forest department, while only the probationary Tehsildar favoring the transfer of land to forest department with a lone dissent vote. Due to its dissent voice the matter went to courts serially as appeals. The district administration did not take any decision to change the status of land but strangely took the sides with the land owner for many years and the matter went to various courts till it was decided by the Supreme Court in favor of canceling the private ownership after a long thirty five years. In every court the government was losing the case without arguing the case effectively. However, routine appeals by the Law department continuously over three decades helped in restoration of forest land.

A Wild Beast in Deputy Commissioner's Bungalow

The new deputy commissioner of Mangalore was not comfortable to stay in the old bungalow built during British collector's days. It had a huge area intended with jungle growth and looked like a thick forest. The bungalow resembled a haunted house and during night times and on rainy days the blowing of monsoon winds, storms, can be very scary if you are staying with a small family with huge rooms and verandas. There were also lots of ghost stories too attached to most of the British days Bungalows and passed on from generations of staff members.

One day I was in the field in a forest range when I received a message from deputy commissioner to send a few forest staff to deputy commissioner's bungalow to shoot the wild animal seen by his staff and was not sure about its exact description. Some thought it to be leopard, or hyena, or a wild dog but deputy commissioner had funnily described it as some kind of wild unexplained beast when he spoke to me. Immediately I rushed back to headquarters and rushed to the deputy commissioner's house with guns and torches to track the beast. We were told that the animal was seen last night by the watchman and was not sure what the animal is. The people were wildly guessing it to be either tiger or leopard. The deputy commissioner was completely shaken and was convinced that there is a beast hiding behind jungle growth inside the compound of bungalow. We combed the entire area with torch light and made huge sounds and opened crackers yet nothing was spotted. The deputy commissioner was happy about our prompt service and felt absolutely assured. We left the team for guarding the bungalow, for a week but nothing was spotted. But the deputy commissioner continued to believe the story and made our staff toil for a long time.

This deputy commissioner was little reserved and did not waste his precious time on jokes or allowed his smiles without rhyme or reason to be exhibited and also did not have the art of exchanging pleasantries. He was quite senior looking in age well as in appearance had come to the district after 12 years of service. He was not friendly to his young assistant commissioners either. Two of his young IAS officers who had come for a monthly meeting decided to halt for the night and go back next day morning to their head quarters. We all decided to go for a movie after dinner and returned to guest house from the movie around 12.30 pm. We were just chatting and mostly the IAS officers were telling about the deputy commissioner's attitude towards other officers. In a matter of joke at midnight I called at the number of one of the Assistant Commissioners and promptly he took the phone. I imitated deputy commissioner voice by slightly halting my speech between words which deputy commissioner was known to do. Calling his name twice on phone I disconnected the phone. However, he called repeatedly the deputy commissioner and when he picked up the call he said he had not called him. Next morning deputy commissioner was very furious that he was called at midnight without fact checking. He did not forget to instruct him to inform police about the prank call.

My experience with civil servants is that they play double roles. In front of politicians they paint a false picture by praising them. I remember once In front of me the deputy commissioner was briefing about the very poor impression people have about a minister who was seeking re-election in few months away. He began to sing paeans about her popularity as soon as she visited and told what a great service she had rendered to society. He further assured that she will win surely the election. He praised her using all possible superlatives and described her as most invincible popular leader. I was surprised to hear this from him as he had told me before we met her that her party and she are going to lose the elections. In the next elections she and her party lost the election miserably contrary to his assurances.

Mr. Veerappa Moily was both State finance minister and the district minister of Dakshina kannada had complete trust and faith in the deputy commissioner and gave full support to him by releasing huge funds and other support. The young deputy commissioner was very hasty and indulged in cheap gimmick and image building exercise than doing anything serious or lasting good honest work. He was also fond of publicity and had kept the media in good humor. The media too played its dirty role and was conveniently reporting anything and everything about the deputy commissioner to built his false image. Many of the political leaders are fooled by these chaps.

Kyasanoor Forest Disease-a Rare Disease Outbreak in a Forest Area

The outbreak of Kyasanoor (KFD) monkey disease which was very infectious and spreading through monkeys living in and around forests were mismanaged by the administration and no preventive measures were done seriously. The forest department too had made a mistake in taking up clear felling the forests without anticipating that monkeys would move towards villages carrying the disease.

The district administration efforts in handling of Kyasanoor forest disease that had taken the heavy toll of the villagers were rather slow and very scanty. It took quite a long time to identify the disease and causes behind it. Many teams of experts began to visit the spot and we were busy organizing their programs to forest areas. It took many days to identify the causes of death and to take measures to contain the disease without further spreading to other areas. The World Health Organization Team arrived on the scene much later and till then only forest department was facing the problem directly in the field without much support. The Chief Minister Sri Ramkrishna Hegde made a hurried visit to the district and held meeting of the district officers and assured the government support to control the epidemic. With lot of courage and conviction the protection of forest wealth was done and very many sensitive cases were unearthed though many a times we were threatened and assaulted by the timber mafia. But the district administration's lack of support and help was very disappointing. In one such timber smuggling cases the lorry carrying the timber was seized in the midnight by me and my staff when it was coming out of the forest. The driver and others in the lorry were apprehended. The lorry owner was a very influential person and a relative of MLA who in a very short time mobilized many people including students who were staying in the nearby hostel and attacked us with threats to burn us along with the vehicle. An identical message was sent to the police head quarters but no support was provided by the district administration to nab the culprits. However, the first posting in a highly developed district had taught me many lessons and I completed my first stint in beautiful Western Ghats forests. We had seized many sandalwood vehicles caught many timber smugglers and had initiated action against corrupt staff. The experience gained was enormous during the Kyasanoor forest disease management.

Diversion of Thick Forests to Grow Plantations

What bothered me most was the speed with which very rich forests was sought to be cleared for raising commercial plantations like cashew, rubber and pulpwood plantations to increase the revenue to the government. The government has established plantation corporations to enable them to borrow money on very high interests to raise these plantations. The burden of loan and degradation of forest was most unfortunate decisions. The State government was promoting cashew plantations in the coastal districts to export the processed cashew nuts to foreign countries to earn foreign exchange. African countries had the monopoly over the cashew trade in the international market owing to cheap labor and raw material availability. India too had cheap labor but there was not sufficient production of the cashew kernels. The State government had created an Independent cashew development corporation to raise plantations on degraded forest lands by clearing the well wooded forests. By the time, I went to Mangalore the plantation activity was in full swing and concomitantly the forest clearance was also in full swing. My immediate job was to go and inspect all the forest areas earmarked for tree felling and to ensure that forests are cleared very fast and land is made available for plantation. I was appalled to see the areas marked were very rich in biodiversity and most of them were located in critical Eco- sensitive zones. I was having tremendous pressure on me to clear the files after field inspections to initiate logging operations and the progress was being monitored by the senior officers from Head office. However, I mustered courage and wrote about the ecological disaster that would occur if we allow the clearances of forests are allowed. I was lucky that the senior management did not find fault with my stand and agreed to delete those area from the proposed list. I must say foresters were under tremendous pressure to do such works which they did not like to do it and at the same time did not have courage to go against the government. Similarly, the rubber plantations were established to rehabilitate Sri Lankan Tamil refugees as per Lal Bahadur Shastri and Sirimao Bandaranayke agreement. The rehabilitation program to provide employment to refugees from Tibet and Sri Lanka has been most unfortunate which has destabilized the most sensitive ecosystem in the rainforest of western Ghats.

During the last three decades foresters had to face the wrath of politicians and civil society while discharging their duties as expected in accordance with laws. The gritty foresters went on fighting and arguing for conservation and they refused to budge to political powers but politicians did not allow the foresters to have their say. They put lot of pressure to make the foresters to yield to release forest land. Most of the foresters were harassed, transferred and sent on leave for refusing to agree with the political masters. Though a few could survive with the caste links and money power, the majority of foresters managed with self controls and playing safe.

Chief Ministers Wrath

In Bangalore Birla house had a very nice guest house in the outskirts of Bangalore city. The guest house is located next to a forest wood lot which has an arboretum conservation located with very rare species. The guest house was used by many VIPs very often including the then Chief Minister Sri Veerendra Patil who was sober and a gentleman politicians would use it to dispose of the files. The guest house had no water supply and was depending on the private bore well located outside its land. Just few months before, I had disconnected the connection by removing the water pipe passing through forest land after one of our senior officer threatened to report to the government for allowing the company to take a pipeline of 4 inch diameter on the forest land. Since I had allowed it on the request made by the company, I thought it must be canceled and accordingly it was done to avoid any future punitive complications under Forest Conservation Act. When, the Chief Minister went to the guest house they were using water from the private source with lot of inconvenience. The water problem was noticed by the CMs staff and found out the reason for the current situation. They contacted and asked the PCCF who was also visiting the guest house to meet the Chief Minister to restore the connection. My boss called me and said he did not expect such a poor decision from me. Then I had to apologize to the PCCF and explained what made me to take such a poor decision. Of course, the agreement was restored and by charging higher rent we allowed them to take the pipeline.

The moral of the story is we were not sure what is legally right and what was irrational and impractical while taking decisions. The same decision was seen by one officer as bad and for another it was gross violation and hence good decision. This was the dilemma foresters faced and were castigated often for utterly failing in their constitutional obligation.

Foresters and Politicians' Nexus

During my service time I did not find IFS service having any political patronage or support in the State as we normally find in other services. One or two had some relations as politician but not in large numbers. Foresters were never considered seriously by politicians as they mattered very little in the power game and for the fact that we always throw rule book on their face and are termed anti development. Moreover, forests are seen as a free resource to be bartered away in vote bank politics. The politicians used their power and muscle power to get these hapless guys who do not agree to their illegal demands. They either are transferred or made to listen to them. Even in very forest rich districts the powerful timber lobby used the politicians to influence the foresters. In many instances it was timber mafia-politician nexus that controlled the forest department as there was no help coming from the top. However whenever there was strong and assertive forest friendly senior cabinet minister the field staff felt protected and asserted their positions and responsibilities. We were lucky to that we had Mr. K.H.Ranganath as forest minister who was a Statesman. He was completely honest and ran the department like a Colossus for five years with iron hand. The period is known as golden age in the history of forest department. Many of us are very lucky to have served under him

Working with Police Department

There is always lot of fun and frolic in the district posting compared to capital postings. The AIS officers do have very cordial relationship with each other with close social interaction. Yet, the coordination and support needed by the field staff in handling field problem is always lacking. Forest department always needs the help of police department on regular basis in handling encroachment eviction timber smuggling, and many other issues. And most of the time the assistance given by police mostly depends upon interpersonal relationship that we maintain with the police department. Especially working with police friends is a different kind of experience. I had a distinct advantage of knowing quite a few police officers due to my IPS training in the IPS Academy. In Mangalore posting my batch mate was posted and had very good working relationship with the police department. But in the field, the staff had always problems in getting the help due to various reasons.

Once I was assaulted by the group of smugglers when we seized their vehicle carrying illegal timber. It was a mob attack the vehicle was forcefully taken away from our custody by threatening us. The arrested smugglers were also freed from our custody. All these things were reported over wireless to the DIG and SP office, but no help was received from them. Even after many days they failed to seize the vehicle and arrest the culprits, who were responsible for attacking the forest department staff who were on official duty. The help from police was never assured and always depended on individual officer's attitude.

There were occasions when police friends created problems by violating the wildlife act provisions. Most of the subordinate police were not aware of simple forests acts and provisions. In one instance, the police had killed a baby elephants that had strayed into a village without getting any permission from the forest department. The mob had gathered out of curiosity to watch the elephant. The superintendent of police informed me over the incident and asked me to join him to visit the spot. I was not given full information about the field situation and was not aware of the animal identity. I was simply informed that a wild animal has entered the village and is creating trouble. I soon alerted my staff and rushed with police superintendent of the district. Before we could reach the spot the police had opened the fire and had shot down the animal. They had kept me in dark by concealing the identity of elephant and had informed me as some wild animal. This was a great shock to me and felt terribly let down by the police department. I was very upset about the whole incident and reported the matter to the Wildlife Warden who was also upset about the shooting. The police are lose canons and would not think twice before opening the fire.

Posting In a Very Drought Prone Dry District

I left Mangalore for taking up my new posting assignment with tons of satisfaction. In my next district posting I had to face another kind of IAS officer who was a promote officer and was on the verge of retirement, who treated All India Services officer like me as a young and imbeciles. After couple of interaction with him I thought he sounded a bit biased towards young officers, except that he treated a young lady district police officer with more respect and cordially in the meetings compared to us! Yet I found him very respectable and warm person and against all odds hoped that I should trust him to work in harmonious relationship. I knew the district has very low forest area and I wanted to work hard to make the difference. I knew the importance of a district collector and his role in the district development work.

Chitradurga is an eastern plain arid area known as drought prone district of the State, where famine was a regular phenomenon. In my three years stint I had to face three drought years and was expected to do greening of barren area in an otherwise perpetually dry district. It was a challenge and nightmare. Now if I look back it was really a great opportunity and learning experience that could test my resilience and mold me into a professional forester. The experience I gained here helped me to work in my next postings especially in Research jobs. Now if I look back at the efforts it was really worth taking the trouble. Chitradurga district was awarded Indira Priyadarshini award for best afforestation works after few years of my stint was very satisfying as the afforestation practices were well institutionalized. Due to many initiatives taken then it is very heartwarming to see the changes it has brought in the district. The district now has more green cover than ever before. Jogimatti is a beautiful hill station situated at an elevation of 1300 meters, spread in an area of about 25000 acres is like a mini mountain. It was described by a British Forester who worked there in Jogimatti guest house register as "A paradise for honey mooning couple". It was unfortunately in a complete degraded state when I first time saw it. Today it has been restored back to its original glory by providing continuous protection and aforestation. The biggest challenge, I had to face and struggle was to cope up with adverse climate condition where the rainfall was very scanty and temperature was very high. Very high speed wind and low moisture regime, with soaring temperature was anathema for raising a successful forest plantation.

During my interaction with a promotee deputy commissioner I understood I might have tough time working with him. His understanding of the climate and droughts were very shallow mainly because he was coming from social welfare sector working his entire service and had no knowledge of other vital sectors. He gave very impractical and unscientific suggestions about greening the district on massive scale. On Many occasions he will support MLAs/politicians and put officers into very awkward position and create very big embarrassment and predicament to officers. I had to suspend few forest officers on corruption charges which were resented by politicians for obvious reasons and very strangely deputy commissioner was sympathetic to them. There were many forestry related problems peculiar to the district which included, grazing rights, Tree lopping for leaves, firewood demand, charcoal burning, encroachments and politicians nexus with some foresters. And I needed very badly the support of politicians and district administration which was completely missing.

A Suspension in Waiting

Kannada Watchdog Committee became angry with me on me for not attending the committee meeting. In one of the meetings convened by the committee Chairman Sri Siddaramaiah, I was unable to attend the meeting, as I had to rush to a village to oversee the medical treatment of two village youths who were attacked by group of bears. The youths were grievously injured when they were inside the forests and needed to be shifted immediately to Bengaluru. I was informed by my field staff in the morning hours of the same fateful day of the meeting fixed to review the implementation of Kannada. My absence was taken as an insult by Watchdog committee Chairman and had resolved to teach me a lesson. I did not understand the logic for taking such an extreme steps to recommend for my suspension for ignoring the Kannada watch dog committee meeting. It was a big joke and conspiracy to shift me out of Chitradurga and the deputy commissioner was a party to this nefarious design. It was also amounted to harassment of an honest officer by the district administration in league with corrupt politicians. The deputy commissioner had created the misunderstanding about me with Sri Siddaramaiah, Chairman of Kannada watchdog committee. He took it as a prestige issue and went on demanding for my blood. He wanted me to be sacrificed at the altar of political expediency.

The reason for my absence for meeting was explained both orally and in writing but did not help in convincing the committee. They went ahead with their decision to get me suspended for prioritizing a medical help over a language meeting. I was already writing articles in Kannada on newspapers. After returning from village, I rushed to attend another important program of celebrating the Ramakrishna Hegde government's first year in office celebration. I met, Sri S.Nijalingappa who visited forestry stall and inaugurated our stall for public and spoke about the need to increase the forest cover in the district. Despite my preoccupation on an important works the absence to a meeting kicked up such a huge storm and big controversy leading to the recommendation for my suspension from service. The matter went before the cabinet for my suspension for no mistake of mine high lights how a few in bureaucracy commit white collar crimes. When the threat of my suspension was hanging on my head like a democles sword it was the political sagacity of Ramakrishna Hegde and other members of cabinet that saved me from such humiliation. The cabinet took mote of Kannada proficiency and the Kannada articles I had written in newspapers and ridiculed the demand for suspension. When, I was Secretary Forest Mr. Siddaramaiah held Public Accounts Committee meeting for continuously for five months in which the pending Paras of Accountant generals on various forestry works were discussed. No explanation could satisfy the Public Accounts Committee after prolonged meetings and a scathing biased report was published criticizing the department officials.

The district was facing severe drought with complete failure of Monsoon. There was no fodder and drinking water to cattle or people and were selling cattle for desperate sales. The forest department was asked to provide shelter home to cattle and to grow fodder, wherever water was available near tank beds. We were working hard to provide relief measures and some succor to the distressed farmers by maintaining more than 20000 cattle in cattle camps and to save them from starvation and death. The cattle camp became a model to the State and many people were sent here to see our work and to provide similar such service. To understand the gravity of the situation and to provide the relief work and to review the situation Prime Minister Rajiv Gandhi was visiting the district. We were all asked to organize the visit and to manage the program to impress the PM on the severity of the drought. I suggested to the deputy commissioner that near the helipad we must put up a small stall to exhibit the drought area photos and few charts to explain the rainfall deficit over the year and people photos showing working in the drought relief work. I only prepared the rainfall chart, and graphs showing the rainfall and crop loss. I was asked to be in charge of the exhibits and explain to the PM and others. When the PM arrived he was taken to the field directly by the local officers. I was too part of the team. The security was so lax and unprofessional that our vehicle was the fourth in the convoy became 6th in the row as the other unidentified vehicle with MP and MLA had made way into the convoy. The Superintendent of Police was sitting in the front car convoy was not aware of what was happening behind the Prime Minister.

In the field a dried up well and drying coconut trees were shown and PM was informed that the owner has incurred Rs 5 lakh loss due to drought. Immediately PM was surprised and remarked "Oh he is a rich farmer". We returned to the helipad, not able to impress the PM but in the makeshift exhibition stall deputy commissioner began to explain the charts and graphs to drive home the message of severe drought. PM spent more time to understand the situation which was a great show. The person who was designated to be doing the job was not allowed to explain. The district administration did not support me when the government was contemplating suspension. If government had taken a decision to suspend me it would have ruined my life. Disappointed with lack of support by the administration I applied for foreign studies and was looking for fellowship for jumping over to overseas for higher studies. I had applied for many fellowships including, Hubert Humphrey fellowship which was very close to becoming reality. I had to get relieved from the government but was delayed enormously and was clubbed with another senior bureaucrat's application. Finally it did not materialize for both of us. I was denied six times the opportunity to go abroad for higher studies or for presenting papers. But all the time both Governments in State and Centre would put some obstacles.

Once again during subsequent drought year, the Chief Minister came for reviewing the drought relief works. Two days before, the Chief Ministers review, a preparatory meeting was held as a dry run or curtain raiser to prepare meeting note. We had a senior IAS officer who had come to assess the drought relief works of the departments and to prepare the agenda notes for Chief Minister's review. The senior officer had extensive field trips and field assessment and was apprehensive about the CMs meeting outcome as many MLAs were dissatisfied with the works. I used to have a running battle with most of the MLAs as they would always find fault with forestry works. In few cases I had suspended few staff which also had created a kind of heart burn in them and dislike towards me. The district administration was aware of this and was siding with politicians. Politicians were bribed by MLAs and were had much to say against me before CM.

The day of the meeting I went in time and sat in a pre-designated seat. I looked at MLAs and felt uneasy and was preparing for a big showdown. Chief Minister already knew about my Kannada related suspension issue which had engaged cabinet for six months as Sri Siddaramaiah was threatening to resign if I was not suspended. The unexpected happened in the meeting was that the first subject in agenda was forest department works. CM asked me to explain the relief works along with financial targets. Fresh in the morning CM and Mr. Devegowda PWD Minister and S.R.Bommai were reviewing my works. CM was pleased to know that I have generated more Man days for every lakh of rupee spent which I was not aware. The meeting went out smoothly with my department and others were found with mismatching figures. I had a narrow escape. MLAs must be wondering. I realized much later that I was used as a punching bag for MLAs to bash me to relieve their stress or to vent out their pent up anger against district administration.

Encounter with Judiciary

There was another serious crisis like situation cropped up suddenly like a bolt from the blue in which I was harassed by the session court Judge for contempt. It was regarding a seizure of sandal wood lorry. I being the authorized officer had the case pending before me. I was informed that the lorry was hired by the district Judge to transport his luggage on his transfer. While returning the lorry was seized on some credible information as the staff found it carrying sandal wood logs. Before I could pass orders the case was filed in session court. I called our public prosecutor and told him why he had not protested in the court as it was not a maintainable case. The public prosecutor was very upset with my reprimand and he shouted at me and called the district bar to pass the resolution against me and held dharma. I was summoned by the court where my own public prosecutor stood against me. I told the court to give me time to hire some lawyers from the next district as no one is taking my case. The Judge called me and shouted at me and threatened me with contempt if I do not apologize. I felt terribly awkward as no lawyer was willing to help me to argue my case I was quite patient and was mentally preparing to face very unusual situation. I was almost isolated in the district administration setup. I was repeatedly called to court and asked to apologize and to release the vehicle. I contacted lawyers in Bangalore and met the Secretary of Law department. I was advised to meet the Registrar of the high court to explain my side of the story. After meeting the officials of the high court I returned to district. The superintendent of police who was my friend at personal level did not bother to help me or speak to the judge There was a sudden change in the heart of Judge after my briefing the Registrar of the high Court. He asked me to meet him in his chamber and there when we spoke to each other one to one he asked me to forget and be his good friend. He must have been cautioned and appropriately advised by the Registrar to be careful.

Policy of Open Discrimination

Overseas Development Agency (ODA) of United Kingdom was providing financial support to Karnataka forest department for Western Ghats development and was keen to extend it for phase ll. They constituted a design team with experts from different backgrounds. They in 2003-04 asked me to join the team for six months on secondment with an offer to pay the usual fees. I was bit hesitating and was not sure whether I would be spared by the government but the well meaning development commissioner an IAS officer insisted that I must join the team. I gave my consent to the government. The Chief Secretary called a special meeting on a Sunday to discuss the policy of sparing government officers to such assignments including finance Secretary and forest secretaries to decide the permission. Later in the evening a letter was issued by the department of personnel informing to join the team with a condition to not to receive any remuneration from ODA as offered and work in addition to my present position. This denial by the government was bit disappointing to me as it was shocking to ODA team and they knew that it was simply due to jealousy that the IAS lobby did not approve the offer. The amount in those days was quite substantial at the rate of Rs 3600 day. For 6 months it was around 7.0 lakh which would have saved the Karnataka government in salary as in that case I would have not drawn the salary. The ODA has been quite active in Karnataka and knew the reasons for deliberate discrimination. The decision to deny permission to draw the consultancy charge affected the working as it was difficult to work full time in the design team and that was very crucial for the success of the project designing. This decision shocked the ODA team and they could not fathom the logic behind very illogical decision of not allowing me on secondment which would have saved the six months salary to the State. *The ODA decided to pull out of the State and the State lost 50 million pound poverty alleviation project.* What is shameful is the fact that in the same meeting without any hesitancy they allowed an IAS officer to take ODA salary for 5 years to work in another forestry project (Karnataka Watershed Development Project (incidentally there were more forestry professionals suitable for this project) He later went on to become Chief Secretary of the State. Shamefully IFS officers were denied legitimate opportunity to work in the project on the ground of remuneration from Over Seas Development Agency. What is interesting to note is the fact that the development commissioner who had advised me to join the team was also in State committee meeting that denied us the offer. Same committee permitted an IAS officer to receive the salary directly from ODA. This open and blatant discrimination and completelt irrational decisions by IAS officers are never ending stories. Now the question is how in a democratic country we will stop such top bosses to play havoc and silently commit white collar crimes by grossly misusing their positions. It also reflects poorly on the Ministers who conveniently ignore such misuse of powers and such events are a threat to the rule of law in a democracy. Should not the government amend the corruption laws to make such actions of civil servants punishable?

Yet Another Discrimination in an United Nation Development Program (UNDP) Posting

I was posted in UNDP "Biomass Energy for Rural India Project" (BERI) by the government to succeed one IAS officer as Project Director (PD) in 2006 which was a very prestigious project for both UNDP and the government of India. The IAS officer I replaced went on to become Chief Secretary soon. This officer despite working PD for five years had failed to produce even one kilowatt electricity from biomass energy project. The UNDP was highly disappointed with the progress and after seeing my successful work in the other UNDP project the UNDP India office contacted me and requested me if I can implement this project. I had replied to them yes I can but State government had to be convinced. In fact this project was becoming a butt of joke for UNDP India in their Washington office. The UNDP India officials met the Chief Secretary and the development commissioner and asked them to post me to head the project so that the project can be salvaged. The IAS lobby got incensed with this and said to UNDP India office well we will advertise and post the best available candidate. However, after the open advertisement making eligible AIS officers as well as scientists; the shortlisted list was again rejected by the UNDP India office and requested that Dr Swaminath should be appointed. But I had not applied because I was sure that the IAS lobby would not allow me the UNDP salary of the IAS officer whom I would be replacing. The UNDP then proposed to withdraw the project. Lo and behold, suddenly one fine morning I was appointed to replace the IAS officer but on my usual pay scales on deputation. I joined the post and worked very hard to get the phase one project commissioned three units of 2 mega watt within six months of my joining. UNDP was very thrilled to get the Biomass gasification project commissioned by inviting UNDP chief Dr Kamal Dervis and they thanked me for saving their reputation and commissioning the project in record time. UNDP was very unhappy with the State government for the blatant discrimination against me. The IAS officer was drawing five times more salary than his usual pay scale. These are some of the unknown facets of serious fault line in our public administration for which no one bothers.

Visiting Fellow at Oxford Great Britain

House of Lords of United Kingdom in 1992 visited the Research project when I was working as State Silviculturist on water use studies of fast growing species funded by ODA now Department of International Development (DFID). They visited our research plots and were highly impressed with the work. The team leader of House of Lords made me travel with him in his car and while discussing with the progress he offered me a fellowship to visit Oxford University for the higher studies.

I joined Oxford University to pursue my PhD. I was asked to share a room with one IAS officer who had come to same Institute for his doctoral work. He later on became planning commission Secretary in government of India. I knew him earlier too when he was faculty member in LBNSA we both shared a room. Nevertheless I was doing my works on little complicated work which required extensive consultation on genotype and environment interactions. However, my senior colleague was most of the time busy talking about his plane tickets, bookings, his wife's London trips etc for long hours. He was not good in statistics which was needed to do doctoral work. He would consult me and called me 'Pundit' to get some statistical help to analyze his research data which I did happily.

There were other half a dozen very senior IAS officers in Queen's college and were quite a gang who looked lost in Oxford University. But unfortunately there was one senior IAS officer from my State Karnataka who was a very funny creature. He visited my house and had borrowed my laptop and had kept it for six months. In his course there were many interesting episodes used to occur and their inter-personal relationship was not at its best. There were many jokes on each other's conduct including some romantic episodes between these people. I was good with everyone and had not taken any sides including my wife who was more close to locals. Funnily my cadre senior officer one day cautioned me to not move with other officers except him because we are from same State. I was sick of petty politics and kept aloof from these guys. My roommate continued to travel frequently to India and would bring Indian goods and sell them. I was wondering what is the great purpose achieved by deputing these old guys at the fag end of their service which does not serve any purpose. What is pathetic is the poor capability of the elected representatives who become ministers to control such trips of bureaucrats.

I used to meet one Indian Foreign Service from Bangaluru who was working in the Indian High commissioner office. He would invite me London on weekends for dinner where I had a chance to meet his Foreign Service friends who would always talk about central secretariat and curse Babus for delaying their promotion or any such matters.

I was very comfortable at Oxford where there was no discrimination in the university. In fact as a visiting fellow I had more privileges than some of our senior IAS officers. After my Oxford studies I returned to India against the advice of the Oxford Forestry Research Institute Director Dr Burley who wanted me to stay in Oxford as long as possible to pursue my interest in the forestry research. After returning to India, I was posted in a research post in the Western Ghats forestry project to meet the research needs of the project. It was both a challenge and opportunity though to lay a strong foundation to forestry research to meet the multiple strategic demands of information to conserve and manage forests in Karnataka. But the lack of institutional support was major hurdle in achieving any substantial progress. The steering committee chairman was the development commissioner who did not understand the need to establish an independent research Institute in Bangalore and he wanted it to be in Dharwad which was not practicable. With all these constraints some tangible work was done in tree improvement and biodiversity mapping.

It was a great opportunity to work with DFID experts in building the research institutional development.

Converting a Non-Existent Post to an Institution of Great Importance

In another example of carelessly choosing senior officers for defunct posts in a shocking development in the year 2002 I was posted as Director-General of an organization which never existed and department of personnel had mislead me to believe that it is a wonderful opportunity to build a great Institute. I do not know how the Chief Secretary could be so naïve to believe on this idea and agreed to post me as Director-General against a non-existent post. Before getting posted to this post I was working in the forest department with a decent job of assisting the head of the department as his staff officer and also simultaneously writing externally aided projects for financial support. The Japan International Cooperation Agency (JICA) project for forest and Biodiversity conservation was prepared by me and approved by JICA for an outlay of Rs 1000 crore. The new post did not have any financial support or government approval for creating a new organization as envisaged. There was neither a building nor staff to run the new office or operate it.

In reality it was a fake high sounding posting order to build and run an imaginary organization that never existed. The idea of creating a new institutional structure was taken by the Chairman of the Karnataka pollution control board by issuing an internal office order to have an Environmental Protection and Training Research Institute (EPTRE) similar to one that was established in Andhra Pradesh. The EPTRI in Andhra Pradesh was headed by a very senior IAS officer who had passion for the environment and had a big clout in the government. I was told that she was doing a good job of preparing annual environmental reports for various States as World Bank sponsored consultant and that was a good source of revenue to the institute. Though the idea was commendable to have an organization like EPTR in Karnataka also there was no strategy, vision or a road map to create an institution of that size and eminence.

In Pollution control Board an existing training facility named Environment Training Institute was converted as EMPRI. The training institute's staffs from pollution control board were also shifted to the new organization. Now it was a greater and excruciating challenge for me to earn their salary and other expenses through consultancy services. I had to spend sleepless nights to earn money by providing consultancy to other States on Environmental Impact Analysis (EIA) and Clean Development Project (CDM) projects and generate our finances till we could stand on our strength. I took up the challenge of creating the Institute and got the new entity registered as a society. We recruited staff on contract assignment and developed the new projects seeking funds, provided services and generated finances for building the new institute. I did not go and ask support from the government. Mostly we took CDM projects related to climate change programs in various States and provided capacity building services and substantial revenue was generated. As the financial position improved, we could get a piece of land on lease within city limits and after clearance under Forest Conservation Act 1980 constructed an independent environmentally friendly building to run the institution. Today the Instituted has grown into a huge organization servicing the State on various environmental issues. It has been recognized as Centre of excellence on climate change.

From a Research Organization to Government Secretariat

As always happens in the government one fine morning in the year 2007 when the BJP came to power the Chief Minister shifted me from energy sector to government as Secretary Forests. I was very new to secretariat posting I had to deal with the Chief Minister directly as he was the forest minister. It was tough time to handle his secretariat staff who always used to handle the power projects and mining files directly. In the secretariat within few says I learnt the ABC of administration which was the guiding principle of bureaucracy. A stood for stood for avoiding the responsibilities. B stood for bypass the responsibility. C stood for create confusion and all these were evident in the day to day administration at the government level. I was supposed to help many political aspirations of the newly elected government. In one incident of forest violation by an IAS deputy commissioner and speaker of State assembly a petition was sent to Central Empowered Committee (CEC) of the Supreme Court to take action against the State government. It was most serious issue as the petitioner was Air Marshal Cariappa who is a well respected man in the country. The Central Empower Committee was very upset with the developments and violation wanted a reply to the petition. The letter was addressed to the Chief Secretary who was shaky and terrified to accept the actual violation which would indict both the deputy commissioner and the Speaker.

I was asked to draft Para wise reply to Air Marshal Cariappa's petition. I narrated the facts in the affidavit and accepted the gross violation on the part of the deputy commissioner and Speaker and expressed regret over the incident. The affidavit was approved by advocate-general who was a decent person and the file was sent to Chief Secretary to sign the affidavit which he refused to sign. He took the advice from one of Central Empowered Committee member who was a forest officer who suggested that the forest secretary can sign the affidavits. Finally I signed the affidavit which agreed with most of the violation narrated in the petition. Speaker was completely in the dock and CEC visited the site of violation and took lenient view and let off the deputy commissioner who went and cried before them.

Wildlife Posting

The mining scam report and subsequent resignation of the Chief Minister I was transferred back to the department in the year 2009. The wildlife posting gave enough opportunity to expand the protected area network. Now Karnataka has one of the largest wildlife area networks in Asia. The man-animal conflict was a huge problem with hundreds of elephants getting electrocuted and also more than two hundred human beings too getting killed by the pachyderms. Many proposals were sent to the government for effective management of elephants. The Mysore citizens were in for a shock when they saw herds of Elephants were on a morning walk in garden city of India. They had already killed one watchman who tried to shoo away the elephant with his lathi. The death of this watch man was beamed live on TV making people terribly afraid of elephants invading Mysore. I rushed to Mysore with fresh tranquilizers and reached the spot which was a coconut garden. The district police chief met me and looked worried and was demanding the capture of elephants soon. I promised him to capture them soon and he must help us in crowd control. The forest staff were struggling against all these odds and trying to tranquilize the two baby elephants of two years of age that were left behind by the group when they were chased away. Baby elephants were completely lost and confused and were running helter-skelter. I was in touch with our Chief Minister and his principal secretary for every ten minutes to brief back the progress. Some politicians too started calling me to not release the captured elephants back in jungle. We tranquilized these baby elephants and finally succeeded in tying them to a tree. They were very sad and refusing to eat or drink. Meanwhile, our secretary hurriedly called a press meet to announce that operation is successfully completed and we are putting the elephants in permanent captivity. I refused to take his words and had clearly told him that it cannot be done. I worked out a plan to leave them in deep forests of Bandipur. Next day before Mysore people could wake up I had transported them quietly to Bandipur forest and let them to safely join the group of distant relatives. I knew these two baby elephants will be happier with their own kind instead of rotting in zoo or animal care Centre or some foreign land.

Mining Mafia

Karnataka mining scams are well known all over the country which resulted in the resignation of the Chief Minister. The bureaucrats were totally responsible on the mismanagement of the mining sector right from Chief Secretary to lower level and were misguiding the new Chief Minister. Some of the forest officers were arrested and kept in jail for years. Many lower level officers were also suspended based on their names mentioned in the dairies of mining owners. When I was secretary forest and environment, I had initiated the process to change the permit system to regulate vehicles carrying ore. According to new regulations the forest department was suppose to keep the permit books and issue permits personally after inspection. We got the approval of the Chief Minister for the change over in the procedure of issuing permits by the forest staff. However, it was not implemented for some reason or the other till I was repatriated. The mining companies were too happy to be in the old system wherein the permits are with the mining companies and they can use as many time as they want in a day and give account at the end of the month. These procedures helped in misusing the permits to transport from illegal sources and was the cause of infamous mining scam of Karnataka which ultimately attracted the attention of the media all over India and Supreme Court intervened.

The new system was introduced by me when I was sent back to the department. Once I was repatriated to the department as Additional Principal Chief Conservators of Forests and had an opportunity to change permits system which involved issuing permits to the mining owners by forest department staff after personally inspecting them. The lorry number was to be personally verified before issuing the permit. It also helped us to track vehicles and seize illegal vehicles. The seizure of vehicles and material created heart burning among mining mafia who brought political pressure on us to switch over to older system. The chief Secretary convened the meeting of mine owners and made us to sit in front of them and asked them to tell their grievances. The mine owners were criticizing the officials of forest department for the enormous delay in issuing permits and harassing them by doing inspections. The government sent a special team to investigate the delay in issuing permits but not to look into irregularities. This was the status of politico-bureaucratic nexus in the mining. Even the Chief Secretary in meetings would side with them. In many instances of forest diversion cases IAS officers in Karnataka did not protect forest conservation instead they liked to distribute forests as a freely available commodity. It is ironical that the responsibility of forest conservation is on the foresters who are criticized by the environmentalist and the public.

Forest Development Tax on Mineral from Forest

Most of the iron ore deposits are found in the most fragile ecosystems of Karnataka. The ore is very rich in Iron content and has very high concentration in the hills and mounds with steep slopes with very sparse vegetation. The mining operations cause heavy damage of soils on the slopes due to soil erosion and land degradation. However, the mining licenses are granted without considering the carrying capacity. The number of leases granted in Sandur taluk alone has exceeded more than a thousand licenses. The sudden rise in the demand for the iron ore from countries like China made the mining companies to indiscriminately mine the ore exceeding their limits and resorting to illegal mining by violating the forest laws and mining guidelines. The politicians and the miner nexus created a kind of situation that the officers were misused and made them to be part of the mining scam. The posting of the officers were arbitrary and the head of the department had no control over their functioning. This led to lot of irregularities and excessive mining which had put the forest department senior management in a very piquant situation. Any amount of requests to change the officers was not agreed and the public and press started blaming the government for allowing the indiscriminate mining to continue with a political patronage. The Chief Minister made an announcement that the government would collect forest development Tax by treating the mineral wealth coming from forest as forest produce.

After the announcement was made there were lots of issues involved in issuing a proper government order to enable the forest development to recover the tax. The issues were more complex, like, value of the mineral, stage of collection and mechanism to fix the rates. We consulted the finance department on the issue with a request to guide us, but there was no satisfactory reply from them. Finally I took the responsibility of fixing rates and formulating mechanism of tax recovery from the mining companies. The department was issued directions to follow the guidelines. The department was able to collect more than Rs 1000.00. crore in about three years time.

When the things became very bad in mining scam the Principal Chief Conservator of Forests (PCCF) and myself as secretary forests confronted the Chief Minister who blamed us for allowing the things to reach such a State of affair. PCCF Dr PJ Dilip Kumar retorted back saying "we are not responsible for what is happening on the ground as we have no control over the postings and transfers of these officers". Therefore, as Chief Minister he must own the responsibility and face the consequences. He further said, when time comes, he will share the stark truth in an appropriate forum. He warned the Chief Minister to see the writing on the wall. The minister of some other department was seen cooling the furious Chief Minister but none of the IAS officers made any effort to tell the CM the wrong doing that he and his office was doing. In fact they kept supporting the illegal activities. Soon Dr PJ Dilip Kumar was removed as PCCF and transferred and in a few months time the Chief Minister too lost his post. Later thanks to Sri Jairam Ramesh who had in 2009 just joined as environment and forest minister in government of India visited Bangalore and interacted with us on the situation and that paved the way for taking a decision to make Dr P J Dilip Kumara as Director- General of Forests.

The Shabby and Shameful Treatment of Icon of Civil Services P Srinivas

P Srinivas out batch mate who was beheaded by brigand Veerappan in November 1991. On the one hand the IAS academy Mussoorie treat P Srinivas as an icon of civil services for his selfless service and every year during the foundation course a memorial lecture is organized in his memory. However, the wretched officers occupying top posts in the secretariat deprived him of his salary and trapped him in bureaucratic red-tapism. His parents were very poor and did not have any means of livelihood after the death of their son they were desperate to get some help from the government for which they had approached the Chief Minister Sri SM Krishna. The Chief Minister was gracious enough to give his approval on the paper given by the parents with instructions to extend the same benefits granted to Sri Hari Krishna IPS officer who was also killed by the Veerappan gang in another encounter. We were happy that the CM was very kind to treat both officers on equal footing but the IAS officers were not happy that the orders was written on the petition paper and they insisted that the orders must be obtained by initiating a separate file by the concerned secretary. However, by the time they moved the file as the luck would have it the CM had demitted his office and the new CM was not approachable and the benefits could never be granted to parents who continued to fight for their justice. His parents struggle went on for years and things were little easier when I was in the secretariat to get some benefits to his parents that included a site and pension. The benefits package for a martyred IPS officer included a petrol pump and site with a job to family member. P Srinivas was also denied salary while he was posted in the task force as the post was created on temporary basis. The department of personal was approached several times for sanction but was not given salary before his death. Two months before his death, he came and asked me for loan as he was not getting his salary. I was terribly upset that an All India Service officer had to struggle for getting his salary even after being appointed to chase Veerappan. Both of us went to personnel department in the secretariat to request the secretary to process his papers to enable him to get his salary. It is shame for the entire civil services that such an officer who put his head on the chopping block to chase Veerappan in the forests as head of the police unit was so shabbily treated by the secretariat people who himself appointed him. It would be desirable if the government can ensure that no such ill treatment is met out to the martyrs like Kirti Chakra P Srinivas.

Funds for Forestry Were Always a Constraint

The get investment in forestry was always challenging task due to inherent bias of IAS officers and the politicians. The department had the onerous responsibility to protect and conserve nearly about 25% land mass of the State was constrained by inadequacy of funds. The finance department would never increase the outlay unless there is a political gain to every rupee spent. Naturally forest was seen as a more of a financial burden and necessary evil as people or politicians always saw foresters as the stumbling block in the decision making. In every successive budget the rise in the budget was always marginal. I had a good finance Secretary as an old friend and very reasonable person. I tried many times to raise the issue of getting increased outlay to many innovative works in the areas of research and information technology but with little success. Our budget outlay was less than 0.5% of the total budget and revenue was around 3 to 3%. During budget finalization there would be always pressure to increase the revenue for which there was always extra funds allocated for taking up logging and similar revenue generating works.

No Money for Feeding Animals in Zoos

It was very frustrating experience to approach each time seeking funds to feed animals in the national parks or paying animal keepers their wages. Once I went and met the finance secretary who was also my good friend with a request to release some as emergency funds for meeting animals' feeds and fodder expenditure. The finance secretary looked highly harassed and looking for sympathy from people being in a very unenviable position. He looked more and more suffering from self pity syndrome. As soon as he heard me he gave me a big sermon on government's ways and means and how the big ticket departments under political pressure have been trying to put pressure on him to squeeze funds from him which is beyond the capacity of the treasury department. It was the Karnataka case of not releasing compensatory aforestation funds to the forest department became the reason for the Supreme Court to order creation of compensatory fund which ultimately led to the setting up of CAMPA.

Development versus Conservation

It was very hard to find any support from the senior IAS officers for conservation issues in any forum. In my entire service period I did not find any one who were responsible for protecting the forests while holding key positions to protect the interest of forest conservation. In one of the wildlife board meeting held under the chairmanship of the Chief Minister, there were two cases that listed for the board's clearances and before the arrival of Chief Minister there was an informal chat on the agenda listed for the day. The principal secretary forests and environment unilaterally declared that he is there in the meeting to argue the case for development need of energy as it was his commitment to the cause of development. When I added who would then argue for conservation he said there are foresters and scientists from botanical survey of India to do the job. The Chief Minister heard both sides and decided to give approval for both the proposals.

Encounter with Cabinet Secretary

Once, one Cabinet Secretary was in the town and he decided to interact with officers in a hurriedly arranged meeting. It was finally only secretaries who were sitting ducks who attended the meeting. There was no agenda set for the meeting and the discussions were mainly on the pending works in the State and vice versa. One senior colleague, working in the energy sector began to express his anguish over the delays in the forest clearances in Delhi. He gave a list of papers pending in ministry of environment and forests and went on suggesting decentralizing the power to give clearances within the State. The Cabinet Secretary was expressing the legal hurdles in the decentralization and promised to look into the matter as there are many projects which are delayed due to pendency in the ministry. Our Chief Secretary looked at me for my opinion on the issue and I just quipped we are following the procedures as per law and as the Supreme Court is monitoring the cases of diversion we cannot take too much risk. It was pity that no one in the meeting was sympathetic to the cause of conservation as the entire bureaucracy from top to bottom.

Hubli-Ankola Railway Project

Hubli-Ankola railway project is pending for government of India clearances for many years under different regimes. The railway line is planned to connect Hubli a commercial town with Ankola a coastal town to promote the regional development of the area. The distance between two towns is approximately 108 km passing through Western Ghats forests. The survey of the proposed line needs more than 1200 ha of forest land and nearly felling of 7 lakh trees. The project is described by environmentalist as a very disastrous project as it is like putting knife into the chest of Western Ghats which would eventually bleed out the Ghats ecosystem. When I was secretary forests Dr PJ Dilip Kumar as PCCF wrote very strongly against the idea of making railway line as it would destroy the biodiversity of the area by fragmenting the landscape. I very strongly opposed to the idea of railway line due to its ecological impacts and destruction of forests and wildlife. Our notes were approved by the Chief Minister and the State did not make any recommendation. But after few years the issue was revived by the State government due to political pressure. The Chief Secretary this time by passed the forest department and asked Indian Institute of Science scientists to give their EIA report justifying the project. The scientists were ready to give any type of report that served the purpose of the government. The report was ready in just two to three months about the feasibility of railway line passing through the pristine forests and the alternatives to mitigate the project impacts.

The report was an eye wash as the scientists had justified the project on the grounds that it would be very climate resilient sustainable project which will save the millions tons of fossil fuels and the carbon emissions as the railway line will be an alternative to the road transportation. The report was obtained to negate the opinion given by the forest department. When the scientists presented the EIA report I was also present in the discussion chaired by the Chief Secretary. As soon as the presentation was over the Chief Secretary congratulated the scientists who had prepared the report justifying the project as planned. The report was sent to MoEF without consulting the forest department. The matter is now pending before the high court on a public interest litigation filed by an NGO.

No Respect for Forest Laws

There are many instances wherein the bureaucrats have shown scant respect to forest laws and have taken arbitrary decisions overlooking the forest department's technical opinions. In one very strange case in Karnataka the Chief Secretary had shown utter contempt to the very forest law by overlooking the opinion of the forest Secretary and principal secretary. This case was a very brazen violation of the forest law by wrongfully encroaching on the forest land by a noted poet who had very high status in the society. He was not questioned by the forest staff despite knowing very well his illegal occupation. After enjoying the possession for more than three decades the encroacher wanted to sell this land to get his daughter married of from the proceeds of the sale. However he had realization about his illegal possession and wanted it to be regularized. He had already developed it by investing money and had well grown commercial crops and plantations on it. He had approached forest officers for regularization many times. He approached the government and in the process he met me and was finding big fault with forest staff. I ordered for the re-survey as per his land grant records and was convinced that he was occupying the forest land. He did not get any help from us and approached the Chief Secretary who had lot of sympathy for the poet called the file and wrote more than a dozen page blaming foresters and threatened to take action against them if they failed to rectify the mistake. We never took his noting and orders seriously.

Civil Service Day Agenda – My Humble Contribution

Every year April 21 is celebrated as civil service day in Delhi. It coincides with the birthday celebration of Iron man of India and the first Home minister of Independent India late Sardar Vallababhai Patel. The events on this day include Inaugural address by the prime minister followed by presentation of awards to distinguished civil servants in various fields. I attended quite a few such civil service day events during UPA Prime Minister Dr Manmohan Singh time. In one of such meeting there were group discussions on burning issues of various civil administrations in the country. I was in the group of civil servants chaired by Sri Subba Rao, who was then secretary finance in government of India. The group's task was to identify the issues, and develop strategies for the pressing problems that India was facing. The group decided to identify and list the challenges. As discussion began officers went on giving their suggestion. The issues were written on the black board as members spoke and in no time the board was filled with issues ranging from economic, environmental energy, governance, poverty corruption water, agriculture, education, electrical reforms, industries, and so on. The listing went on for nearly two hours and still it was growing and there was no consensus on prioritizing most burning issues

We dispersed for lunch and during lunch time we were told that we must complete the discussion by tea time and ready for group presentation in front of Prime Minister. After lunch we reassembled and continued our discussion. I was somehow disappointed with our failures to identify five key issues for discussion. I stood up and expressed my disappointment over our collective failure to zero on few issues and told that we as civil service are trying to assume that only bureaucracy is competent enough to address all the issues nation is facing forgetting that there are many other actors, institutions, agencies and individuals who are playing key role in addressing and helping people to solve their problems. I told them we must try to restrict our role to simply on policy and promotion in partnership with others by sharing both powers and responsibility. My frank opinion and open criticism was attentively listened by all and did not try to stop me. Chairman agreed with my suggestions and suggested to focus on decentralization and strengthening delivery mechanism aspect of governance and to free civil service from politically embedded structure.

The group finally recommended to decentralize the decision making process by making it more transparent and participatory. The civil service must be reoriented to make it people friendly institution was also recommended. Another major recommendation was to make civil service a more flexible instrument with its own independent autonomy free from political influence. However, nothing comes out of such meetings as they end up ceremonials.

Is Civil Service Indispensable?

The civil services have become a necessary evil which cannot be easily replaced or an alternative system can be found in immediate future. The country's governance is very intricately embedded with civil service. I have been observing the bureaucracy for last forty years day in and day out and interacting and working with them in various sectors. I honestly feel the same job could have been better handled by some other person who is more competent and well qualified than an IAS officer or any other civil servant. The country is somehow has more trust and faith in these people who have as a group not delivered in any sector they have been handling. Though there are exceptions but my experience in Karnataka is otherwise is not very good. The bureaucracy has completely failed India in many respects and this disease inflicts all the civil services which have completely let down the people. Unless there is a paradigm shift in our attitude, functions and style, we continue to perform poorer and poorer. The day has come when government should look for alternative system.

Disclaimer

The narrative in this chapter is to bring some of the hidden aspects of civil services before the readers and the write up is with malice towards none. I have best friends among all the AIS and other civil services but we need to reform ourselves to get back the confidence of the people. Hope this write up as part of this wonderful book brings more civility among the civil servants.

Epilogue

16

The first hand experiences narrated by me in the preceding pages as being part of the civil services, clearly underscore the need for rewriting our norms of governance sooner than the later. The enlightened leadership of the country, opinion makers like intelligentsia, academics, social reformers, informed media and people in general do feel the dire need for reforms in our governing systems but so far unable to articulate strongly. After more than seventy years of independence we have not fully won the confidence of our citizens at the grass root level in providing world class developmental opportunities like good health, education and jobs though we have amended the constitution for more than 100 times. The political leaders and our civil servants though did some outstanding works in some fields but over the years the prevalent '***mai-baap*** culture, wherein the poor or the less powerful bend over backwards to please a few political leaders and civil servants but get nothing substantial in return is creating resentments in many sections of people. This is not acceptable for a nation in the quest of world leadership.

As a conscious people centric civil servant during my career in the government my mind always used to get agitated whenever I found that many highly placed civil servants are behaving in utter disregards to the basic guiding norms for the civil servants. A civil servant has to be above board on his integrity and devotion to duty because their actions directly affect the people as they are crucial for smooth execution of government policies and ensuring prompt justice to people. A civil servant should all the time during his or her career be fair, impartial, accountable, and courteous and should never use dilatory tactics nor misuse his or her power for selfish ends in dealing with people while performing his or her duties. When I entered the service four decades ago the situation was not so bad especially whenever we used to find a corrupt officer he or she used to be ignored, sidelined and looked down in the social gatherings. However, after three decades there has been a sea change in the conducts of civil servants as a result of which the society is noticing increasing criticism of civil servants on various counts. Now many civil servants brazenly misuse their powers openly side with political leaders and many even did not bother to listen to their superiors. However, there is quite a good smattering of good civil servants even today in all the services which is needed to be promoted and rewarded. At the same time there is dire need to enforce accountability for the actions of civil servants and weeding out the corrupt and the deadwood. The power and position of civil servant has to be used in the service of the people hence changes in the format and structure of civil services are necessary and should mirror the needs and aspirations of changing society. In the entire process it is also necessary to acknowledge that the conduct of falling standards among the politicians of the country has exacerbated the problems in our civil services so reforms in the political arena are also equally important if not primary concern for an impartial and efficient civil service.

A vibrant democracy requires honest and dedicated public servants for the three wings of the government and the recommendations by the author should be treated as illustrative feedback to be debated by the public and policy makers. In many spheres we have done well but in many other fields our institutions lack proper accountability and innovations. Efficient, honest and transparent people centric civil services have always been and shall always be admired by the people. In this book the author has brought to public domain some of the facts relating to the way some civil servants behave and their actions remain suppressed in the files of the government and thus never come into the notice of general public. Such civil servants are parasites on the system and must be weeded out. When truth is suppressed justice is the victim and when justice is victim then the foundations of rule of law gets uprooted and history is replete with instances when the societies world over are in turmoil due to this. It is also a fact that when the truth is suppressed it will in some way or the other will resurface in one form of anger or the other and destabilize the society. The critical statements made in the book by me and Dr MH Swaminath on governance are purely for improvement purposes with no malice or rancour against any cadre or any individual or people in power.

The issues raised in this book are genuine and the suggestions given for improvement are only illustrative. Some of the recommendations can easily be adopted. The government can at least take action within the existing framework for the civil services and on some judicial and legislative matters. The Hon'ble Prime Minister Shri Narendra Modi is concerned with the falling standards of our governance and has severely criticized the lackadaisical attitude of civil services both inside and outside the Parliament and is also trying to get people in the central secretariat through lateral entry. I would earnestly hope that he and his colleagues read the book and take some positive actions on the suggestions made by me in preceding pages for all the three wings of government i.e. the executive, legislature and the judiciary. Similarly, I would hope that other political leaders of different national/regional parties as well as the media read this book and look at the suggestions. If the book can generate some discussion on these subjects and cajole the conscience of policymakers, informed citizens, media and intellectuals of the country the purpose of writing this book will be achieved.

"The best way to find yourself is to lose yourself in the service of people".
– Mahatma Gandhi
Jai Hind!

Bibliography

Serial No	Reference

1. Anonymous: Various reports and orders, notifications of Government of India/ Expert Committees on the functioning of Forest Research Institute and ICFRE.
2. Ancient and Medieval India. by Poonam Dalal Dahiya
3. A History of Ancient and Early Medieval India: From the Stone Age to the 12th Century. Pearson Education India.By Upinder Singh (2008).
4. Constitution of India, Ministry of Law and Justice, Legislative Department.
5. Constitution of India by VN Shukla
6. Government of India Act 1935
7. India's Struggle for Independence By Bipin Chandra
8. Indira Gandhi National Open University, School pf Social Sciences ERA-04, Personal Administration, July 1991.
9. Kautiliya Arthasastra By RP Kangle Volume2 and 3
10. Lecture by LP Singh on 15th December 1986 in South Gujarat University.
11. Modern India. By Sumit Sarkar
12. Article Entitled "India's Civil Service Needs to Reinvent Itself" dated 5th November 2020 by Moin Qazi in LEAFLET (constitution First)
13. National Commission of Agriculture Report 1976

14. National Commission to Review the working of Constitution Report 2002
15. National Forest Commission Report 2006
16. Our Parliament. By Subhash Kashyap.
17. Reports of the First and Second Administrative Reform Commissions
18. Representation of the People Act 1951
19. Sardar Patel and the Indian Administration. Lecture delivered by Warren Hastings, British Colonial Administrator by PJ Marshal, Encyclopaedia Britannica
20. The Framing of India's Constitution, Select Documents, Volume 4, By B. Shiva Rao, Universal Law Publishing Co. Private Limited, Delhi, Pages: 332-333).
21. Wonder that was India. By AL Basham

www.ingramcontent.com/pod-product-compliance
Lightning Source LLC
Chambersburg PA
CBHW051041250726
48656CB00001B/78